Praise for *The Most Human*

"It was not easy being the son of such an icon as Leonard Nimoy, a man wrestling with his own demons, but Adam Nimoy has succeeded brilliantly in capturing the story of his struggle to function in the chilly shadow of his famous father in simple but evocative prose. The lacerating father-and-son saga bristles with acute observations and painful memories, but remarkably never loses its tender heart. Readers will get much more than they bargained for."

—**Nicholas Meyer**, director of *Star Trek II: The Wrath of Khan*, cowriter of *Star Trek IV: The Voyage Home*, and cowriter-director of *Star Trek VI: The Undiscovered Country*

"Adam Nimoy tells a vibrant, difficult, loving story of growing wiser and kinder, smarter and more spiritually fit through life with his famous father, with his children, his wives. He relates for all of us how both life's experiences and our relationships give us paths for growing, understanding, and loving in ways we never thought possible. This book weaves together Torah and twelve-steps, makes amends and T'Shuvah for Jonah the prophet and Adam's missteps. Adam Nimoy tells the story of redemption through his relationship with his father, his family, and God. This book epitomizes what God wants for us all: to return to our soul's calling and to live our spiritual life and growth out loud."

—**Rabbi Mark Borovitz**, author of
Finding Recovery and Yourself in Torah

And about bigger things.

"John Lennon's been shot," Dad told me one December night as I was cramming for a final in Civil Procedure.

"What do you mean he's been shot?"

"They just announced it on the news."

I got up from my desk and ran to the family room to turn on the TV. I flipped through the channels looking for the news, not quite believing it. Or more like believing it but assuming that John was just injured. Nope. My favorite Beatle was dead. I turned toward Dad, who was standing behind me.

"He's dead," I choked out. "Some idiot killed him."

"I know," he said, "I was just talking to Harold about it."

(Harold Livingston. The screenwriter of *Star Trek: The Mediocre Motion Picture*.)

"Harold said John Lennon was responsible for the entire drug culture in this country."

The lighting was low in the family room as the TV flickered and the newscaster droned on about the tragedy that had taken place in front of the Dakota Apartments in New York City. Dad stood right in front of me, challenging me, my idol, my life. One of my all-time favorite heroes had just been shot dead on the street in front of his home, and this was my father's response. He knew how much I admired John, how much I loved him. I still had an old, tattered Beatles poster on the door to my room, the one of them at the blue wall advertising the Royal Command Performance.

"Yeah, well, Harold Livingston's an asshole," I said, then stormed off to my room, slammed the door, and lit up a bowl.

The LORD provided a huge fish to swallow Jonah; and Jonah remained in the fish's belly three days and three nights.

Dad was mesmerizing as he continued with the story of how God prevented Jonah from sailing away by throwing a tempest on the sea and how on Jonah's suggestion the terrified sailors threw him overboard to stop the sea from raging. The whale showed up out of nowhere to save

Jonah from drowning, which all seemed well and good except that Jonah then found himself stuck inside the whale with nowhere to go. Just like I was back in L.A. stuck in my room. Stuck in my addiction. Stuck.

Dad gave it his all. His voice was full and committed as if he were recounting events he himself had witnessed. The octogenarians in the congregation sat up straight. We were all there with Jonah, trapped in the belly of the whale, trapped inside the synagogue, forced to reflect on our own sins, the things we needed to atone for, the things we had run away from.

I turned in my seat to look at the sea of traffic flowing outside the open door of the synagogue. Despite the trouble I had connecting to my dad, a problem we had experienced off and on since I was very young, I was always proud of him. It didn't matter that he was playing to a near empty house, he was a class act, as he would say of others he admired. Dad was a born actor. He knew his craft and he gave it his all. I started thinking that if *Trek* fans knew they could walk straight into the shul and watch Leonard Nimoy recount the trials and tribble-ations of Jonah and the Whale, the place would be packed.

The fans. By the time I was ten and *Star Trek* was in its first season, it was impossible for me and Dad to be in public together—people would swarm him asking for autographs, telling him how much they loved Spock and *Star Trek*. They'd get so excited I often heard them say, "You're my biggest fan." Dad always tried to oblige the fans. He had a deep appreciation for them, which I admired. Then again, there were times when the attention he gave the fans was frustrating—just another distraction from our relationship, a relationship which was often distant and awkward.

By my teen years, the awkwardness I had experienced with my father during my childhood turned to conflict. Throughout our lives my dad and I experienced many great moments together, mostly celebrating his incredible career. Along with those positive experiences came some serious head-banging that would periodically plague us. Now here we were on the holiest day of the Jewish year, the Day of Atonement, the day of apologies and forgiveness, all of which eluded us.

> *Jonah prayed to the LORD his God from the belly of the fish.*
> *He said: "In my trouble I called to the LORD, who answered*
> *me; From the belly of Sheol I cried out, and You heard my*

THE MOST HUMAN

RECONCILING WITH MY FATHER, LEONARD NIMOY

ADAM NIMOY

CHICAGO
REVIEW
PRESS

Copyright © 2024 by Adam Nimoy
All rights reserved
Published by Chicago Review Press Incorporated
814 North Franklin Street
Chicago, Illinois 60610
ISBN 978-0-915864-73-7

Library of Congress Control Number: 2024931791

Typesetting: Jonathan Hahn
All images are from the author's collection

Printed in the United States of America
5 4 3 2 1

For Mom and Dad
and
For Martha

"Of my friend I can only say this: of all the souls I have encountered in my travels, his was the most human."

—Kirk's eulogy for Spock, *Star Trek II: The Wrath of Khan*

CONTENTS

Part II: Things Change

Part III: The Dad I Needed

AUTHOR'S NOTE

Some names of individuals and identifying details mentioned in this book have been fictionalized. Any similarity between the fictionalized names and the names of real people is strictly coincidental.

Some text passages originally appeared in my book *My Incredibly Wonderful, Miserable Life*, published by Pocket Books in 2008. Others are from my short story "My Father the Vulcan" in *To Me, He Was Just Dad* from Joshua David Stein and the editors of Fatherly; they are reprinted by permission of Artisan Books © 2020. Additional material appeared in the article "I Absolutely Adored Spock. Loving Dad Was Much More Complicated," *Boston Globe*, June 17, 2021.

The title to chapter 25, "My Cinnamon Girl," was inspired by Neil Young's rock anthem "Cinnamon Girl." The reference in chapter 32 to dragging "a comb across my head" was derived from a line in the Lennon/McCartney epic "A Day in the Life." The words "cellophane flowers of yellow and green" in chapter 33 is an echo of John Lennon's psychedelic classic "Lucy in the Sky with Diamonds." And the sentence "The doctor came in, stinking of gin" in chapter 35 was borrowed from Paul McCartney's quintessential ballad "Rocky Raccoon."

Much gratitude to Brenda Copeland for her tireless efforts in helping me figure out what this book should be about and how best to write it. Many thanks to BJ Robbins for believing in this project and to Cynthia Sherry and Jerry Pohlen at Chicago Review Press for their support in publishing it. Special thanks to CRP managing editor Devon Freeny for his meticulous work in copyediting. Finally, I'm so grateful for Harriet Rossetto and Rabbi Mark Borovitz, the founders of Beit T'Shuvah, and for my fellow board members, the staff, and the residents at Beit T'Shuvah, all of whom carry on our mission to heal broken souls and save the lives of those wrestling with addiction.

Part I

IN THE BEGINNING

1

SINS OF OUR FATHERS

We were sitting in the last row of the synagogue when Dad was called up to the bimah—the stage at the front of the congregation where he would be reading from the Book of Jonah. Dad and I liked sitting in the back. It was something we had in common—Dad because he normally didn't want to be recognized, me because I didn't want to be noticed. It was a weekday afternoon and the temple was almost empty, typical of Yom Kippur—the Day of Atonement.

The morning services are always packed on this, the holiest day of the Jewish year. Everyone shows up to ask God for forgiveness—for the sin of lying, for the sin of hatred, for the sin of wanton glances. All the sins. We fast all day on Yom Kippur, so when the morning program is over almost everyone heads straight home to distract themselves from thinking about food (or to eat). Most return just before sunset, when we stand for an excruciating hour as the ark remains open for one last chance to seek forgiveness. Before that, the shul is near empty during the least popular afternoon service, the Mincha. This didn't bother my father. Always the professional, he would give the few die-hard congregants something to remember. With his deep, resonant voice, he began:

> The word of the LORD came to Jonah the son of Amittai: "Go at once to Nineveh, that great city, and proclaim judgment against it; for their wickedness has come before Me."

Instead of schlepping to Nineveh, which sits in what is now northern Iraq, Jonah boarded a ship headed in the opposite direction. Of course, you can't flee from the service of the Lord. It's like trying to run from yourself. I knew something about that, having for years hidden myself in a cloud of pot smoke as a way to flee from the challenges in my life— the challenge of college, the challenge of dating, the challenge of having a complicated relationship with my famous father. All the challenges.

When I started smoking in high school at age seventeen, it was fun. You have an instant community when you start smoking pot, and I liked hanging with the stoners because before that, I was eating my lunch alone in a high school bungalow. Five years later I was smoking daily by myself, and it had become a lonely, isolated experience. I was a pretty high-functioning substance abuser and was always able to keep up with my college coursework. But I couldn't shake the need to be stoned all the time. In the words of my college roommate, "Sure, I smoke pot. But you, Nimoy, are a pothead."

I wasn't the only one in the family who fled from life's challenges. Every night I'd hear the ice hit the glass, followed by a pour of Johnnie Walker or a dry Bombay martini with a twist, depending on Dad's mood. There was a built-in bar in the family room next to my bedroom, and I could hear my dad whenever he was in there. My father was the epitome of a high-functioning alcoholic. He made every early morning call, every meeting, every personal appearance. Years later, when he was sober and being interviewed by none other than Bill Shatner, Dad admitted his habitual drinking began in the 1960s to cope with the pressures of making *Star Trek*. What he didn't say during that segment—and later confided in me—was that his drinking was the result of long hours on the set, the difficult producers, and his problems with Bill Shatner.

During my college years there were times when I wanted to quit smoking pot but was clueless as to how to do it—my willpower having repeatedly failed me. Now I was back in L.A. living with my parents under the misguided notion that being home was a safe, supportive place to be as I took on the challenges of a first-year law student. Dad's drinking and my pot-smoking were a combustible combination, which was why at night I would hide in my room to smoke, study, and stay the hell out of his way. Still, there were skirmishes about little things.

"Were you in my toolbox?" Dad asked. "Because I'm missing an awl."

"Why would I need an awl?"

voice. You cast me into the depths, into the heart of the sea, the floods engulfed me; All Your breakers and billows swept over me. . . . Would I ever gaze again upon Your holy Temple?"

Jonah had really hit bottom. He prayed mightily, admitting that he was sinking to his lowest depths, that weeds wrapped around his head, that his soul was fainting away, when suddenly he remembered the Lord and promised to do what the hell he was told. It's a heartfelt story of repentance and forgiveness, which is why we read it every year on Yom Kippur.

The LORD commanded the fish, and it spewed Jonah out upon dry land. The word of the LORD came to Jonah a second time: "Go at once to Nineveh, that great city, and proclaim to it what I tell you."

Our synagogue was modest compared to the monumental structures of Sinai Temple a few miles north or Wilshire Boulevard Temple, the oldest congregation in Los Angeles. Adat Shalom was a basic rectangular structure much like the Tabernacle the Jews dragged around the desert for forty years, ours a rectangle with parquet wood floors and modest stained-glass windows. Halfway up the aisle was where my mother's parents used to sit every Saturday morning for the Shabbat service, Grandpa Archie in his best suit and cuff links, Grandma Ann always wearing a pillbox hat, always lost in prayer. Not much had changed since my bar mitzvah in 1969, when I stood on the bimah where my father stood now.

Beautiful mosaics hung on the walls, depicting Bible stories: Sarah and Abraham being visited by three strangers, Rebekah drawing water from the well, and a picture behind me of a boy dressed in a plain white tunic lying blindfolded on top of a woodpile. His feet and hands were tied together, and behind him was all blue sky, giving the sense that he was high up on a mountain. The woodpile was firewood, the round logs neatly stacked under the boy's body. As my father continued to read, I felt sick as I realized what I was looking at. The blue mountain sky, the blindfolded boy, the firewood. This was the Akedah, the Binding of Isaac, in which Isaac's father, Abraham, prepared to sacrifice his son as an offering to God. As the story goes, just as Abraham grabbed the butcher's knife to slit Isaac's throat, an angel appeared and stopped him.

I looked back out the front door to catch my breath. The intersection of Westwood and National Boulevards is one of the unsightly cross streets in West L.A., with a strip mall on one corner and a gas station on the other. A freeway overpass connects the two. In that moment, with the view of all that grotesque concrete and the noise of the street traffic, it seemed as if Adat Shalom was nothing more than a giant shoebox built at an ugly intersection, adorned on the inside with the mural of a boy about to be murdered by his father.

It's in Genesis 22 where God puts Abraham's faith to the test by telling him to take his son up to the mountain and offer him as a sacrifice. Biblical commentary explains this as Abraham passing the test of his faith in God, but there's been some debate as to whether he would have gone through with it, whether he really would have killed Isaac. Then again, why else go through all the trouble of calling Isaac, collecting the firewood, and schlepping all the way up the mountain?

Rabbi Mark Borovitz, with whom I later studied the Bible, would tell me that Abraham failed the test because of his resentment toward Isaac. Isaac was not his only son. Because Abraham's wife, Sarah, was too old to have children, she gave him her handmaiden Hagar, and soon Ishmael was born. Sarah did eventually give birth to Isaac, but to protect Isaac's interests, she told Abraham to get rid of Hagar and Ishmael, and this hurt Abraham deeply. Rabbi Mark explained that Abraham resented Isaac because he was forced to send Ishmael into the wilderness. He was acting on this resentment when he willingly took Isaac up to the mountain, thereby failing the real test presented by the story.

But at that moment, sitting alone in that sanctuary as my father's voice commanded the space, I couldn't understand why the synagogue would prominently display one of the most hideous scenes in the Bible. I only knew that it seemed personal—like in-my-face personal.

The Akedah is a horror show, a reminder to all young men that if they don't stand up to their fathers, they might be destroyed. This is a running theme throughout Torah, the first five books of the Bible: ancient stories of fathers and sons struggling with one another. Abraham with his son Isaac, Isaac's problems with his son Jacob, Jacob's problems with his twelve sons. And now here I was back in L.A., living in my father's house, repeating the cycle of dysfunction all over again, not knowing if anything could ever be done about it.

2

SPOCK AND SPIDEY

ON A SATURDAY MORNING IN THE FALL OF 1966, when I was ten and *Star Trek* had just gone on the air, I went with my dad to Hollywood on one of our father-son outings. It was an annual tradition we'd started the year before where we'd drive to M'Goos—an old-school pizza parlor on Hollywood Boulevard—then head over to the Cherokee Book Shop, where Dad would buy me some vintage comics. It was a tradition that occurred exactly twice before being abandoned, which was something of a relief, as I never knew what to say to him when we were alone, and he barely said anything to me. In this respect, my dad was exactly like *his* father, my grandfather Max, a man of few words if any. Oftentimes it felt like Dad and I were strangers, always struggling for something to say.

"I like the sawdust on the floor," I said.

"Yeah, it's good," Dad replied. Then, nodding toward the waiters in their straw hats and red vests, "What do you think of their uniforms?"

"Yeah, they're neat," I replied.

Despite our discomfort, I loved M'Goos—it had an authentic old Hollywood feel to it not unlike Musso & Frank, a dining landmark right down the street. We were at M'Goos in the late morning before the lunch hour, and the place was practically empty. Had it been busier, people would've been coming up to the table to ask for autographs, something that had been happening regularly over the past few months as Spock's popularity grew. One time Dad took me to a carnival at St. Timothy's Church on Pico and Beverly Glen. He was immediately mobbed, and that was the end of that. With no fans around at M'Goos, we just sat there in our awkwardness. I was glad when the pizza finally arrived because it gave us something to do. And it was delicious.

After we ate, it was off to the Cherokee Book Shop. Finding the collectible comics section at Cherokee was like discovering hidden treasure. You had to walk to the back of the store, then up a narrow staircase that led to a secret attic hideout. A humorless hippie named Burt ran the comics section, which was a small room of wooden bookshelves stacked with cardboard boxes filled with classic, colorful editions from DC and Marvel. There were sample comics in plastic bags taped to the front of each box—*Batman*, *Justice League of America*, *The Atom*, *The Fantastic Four*. The place was a mecca of comic book art and storytelling. It was there that I picked up old copies of *Daredevil* and *Green Lantern*, and my all-time favorite—*The Amazing Spider-Man*. So satisfying to sift through those boxes and find back issues with killer covers of Spidey being tormented by Green Goblin, Sandman, and Doc Ock. I could relate to that fatherless loner Peter Parker.

Dad and I didn't spend much time together in those early days. Before *Star Trek* he was constantly working odd jobs and pursuing bit roles in TV shows, a remnant of the work ethic forged on the Depression-era streets of Boston, where he was born and raised. My dad was a man obsessed with paying the bills while pursuing his passion. When he got his big break costarring on a new science fiction TV series on NBC, I barely saw him at all. I knew Dad had brought me on a father-son outing to Hollywood because he felt he should, because he wanted to be a good dad. But as was typical, he was distracted and withdrawn that day at the Cherokee Book Shop. We were in a room filled with one of the best sci-fi/fantasy comic book collections in the country, and the man who had appeared on *The Outer Limits* and *The Twilight Zone*, and was now making a splash as Mr. Spock on *Star Trek*, leaned against a wall and waited in detached silence. Sometimes, I simply could not figure the guy out. I remember feeling this unspoken pressure to decide what I wanted so we could get the hell out of there.

"And his own sensibility, it seems safe to say, informed [his] character." So read the obit in the *New Yorker* after Dad died in 2015.

It was definitely safe to say. Like Spock, my father was often inscrutable—it was hard to know what he was thinking or feeling. The similarity to the half-human, half-Vulcan science officer didn't end there. Like Spock, Dad was not the warm and fuzzy type. One of my earliest memories of him was when we were living in our tiny first house on Palms Boulevard in the Mar Vista neighborhood of L.A. I must have been five or six years old. It was morning, and Dad was wearing a suit because we were going to High Holy Day services. We were waiting for my sister and my mother when dad showed me a magic trick. He tucked a small rubber ball into the upper part of his sock and, with a wave of his hand, made it disappear.

Wow, I thought. *Daddy can do magic!* Then I had this weird sensation. While I was standing there in awe, I was waiting for him to give me a hug or a kiss. My mother would have done it. Her parents, Grandpa Archie and Grandma Ann, would have done it. But Dad didn't. I had this feeling that he was almost like a stranger to me, as if he were a long-lost uncle who came to visit and showed me a little magic and that was that. My mom would later tell me that when my sister and I were babies—my sister Julie is a year and a half older than me—Dad was much more hands-on helping to take care of us. We even have some old 8 mm film showing Dad giving us baths and holding us during outings. But by the time I was old enough to start remembering things, I felt this distance from him.

There's another memory about my dad that's stuck in my mind, something that happened when I was a little older, probably when I was seven or eight. I was standing in the kitchen of our second house, on Comstock Avenue in West L.A., while my mother was looking for something in the refrigerator. Dad came in to fix himself a drink. It was the afternoon, and I watched as he made himself a martini with a lemon peel. He then shuffled off to the bedroom, drink in hand, leaving the bottles and the lemon and the knife on the counter. It was just an ordinary weekend afternoon that I never would have remembered, except for the fact that, seeing the mess he left behind, my mother pulled a milk bottle out of the refrigerator, lifted it over her head, yelled my father's name, and threw it against the countertop. It shattered on the avocado-green tile. I ran out of the kitchen and into the living room, where I hid under the coffee table, whimpering. My father came into the room and sat in a chair. He sat there and said nothing. I crawled out from under the table and into his lap. He reluctantly put his arms around me. Years later when I read about Dr. Harry Harlow's "monkey love experiment" for some psychology class, I flashed back to that day, because it felt like I was one of Dr. Harlow's baby monkeys trying to get comfort from a parent made of bare wire.

I had so much trouble bonding with Dad when I was a kid, which isn't to say he didn't try. In the winter of 1968–69, not long after we moved into our third and final house in the neighborhood of Westwood, Dad returned home from an out-of-state personal appearance, which was something he often did on weekends, because it gave him a chance to interact with the fans. And it generated fast cash. I was in my room when he came in and handed me a small box containing a colorful set of Mr. Toad cuff links and tie clip. The set was clearly made for a little boy, but I was twelve at the time. It didn't matter, because I was so grateful for the gift. My father had thought to buy me something while he was away. I never wore the Mr. Toad cuff links or tie clip, but I adored them.

Dad also took me fishing back in the day when there was a huge barge anchored way out in the Santa Monica Bay. And sometimes we'd go sailing. He was an excellent sailor from his years growing up on the Charles River in Boston. He had a natural feel for the wind and the water and would give me clear orders when to switch the jib sail when he was turning the boat. I remember one day we were at the rental office at Marina del Rey and it was windy as hell. The guy at the desk had just said to the people in front of us that he was only outfitting the boats with mainsails. Then he turned to Dad and said, "Mr. Nimoy, you know how to handle yourself out there, so I'm going to also give you a jib."

I always felt secure with Dad when we were doing these kinds of activities, whether we were sailing a boat in rough conditions or he was flying his single-engine Piper aircraft through a rainstorm.* He had a focus and a confidence that put me at ease. Then again, sailing with him was more of a meditative experience than an opportunity for us to connect. And sitting for hours in a noisy cockpit with his eyes fixed on

---

* Dad learned to fly in London in 1972 while making a forgettable TV movie. Once he earned his instrument rating, I could never get him back in a boat. *Star Trek III* actually grounded him for a while, when the insurance company said no to the film's director and star tooling around in the air. Years later, when his plane's retractable nose gear refused to go down and he had to skid to a stop on the landing strip, that's when he hung up his pilot's goggles.

the controls or searching the sky at ten thousand feet was not exactly conducive to conversation. This was the difficulty I had with my father: there was always an emptiness between us—we were missing a deep emotional connection. He sometimes told me that he loved me, but it was so hard to feel it. We never watched TV together, never played catch. He never came to my Little League games. Except for our occasional excursions, we never hung out together. It just wasn't his thing. But I was always proud of him.

Even before *Star Trek*, I'd see him popping up in bit roles on my favorite TV shows like *Get Smart, Sea Hunt,* and *The Man from U.N.C.L.E. Wow,* I'd think. *That's Dad!* I remember one Saturday afternoon in the early '60s, I was at home watching a low-budget thriller called *The Brain Eaters.* I could tell it was a cheesy film, but there were only six channels back then and there was nothing else worth watching. Roger Corman, the king of cult movies, was one of the producers, as was Edwin Nelson, a friend of Dad's. Ed had brought his family to a party my parents threw when we were living on Palms Boulevard. He would go on to costar in the highly successful prime-time soap *Peyton Place,* but in those early days, in the "struggling actor" days when Dad was hustling all sorts of odd jobs, Ed got him a job as a process server. The two of them would hide in the bushes then jump out and serve people with court papers.

In *The Brain Eaters,* alien parasites have infiltrated the small town of Riverdale, Illinois, and have managed to attach themselves to—wait for it—people's brains. It was a typical black-and-white horror movie featuring "crawling, slimy things terror-bent on destroying the world!" Ed coproduced and starred in the film as Dr. Kettering, the lead investigator who finds a spaceship-type structure that has let loose the parasites. Fearlessly climbing inside, he finds a bearded man named Cole who seems to be in control of the brain eaters. The actor is wearing so much makeup he's unrecognizable, but the minute Cole spoke I was shocked to discover that it was Dad. I thought to myself, *Holy cow, Dad is the king of the brain eaters!* Then I yelled for my mother. "Mom! You gotta come see this!!"

That's the kind of acting work Dad was doing in the late '50s and early '60s: small parts in a few films and dozens of TV episodes. Then, one December night in 1964, he brought home some Polaroids of himself in makeup and wardrobe for a pilot episode he was working on. It was one of those *I'll never forget this moment* moments, as he handed me the pictures, front and back shots of Mr. Spock. It was the early Spock, the primitive Spock: rough, uneven haircut, bushy eyebrows—and those ears. (Many years later Dad would explain to me that it was Charles Schram at the MGM makeup department who created the first foam latex prosthetics for Spock's ears. Mr. Schram was best known for his work creating the prosthetic makeup for the Cowardly Lion and the Wicked Witch in *The Wizard of Oz*.)

Even in 1964, when nobody had heard of *Star Trek*, the eight-year-old me had watched enough *Outer Limits* and *My Favorite Martian* episodes to understand exactly what I was looking at. I mean, "The Galaxy Being," the first *Outer Limits* episode, had a huge impact on me. A scary but benevolent alien accidentally arrives on Earth and is misunderstood and treated badly—a sci-fi trope that always appeals to us outsiders and social misfits trying to find our way in a sometimes unwelcoming world. And now here was Dad playing the half-human, half-alien Mr. Spock, soon to take that trope to a whole new level. All these years later I can still feel the excitement I felt that night when I was given my first glimpse of this strange-looking man from outer space. (Miraculously, I still have one of those Polaroids of Spock backed with the inscription LEONARD NIMOY DEC 1964.)

"This is what I've been working on all week," Dad said, obviously pleased by my reaction. It was a big moment for him, a costarring role in the pilot of a potential new TV series. In Dad's family his older brother Melvin was the star because of his academic career—something my father had no intention of pursuing. When Dad told his parents he wanted to be an actor, they were devastated. It was as if he had told them he wanted to join the circus. Dad always played a supporting role to my uncle, but now he was coming into his own, and I shared in the excitement of this new development. It was a way for us to connect on a deeper level, to have something that appealed to me as an avid fan of science fiction and to my dad as an artist striving to get to another level in his career.

There would be many more shared experiences related to *Star Trek*, like the time I was visiting the set and the crew decided to pull a prank on Dad by putting me in Fred Phillips's makeup chair, where he cut my hair, shaved my eyebrows, and glued on a pair of Spock ears. While Kirk was on the planet of the week and Spock was in the captain's chair, the turbolift opened and out I walked onto the bridge. While I was in the turbolift waiting for those doors to open, I remember having another one of those *I'll never forget this moment* moments. The episode was "What Are Little Girls Made Of?"—which was shooting in July and August 1966, over a month before the show even aired. Let the cosplay begin!

When I walked onto the bridge and kissed my father on the cheek, everyone on the crew started laughing. Dad smiled as if to say, *Ha-ha, you got me again*, because they were always pulling pranks on set, all of which showed up in the immensely entertaining blooper reels they screened at the Christmas parties. After our little prank, the crew broke for lunch and Dad and I went off to one of the *Enterprise* corridors to have our picture taken. It was a nice moment between us, because whenever I visited the set, he was otherwise typically all Spock, all remote, all distant.

Then there was the much-anticipated night of September 8, 1966, when *Star Trek* premiered. Our family drove to a friend's house in Beverly Hills to watch the first episode, "The Man Trap," on a color TV. (The fall of 1966 was the first time all three networks aired their prime-time schedules in color.) It was so powerful to see that first glimpse of Spock in the scene on the bridge with Lieutenant Uhura. She challenges him to lighten up and let his hair down while Captain Kirk's away on the planet, but Spock remains all business.

Not only was the *New Yorker* right that my father's own sensibility informed his character, but while they were shooting the original series there would also be this feedback loop. Dad later admitted that he found it difficult to get in and out of character during his three years on the original *Trek* series, which meant that during those years the withdrawn and detached attitude I had experienced from my father was now being amplified because of the character he was playing on television. As my sister Julie succinctly pointed out, during the *Trek* years Dad was simply unavailable.

After the premiere, the producers would regularly let the cast and crew out early on the day the show was airing so that they could all get home in time to see it. And so, on Thursday nights at 8:30 PM, my family would gather on my parents' bed to watch Dad in the breakthrough role that would change our lives—on our portable black-and-white TV.

Spock's immediate popularity prompted the fanzines to start writing about Dad's personal life, characterizing us as a "close family." Julie and

I smiled for photos meant for thought-provoking articles such as WHY LEONARD NIMOY HIDES HIS TWO CHILDREN and LEONARD NIMOY: IS MY WIFE'S LOVE ENOUGH FOR ME? My favorite was a headline splashed over a two-page picture of me and Dad: HOW LEONARD NIMOY TRIES TO COPE WITH TEENAGE SEX AND DOPE.

Star Trek was canceled after three seasons in 1969, but that same year Dad replaced Martin Landau on *Mission: Impossible*, playing Paris, the master of disguise, for two seasons. So from 1966 to 1971, he was rarely around. At the end of each shooting day, he'd come home for dinner, learn his lines, and then crash before getting up at five thirty the next morning. That first season of *Star Trek*, he woke up to the sound and smell of coffee brewing. It was this ridiculous setup—a large coffee pot plugged into an old clock radio, all of which sat on a flimsy aluminum folding table next to my parents' bed.

On the weekends, Dad was often out of town making personal appearances. He was also busy with his recording career, which all started with *Mr. Spock's Music from Outer Space*, a kitschy album that I just loved. Weekends were also made for recovering from the work-week or working on home improvement projects, like the brick wall he built between the driveway and backyard. When Dad decided to leave *Mission: Impossible* in 1971, we were living in our last home in West-wood where he suddenly found himself with a little more time on his hands—just when I was entering the angst and angry phase of my teen years. That's when the awkwardness between us and our failure to find any deep connection led to bigger problems.

3

THAT'S HOW IT'S DONE

THERE WAS A SMALL STORAGE ROOM in the far corner of our house on Cashmere Street in Westwood, accessible only from the backyard. We always referred to it as "the darkroom," because it's where my father jump-started his photography career by developing film and making prints. The room is next to what was my bedroom, my bed right up against the common wall. At night I'd fall asleep while Dad was out there working. I'd drift off to the sound of him pushing the enlarger timer button that hung on the darkroom wall.

It was reassuring to hear that little beep, to fall asleep knowing he was back there. This was all in my early teen years, before the rebelliousness kicked in, before I discovered pot, before I found refuge away at college. I always admired and respected the discipline my father brought to his craft, whether it be acting or photography. Night after night I'd hear him spend hours back there producing some very cool black-and-white prints, many of which I still have in my collection. That inspired me to start borrowing Dad's camera (the Minolta SR-T 101 was the rage for us amateur photographers) and to experiment with my own processing and printing in the darkroom. I was following in Dad's footsteps based on some rudimentary instruction he had given me when I was starting out.

In 1973 my father published *You and I*, his first of many books of poetry and photography. When he came home with a copy of the first printing, he was grinning when he showed it to me, because he had included two photos I had taken when we were in Spain during the spring of 1971. He was clearly trying to do something nice for me, but it was actually a very difficult moment. Dad hadn't asked my permission to use the photos, and I had mixed feelings about them being included in a book containing my father's love poems. I was seventeen and struggling to create my own identity separate from my famous father, and this was going in the wrong direction. He did credit me for one of the pictures, which he was proud to point out, but the credit read "Photograph on page 124 by Adam Nimoy," which wasn't much use, because there were no page numbers in the book. The only way you could tell which image was mine was to count through 124 pages. (As it turned out, it was the very last page of the book.)

By this point in our lives there had been a lot of trouble. While we were on that trip to Spain, I said something sarcastic to Dad at the dinner table in the restaurant at Hotel Aguadulce, and he became very angry. "Don't smart mouth me," he said. It was an embarrassing moment, and the next morning I apologized, because I so badly wanted to make things right with him. Around the same time, there was an unfortunate joyriding episode with some of my classmates at Emerson Junior High School. I had a lot of trouble fitting into middle school. None of my friends from elementary school went to Emerson, and I didn't know a single person when I started the seventh grade. So at age fourteen I tried to impress some girls by taking them for a ride in my mother's car, the 1964 Buick Riviera, Dad's first luxury car, which he bought used then gave to my mother when he bought himself a new '68 Riviera. Everything was going quite well until the cops picked us up. Dad was pissed, and rightfully so, but he was angry for weeks over that episode—there was this constant unbearable coldness between us.

Thankfully my mother was able to forgive me and could eventually see the humor in it. Two years later, when I was taking driving lessons, she laughed when the instructor asked if I had any previous driving experience.

What was becoming clear to me, and I think this may be true of a lot of men from my father's generation, was that Dad had trouble expressing his feelings toward me except when it came to disappointment and anger. When at seventeen I started smoking pot and made a whole new community of friends in the party crowd, things went from bad to worse.

Normally he showed little interest in who I hung out with. Then one day he called me into the living room. "Adam!" he yelled.

"What?" I yelled back. Then silence. This was typical. It was his way of letting me know I was being summoned. Resistance was futile, so I walked into the living room and sat down on the couch opposite him.

"Let's talk about your friends Chris and Matthew," he said. He was sitting in a large antique wood and leather chair with a window behind him, all majestic and safe and sure of himself.

His cross-examination began: "What can you tell me about them?"

I knew it was a trap. It was like, *Wow, you suddenly noticed I've been hanging out with a couple of stoners, which has been going on for like the past year. And now you want to know about them?*

"What do you want to know?" I asked in defiance.

"I called the school about those boys," he said. It went downhill from there.

All conflict ended up in anger, resentment, and frustration. We simply had no constructive way to talk about stuff, and I could often sense his disappointment with me, that in his eyes, I didn't measure up. There was never any calm discussion, no meaningful resolution, no feelings of love. My father had trouble understanding me; I had trouble getting through to him. It was difficult for him to express positive feelings toward me; I never felt safe expressing any of my concerns or reservations around him. It was an impossible situation—which is why the poetry book was so loaded for me.

Dad showed me the book the minute he walked in the door. We were standing in the foyer of our house in Westwood, a small, square entryway with peg-and-groove floors and a vintage brass pendant light hanging overhead. There were white painted louvered French doors on one side that led to our beautiful dining room with an oval oak table and wallpaper adorned with purple irises. On the opposite side of the foyer were solid French doors that opened into the living room and my mother's orange-and-blue Indian printed couches. Dad thought he was doing something special for me—using my photos in his book—and even though I was experiencing all these mixed emotions, even though I felt he had made a mistake, I simply could not risk any more conflict. I knew that if I spoke up, if I said anything about what I was feeling, he would be crushed and then angry. So I thanked him and let it go.

My father was born in Boston during the Depression to Mordko ("Max") and Dvora (Dora) Nimoy, both Russian immigrants. (My grandparents came from Zaslav, a village in what is now Ukraine, but back then they considered themselves Russian.) In 1941, when he was ten years old, he was selling newspapers on the Boston Common in the freezing dead of winter. During his teens, he worked a series of odd jobs—in a card shop, a camera store, folding chairs after summer concerts for the Boston Pops. When he was seventeen, he sold vacuum cleaners.

Dad grew up fast. His parents were able to save enough for him to go to college, but when he said he wanted to go to Hollywood to study acting, they were so disappointed that they refused to help. A determined eighteen-year-old Leonard took a three-day train trip across the country and arrived in L.A. in 1949. He worked several odd jobs to support himself and, seven years later, when he was only twenty-five, he had to hustle faster and harder to support our family of four. He set up fish tanks, he serviced gumball machines, he sold insurance, he scooped ice cream, he drove a cab. He taught acting class, he managed an apartment building, he served court papers with Ed Nelson. Every dollar in Leonard's pocket was his. "You can take the boy out of Boston, but you can't take Boston out of the boy," Uncle Mel, my father's older brother, would tell me years later.

All the while Dad was pushing to get bit parts in TV shows and feature films. When he landed a costarring role in a quirky little science fiction series that was catching people's attention, his parents were amazed by the extent of his success. They were a little embarrassed when the fans began to shower them with attention as well, but they welcomed it, even showing us some of the many adoring letters the fans had written. Still, I never once heard Nana and Papa say that they were proud of my father or that they loved him. As my father once said, "My parents were not demonstrative."

In stark contrast to my father's upbringing, I was born in sunny Southern California. When *I* was ten years old, I was reading Spider-Man comics, listening to the Beatles, and watching '60s TV. There was no need for me to take on a paper route or to find odd jobs. Maybe I was lucky. Then again, maybe I could have used a few lessons from my enterprising father about how to generate fast cash. Maybe I should have had a little job to learn about earning and saving. Whatever the case, much like my friends at the time, I was enjoying my afterschool life just being a kid, and in that respect my dad and I were worlds apart—like from Earth to Vulcan.

I think Dad envied the fact that I didn't have to scramble to generate income. He was proud that he could send me to college and to law school, and I was grateful to have had those experiences without needing to carry any student loans. But I could never quite shake the feeling that deep down, he harbored some resentment that I was able to pursue my passion with his financial help, whereas he had not been accorded the same privilege.

Dad was sort of odd man out compared to my close relationships with my mother and her parents, Ann and Archie. Any conflict with them was always resolved with apologies and hugs and kisses. Weirdly enough, despite experiencing those differences, when I was younger I wasn't really sure my strained relationship with my dad was any different from what my friends were experiencing. That perception began to change when I witnessed firsthand how my friend Alan's dad regularly showed affection for his son. Then there was my friend Gregg, who voluntarily confessed to his dad that we'd been jumping off the top bunk, which he knew wasn't allowed. I would never have mentioned it to my dad, or I would have just lied to stay out of trouble, and I thought for sure Gregg was gonna get it.

"Buddy, we talked about this. I'm worried somebody's going to break an arm. Having a cast is not as much fun as you think," his father said.

Buddy . . . I'm worried . . . That was a real eye-opener for an eight-year-old boy. And then, years later, there was Gregg's eleventh birthday party.

From kindergarten to the sixth grade, I attended the University Elementary School (UES). A "lab school" run by UCLA's Graduate School of Education, UES is located on the north side of the university's campus, on four acres with trees everywhere and a stream running through the length of the campus. The students at UES were a mix of kids from all socioeconomic backgrounds, including me, the son of a once-struggling actor. My friend Gregg's father was also an actor. Byron Morrow was not a name most people would know, but if you were watching television or went to the movies during that era you would immediately recognize him. He was even in *Star Trek: The Original Series*, appearing as Admiral Komack in "Amok Time," the second-season episode in which Spock introduces the Vulcan salute for the first time.

It was Gregg's eleventh birthday, and we were all meeting on a Saturday afternoon at the entrance to UES before caravanning off to a bowling alley. All of my friends were there, including Danny, a sweet, soft-spoken kid, and Tommy, the class bully. For some reason Danny and Tommy got into a tussle, and Tommy flung Danny's present for Gregg into the bushes. Tommy had jumped me once on the schoolyard, and it was incredibly humiliating as the other kids watched him push my face into the grass. Now Danny was the target, and his perfectly wrapped present ended up in the mud. Danny started crying, and Gregg's dad stepped in. He picked up the present and sat down with Danny on one of the benches at the entrance to the school. He found a leaf on the ground and used it to clean the mud off the gift wrapping while explaining to Danny that it was like magic—you could use the leaf to wipe off the mud and anything left over would fade into the background. We all stood around watching Byron Morrow do this for Danny. It was obvious that the mud had not totally disappeared, because the background of the wrapping paper was white. It didn't matter.

Wow, I thought to myself. *So that's how it's done.*

4

A CASTLE OF OUR OWN

I WAS LEANING AGAINST A WALL, peeling the label off my third bottle of beer and wondering if dragging myself to my ten-year high school reunion had been a mistake, when Nancy Plotkin walked in. It took me a minute to recognize her. She looked ultra cool with her short haircut, black leather jacket, and black skinny jeans. I tossed my beer bottle and walked over.

Until then, the University High class of 1974 reunion had been a tedious affair filled with real estate agents, attorneys (like me), and accountants. Learning about Josh Rosen's conversion to Hasidism was probably the most memorable highlight of the evening. While some of my classmates shared pictures of their kids, the former varsity superstar showed off his wooden box containing an etrog, a yellow citrus imported from Israel. That excitement was enough to send me out to the foyer for a needed break and some label peeling.

Since moving back to L.A., I managed to survive law school and pass the state bar exam (I was relieved) and find a position in a law firm (my father was thrilled). The 1980s started looking even better when Nancy walked in. She'd been working as a freelance illustrator in New York, which immediately led to a discussion of our favorite artists. Talking to her was easy, as if we had just picked up from where we left off in Mr. Simcox's biology class. We would have continued the banter had she not been called away by a pack of her girlfriends, leaving me to grab another beer. Twenty minutes later she reappeared, and we made the rounds. I was buzzed enough to introduce her as my wife, which didn't seem to faze her as she continued to smile and shake hands as Nancy Nimoy.

Introducing her around as my wife just slipped out of my mouth as a joke. Then again, I was twenty-seven and like some of my other high school colleagues was thinking about settling down. I'd dated all through law school, then took the bar exam and headed off to the Costa del Sol in Spain with a couple of buddies. Everything seemed different when I came home. I was starting to think about my future and about finding a serious relationship. I wasn't going to pick up with the women I knew before I left town. They just didn't seem to be good matches for me. I was looking for something different.

A friend had suggested making a list of what I was looking for in a significant other, that I needed to be specific and put that energy out there because it was the only way I was ever going to find someone I liked.

So I made a list.

Another friend said that a list was ridiculous, because the minute you specify what you're looking for, you limit yourself and turn a blind eye to someone who could be just what you need. As a compromise, I finished my list then threw it away.

Nancy certainly checked a lot of boxes: college educated, artistic, Jewish. (Membership in one of the Twelve Tribes of Israel wasn't a must-have for me, but it was nice nonetheless.) My parents approved; my grandparents were smitten. By October, we were engaged. She fit right in with the rest of the family, which was certainly true on the cool and sunny morning of January 16, 1985. Spirits were high on that day as we all stood on Hollywood Boulevard just east of Highland Avenue. Dad was about to receive a star on the Hollywood Walk of Fame. I have a box full of photos of the event. We were all there: my sister Julie and her husband; my mother, Sandi; Dad's parents, Max and Dora; my fiancée, Nancy Plotkin. Grandpa Archie was gone, and Grandma Ann, suffering from dementia, clung to Dora. *Star Trek* creator Gene Roddenberry and members of the cast also attended, although for some reason I don't have a picture with Bill Shatner. There were plenty of fans and press on hand. It was a good day for Dad, and the star was well deserved.

One of the things I especially love about that day was that Nancy was giddy with excitement. She was all smiles in her red wool dress with black plaid. The *Trek* cast, the fans, the paparazzi—Julie and I had seen it all before. Nancy as a newbie was just beside herself from all the attention—a sweet reminder of what my family had been feeling almost twenty years before in 1966, when Mr. Spock and *Star Trek* quickly transformed our lives. The other interesting detail about that day is that Dad's star happened to be located right at the corner of Hollywood and Cherokee Avenue, just steps away from the Cherokee Book Shop.

In June of that year, eleven months after the Uni High reunion, Nancy and I were walking down the aisle. Her parents insisted on a hideous wedding of two hundred people at the Beverly Wilshire Hotel. We were children of the '70s and wanted to celebrate our union in a more natural setting. Her father made clear that a wedding is basically the bride's parents' party. In retaliation, we invited everyone we could think of, pushing the total to 325. And we each brought our own rabbi.

We were already living together, having months before squeezed Nancy's stuff into my one-bedroom Westwood apartment. We even made space for her drafting table so she could continue her illustration work while I went off each morning to the firm where I had started my legal career. Many weeknights were spent at that Century City law office, where Nancy tested the limits of the photocopy machines as she created mind-blowing collages and illustrations that were regularly featured in *LA Weekly*.

After we were married, we were ready to find more suitable living space so we could think about starting a family.

For weeks we drove around West Los Angeles neighborhoods looking for a home. There was very little inventory, and the houses that were for sale were beyond our means. Most of West L.A. had been developed in the 1930s during a revival of the Spanish Colonial tradition—small but quaint homes with white stucco walls, red clay tile roofs, and wood floors. The streets were lined with magnolias, jacarandas, and pine trees, and the public schools were good, which was why these neighborhoods were so popular and expensive.

Undeterred, we scoured the listings and spent our evenings driving around, looking for something trashed enough to be affordable. Then my mother told me that Joe, her hairdresser, and his girlfriend were breaking up and wanted to sell their rental property pronto. That's the way it goes sometimes—you do all that legwork, and in the end it comes down to your mother's hairdresser.

It was a hot summer morning when I met Joe Veltri at the white stucco house on Clarkson Road. This was the neighborhood south of Pico Boulevard and west of Rancho Park. I knew it well, because

Grandma Ann and Grandpa Archie had lived near there when I was a kid. The house sat up from the street on a small hill. Several roof tiles were cracked or missing, paint was peeling off the stucco facade, the faded canvas awnings were tattered, the front lawn was dead. So far so good.

The tenants were away and we weren't supposed to go in, but Joe was a New York tough guy turned L.A. hairdresser who couldn't care less. The stench hit us the second we walked through the door.

"Smells like somebody hasn't been using their kitty litter," I said. Joe shrugged.

Three well-fed cats came out to greet us. One got spooked, jumped up on the mantel, and knocked over a glass bowl full of marbles that shattered, colored glass rolling everywhere. I tried to corral them with my foot.

"Don't worry about it," said Joe.

The house had that typical run-down-rental look: the walls were yellowing, the wood floors were scratched and discolored. The dirty yellow kitchen screamed for a grease cleaning. The purple tile on the bathroom floor had a long crack like an earthquake fault running right down the middle. It was a small house with two bedrooms and one bath that most people would have written off as a dump. My excitement was growing.

Muttering something about cats and fleas, Joe led me outside up the slight incline through the backyard, past the weeds and the mangled fruit trees. When we turned around, I was struck by the way the back of the house glowed in the morning sun. There was a pathetic homemade back patio that only a sledgehammer could fix, but it didn't hide the charm of this modest but exquisite old Spanish home that had suffered years of neglect.

Looking at the house from the yard gave me a feeling of déjà vu I occasionally get when I see things that remind me of old L.A. Sometimes when I'm driving around town and come across Spanish houses or old railroad tracks or oil wells, I get this flashback to the city of my youth. It's like I'm looking through a portal back in time. I get goosebumps when this happens, because I love L.A. from that period—when there were still pony rides on Pico Boulevard, when traffic would stop for long freight trains crossing Sawtelle, and the Olympic Drive-In Theatre was still standing with its huge, goofy mural of the perfect California couple surfing the perfect wave.

Standing in that backyard also brought back nostalgic feelings for my grandparents, because their backyard had the exact same layout, with a detached garage that had a walk-through side door. Suddenly I was overcome with childhood feelings of safeness and family and love.

I struggled to stay cool, because I didn't want Joe to sense my excitement. I'd been one of the worst mock negotiators in law school, always giving away the store by playing my hand too early—it was downright embarrassing. But I did have the benefit of knowing that Joe and his girlfriend were done and in a hurry to sell.

"Joe, the place needs so much work. The floors have to be refinished, it needs paint inside and out, the kitchen hasn't been updated, and what's the deal with the plumbing and electrical?"

"I don't have time for all that shit. We're selling it as is. Are you interested or not?"

You can't take the hustler out of the hairdresser.

"Jesus, Joe. I dunno. It's just so run down I'm not sure Nancy's gonna go for it. Even if she did, it's gonna take some serious cash just to fix it. Let me know what you can do on the price, and I'll see if I can make it happen."

Having repeatedly driven that neighborhood with Nancy, I knew exactly what the Clarkson Road house was worth, even as a distressed sale, but I wanted to see if Joe knew.

He didn't.

Escrow closed quickly, and with a minimum of expense we fixed the floors, installed a skylight in the kitchen, and painted the place. The plumbing and electrical upgrades would have to wait. The stove was trashed, so I brought over a vintage Gaffers and Sattler I acquired from the owner of my apartment building in Westwood. We bought a golden retriever puppy and named her Birdy. We rescued a calico kitten and named her Stella. We threw a barbecue where friends came to help dig the trenches needed to install sprinklers and a drip system. It took us all day with pickaxes and shovels. My hands were beat to hell when we were done. After the gardener's crew installed the plumbing, it took only weeks before the lawn and the fruit trees showed signs of life.

It was a dream house, and we were incredibly happy to be living there. At night Nancy and I would watch *Star Trek* reruns, as she had never seen the show. Then we'd lie in bed holding each other, repeating how lucky we were—lucky to have found each other, to have good families and good careers, to have found such an incredible place to call home. It seemed as if anything was possible . . .

Except getting pregnant. It was three years and a pile of money to the fertility doctors for the scans, the ultrasounds, the injections, the inseminations. It's such a racket when there's no clear medical diagnosis to account for the problem. One doctor suggested I stop smoking pot, which I was then using to deal with the stress of working at the law firm. Another doctor said there were plenty of people smoking too much pot and having plenty of children, so I didn't see it as an issue. The pressure and the tension brought on by our inability to conceive was straining our marriage.

We finally took a break from all the hassle and presto! Nine months later our daughter Maddy was delivered into my arms on a Wednesday afternoon in April 1990. We brought home Jonah (yes, we named him Jonah!) almost exactly two years later. My parents were divorced by this time and were no longer communicating with each other, so we would regularly take the kids to see each one or have them over on separate occasions. My mother doted on them. Dad was less comfortable holding or interacting with them, though always willing to try.

Thankfully Maddy wasn't the least bit jealous when Jonah arrived. She liked to hold him in her lap while he slept. I have Polaroid pictures of her snuggling him with her lopsided smile and curly brown hair. When we tried to take him away, she threw a fit. "My baby!"

For the most part I was able to balance my career and parenting responsibilities. I enjoyed my time with the kids, who were just so freaking cute and fun and squeezable. Maddy with her curls and adorable outfits. Jonah with his fat head and happy-go-lucky attitude. I just wanted to hug and kiss those guys all the time. "Look what I got, Ma. Look what I got!" I said to my mother as I bent down and squeezed Maddy in my arms. But there were also times when I would be sitting in Daddy and Me classes thinking I needed to get back to my office to catch up on piles of paperwork.

When Maddy was six and Jonah was four, we temporarily moved out of Clarkson Road so that we could add a bedroom, a bathroom, and a family room on the backside of the house. (That hideous homemade back patio collapsed in minutes.) We converted the garage into an art studio for Nancy and a music room for me—and, in the years to come, for me and Jonah. The week we moved back in, the kids kept playing a video of the Who's performance at the Rock and Roll Circus. They played it over and over on our new TV in our new family room as they laughed and sang and jumped and somersaulted on the couch. Their favorite song was, of all things, "A Quick One, While He's Away" a ten-minute, mostly frantic, high-energy opus that perfectly fit our excitement of having just moved back in. Jonah told me years later it was Keith Moon's supercharged performance that inspired him to become a drummer.

Everything was fresh and new on Clarkson Road. With the help of my father, I had even managed to move on from seven years of entertainment law to a television directing career. By the '90s, Dad and I were getting along pretty well, which I knew had a lot to do with the new life he was enjoying with his second wife, Susan. He was also supportive of my desire to move on from my career in law and pursue a more creative and satisfying professional life.

After the demise of EMI America, a record label I had been working for, I spent some time attending acting classes with Jeff Corey, a terrific actor and dad's former acting instructor. The class turned on something deep inside of me—I could've jumped out of my skin I was so excited about the work the students were putting up and the way Jeff coached them. Before long I realized there was no way I was going to spend the rest of my working life negotiating deals and pushing paperwork. Dad was all about having passion for one's work. I spent months in Jeff's class putting up plenty of work myself, though I knew that directing actors from behind the camera was what I really hungered to do. (One actor in the family was enough).

While taking night classes in filmmaking, weekends were sometimes spent with Dad breaking down scripts I was about to direct. He helped me secure assignments on *Star Trek: The Next Generation*, and after that the hustle was on to find and create more work. We even made a new *Outer Limits* episode together: "I, Robot," a remake of an episode Dad was in back in '64, only this time Dad was playing the starring role and I was directing. In just a few years I was lucky enough to be working on soundstages with groups of talented people creating one-hour dramas for every major studio. Life at home was filled with family gatherings and parties, sleepovers and jam sessions, the kids, the animals, and the fruit trees.

And the slow but steady decline of our marriage. When the kids came along the focus was more and more on them and less on Nancy and Adam. And then there was the intensity of my new career and my continued use of cannabis to deal with all the stress.

Directing single-camera one-hour dramas translates to long days on set and months on location, all of which took its toll. I worked in Vancouver, Toronto, San Francisco, San Diego, Chicago, New York, Miami, and Auckland, New Zealand. Nancy and the kids were at home in L.A. When I was away Nancy struggled to keep it all together. When I was home we didn't talk about the important things. There were fights and misunderstandings over issues with extended family and financial matters. There was mutual neglect. Nancy and I grew further apart. She focused on the kids, her friends, her illustration career. I focused on my job. Two years and three marriage counselors later, it was clear we were living totally separate lives.

Maddy was nine by then; Jonah was seven. Even though the situation was miserable, there was no way I was going to leave. I simply wasn't ready to walk away from our house on Clarkson Road. I wanted to be there with the kids, to watch them grow, to help them and to hang with them. I stuck it out for five more years, to the point where I was high on weed all the time trying to kill the pain or fill an empty hole or flee from my problems or whatever it is that turns people into potheads, drug addicts, and alcoholics.

I always started my day with the best of intentions. If I was in between directing jobs, I would wake up, exercise, get the kids up and off to school, shower, eat breakfast, then go out to my backyard office. Once there I would start the phone calls to my agents and producers to push for more directing work, which by then was starting to taper off due in no small part to my pot problem. By noon I often found myself high, again, not quite knowing how that happened. Why was I constantly picking up my pipe or the bong or a joint when I needed to be clearheaded? My failing marriage, a downturn in my directing career, my pot addiction. My life had become unmanageable. And then one day, while I was stoned and the kids were eleven and thirteen, they were finally old enough to notice that there was something wrong with Dad.

5

THE ROAD OF HAPPY DESTINY

THE VERY FIRST ALCOHOLICS ANONYMOUS MEETING I ever attended was with my father, when he was newly sober. This was in the mid-'90s, when Dad was well into his second marriage. He told me he was happier than he'd been in years, yet he couldn't understand why he was still drinking. So he called someone he knew in AA and started going to meetings. One day he invited me to go with him to a Saturday men's meeting at the community center in La Cienega Park. It wasn't clear why he invited me. Maybe he was proud of the work he was doing in the program and wanted to show me. Maybe this was his way of saying I too should join the program. Or maybe he just thought this would be a good father-son outing, as it had been thirty years since the good ole days of M'Goos pizza on Hollywood Boulevard.

The meeting took place in a well-lit room with lots of windows, linoleum floors, and rows of plastic chairs facing the speaker's podium. There must have been thirty guys there, mostly an older crowd. Dad introduced me to some guy in a sport coat, a heavyset man who was all smiles and seemed to take an interest in me. Maybe this was Dad's sponsor? Or maybe it was some kind of intervention and Dad sought his help to bring me into the program? Or maybe the guy just liked me? In any case, he gave me the creeps.

As usual, Dad and I sat in the back. We listened to someone at the podium sharing about his "experience, strength, and hope." Years later I would learn what those three elements translated to: what it was like while they were out there drinking and/or using (the "drunkalog"), what happened to make them decide to go sober, and what their life was like now in recovery. Then the meeting opened up to group sharing, in which guys raised their hands and shared about their own experience or commented on something the speaker had said that resonated with them.

This was all foreign to me, all these men sharing about their lives in recovery. Dad didn't share. I probably should have been impressed by their vulnerability and openness, but I wasn't paying too much attention, because I was fuming about something that happened at the beginning of the meeting—that something being the recitation of the twelve steps of recovery. I had heard about the twelve steps but never knew what they were. I listened with half interest when someone read them out loud. When he got to steps eight and nine—*Made a list of all persons we had harmed, and became willing to make amends to them all* and *Made direct amends to such people wherever possible, except when to do so would injure them or others*—I was furious.

This program is such bullshit, I thought. My dad was pretending to be in AA, but apparently he got to skip the steps in which he was supposed to apologize for all the stuff he pulled, all the arguments we had, all the times we knocked heads when Johnnie Walker was in the room. I was thinking in particular about the time back in '85 when we were arguing in the living room of the house on Cashmere Street in Westwood. Dad had been drinking, and to emphasize a point he was making he stood up and got in my face. The resentment of Abraham was definitely present during that episode.

"Step back, Dad."

"Why should I?"

"Because I'm not comfortable with you this close to me. Step away from me."

We were standing in a dark corner, and I could smell the whiskey. Up to that moment, I had always believed there was no comparison between pot and alcohol: you can maintain while under the influence of weed more so than you can on booze. While we were standing there, I could see that it really didn't make any difference, that Dad was just like me—trying to fill some big black hole or trying to escape from some unpleasant feelings.

He finally moved away and sat back down. Then I pleaded with him to take some responsibility for the trouble between us. "Just give me an inch, Dad. That's all I'm asking for. Just take an inch of responsibility for what's happening here. I'm begging you." He refused.

Then there was our telephone conversation in '88 when he was in Toronto directing *The Good Mother*. He was sticking it to me, because I was still practicing law at the time but was in between jobs and having trouble finding another gig. (There were too many damn attorneys in this town chasing too few openings in entertainment law.) Throughout the whole conversation I could hear the ice sloshing around in the glass. He was feeling low during this period, because he was finalizing the divorce from my mother and things hadn't gone well. That, plus the fact that he was making a bummer of a movie about a mother who loses custody of her daughter. I was trying to explain what I was doing, all the contacts I was running down, all the meetings and interviews I had lined up, but he wasn't impressed. He kept insisting people were "blowing smoke up my ass."

It went on like this for some time until I finally said, "Dad, when you start in like this, you're not being helpful."

"You're my son and you will stand up and take it."

On that occasion I had no intention of allowing myself to be tied up and blindfolded. "I don't think so, Dad. I think you've got the wrong guy. I think you're just being mean because you're so miserable. I feel sorry for you."

"Sorry for me? Why?"

"Because you're obviously in so much pain."

"What are you talking about? I'm sitting on top of the world!"

"I don't think I've ever seen you this miserable."

It was all so sad, and I just had to move on. After these kinds of exchanges, I would hide away and light up so I could let it all go. Then, of course, in the days and weeks that followed, an image of Spock would inevitably pop up somewhere—in an article or on a magazine cover or on someone's windshield sunshade. Instead of the pride I'd always felt for Spock, I would have these mixed feelings about him. Now here I was at an AA meeting, finding out about the ninth step, which caused all those memories to start rattling around in my head. *This is complete and total bullshit. What kind of phony program is this? Where do I file a complaint? Who do I talk to at "the central office"?* I was so angry I felt nauseated and started sweating.

After the meeting, Dad turned to me and said, "So, what did you think?"

"It was great."

It would be many years later, when I was deep into my own recovery, that it became perfectly clear there was no way my dad could ever make a ninth-step amends to me. No way. That conclusion would also become perfectly acceptable, although it would take years of work before I could get to that place in my head.

It was in 2004, just about eight years after I went with my father to that meeting, that I decided to go sober. I immediately moved out of our house on Clarkson Road and into a nearby apartment. In addition to drying out, it was also time to move on from a marriage that was long over. It seems to be commonly accepted that making major life decisions should be avoided in the first year of recovery, but I didn't know that at the time, and it just felt like something I needed to do. Unfortunately, I was also separated from the cutest kids on the planet. They were so angry and upset that they refused to come visit me let alone stay with me. I was in so much pain that going to a twelve-step meeting suddenly seemed like a good idea. There was an MA meeting for marijuanaholics in my neighborhood at a local church, but once I got hold of a meeting directory, I discovered there were one-hour AA meetings, all day long, seven days a week, all over L.A. Even though I never considered myself an alcoholic, it soon became obvious there were a lot of people at those meetings whose DOC (drug of choice) was something other than booze.

That first twelve-step meeting I attended when I started my recovery was at St. Bede's Church, located near my new apartment and just blocks from the first house Dad bought on Palms Boulevard in Mar Vista. The meeting room at St. Bede's was fairly similar to the meeting at La Cienega Park all those years before—linoleum floors, overhead fluorescents, and picnic chairs, this time arranged in semicircle rows facing each other. And there was also a guy in a sport coat. Otherwise, there were no professional-looking types, no celebrity alcoholics or addicts you read about in the magazines. (I heard that Ringo hosted a private meeting with other celebrities. I was sure it was in some beautiful home up in Bel Air or maybe Beverly Hills. I'm pretty sure this meeting was nothing like Ringo's.)

When I walked in, a bald guy came up and said hello. I soon learned "greeter" was a commitment that people took to welcome others into the meeting. I told him I was new, and he said to take down phone numbers and get to know people. I wasn't sure I was ready for all that.

"Does anyone want to take a newcomer chip for their first thirty days of sobriety?" said Danny, a heavyset, scruffy-looking guy who had a box full of what looked like poker chips. A woman stood up and said, "Hi, I'm Sarah." Everyone repeated back, "Hi Sarah. Welcome!" and started clapping. She went over to Danny, who gave her the chip and an awkward hug. "Anyone else?"

I figured it was my turn, so I stood up. "Hi, I'm Adam." "Hi Adam. Welcome!" I walked over to Danny, took the chip, and let him hug me. Other people took chips for sixty days, ninety days, and six months of continuous sobriety. Then they celebrated birthdays for continuous years of sobriety, brought out a cake with candles, and sang the birthday song.

After the chips and the cake, a surfer named Jason spoke for twenty minutes about what it was like to be a pothead, how he hit bottom and found sobriety, and what his life was like now. Other than the fact that he no longer wanted to smoke pot, very little of what he said resonated with me.

It was only weeks later, when a young woman was the guest speaker at an AA meeting in West Hollywood, that I finally heard something that made a lasting impression. "Whether you stay sober or not," she said, "the twelve steps of recovery are tools you can use to help you live your life when challenging situations come your way."

This totally appealed to me; it was something I could relate to; it was part of my Master Plan. I didn't consider myself an alcoholic or a die-hard drug user, so what I was looking for was "AA Lite." I probably didn't need to follow all the rules. I'd only be there until things settled down and I was back on my feet. My plan was to dry out for a while, get the tools I needed from the program, then return to a life of more moderate recreational weed and alcohol use.

I've been modifying that plan one day at a time for the past twenty years as I've continued to stay sober.

During my first year of sobriety, my new BFF in recovery, Justin Valdivia, took me to some of the hipper meetings in town. I had met Justin in a writing class. There were five guys and fifteen women in that class, and I was feeling pretty comfortable being the only person writing about recovery. Then Justin joined the group, and in his first class, he brought in material about his own drug use and recovery. Midthirties, longish dark hair, black Dickies pants, black Converse, no socks. He immediately annoyed me, because he read a funny story about the ways he would fake prescriptions to feed his opioid habit. He would impersonate doctors over the phone, and the personas were hilarious, especially the Russian doctor. I really wanted to hate this guy for moving in on my territory, but I couldn't stop laughing.

After class, he invited me to go to a meeting. He'd been sober for four years, and I soon followed him to mixed AA meetings in Santa Monica, Brentwood, and Beverly Hills. These weren't like the meetings at La Cienega Park or St. Bede's. They were packed with some pretty good-looking addicts and alcoholics. Sometimes they had the feeling of a fashion show—a place to see and be seen. At other times they also had heartbreaking shares from young moms who talked about losing custody of their kids because of their drug and alcohol problems. Some had been incarcerated and had to release their kids to adoption never to see them again. This always put things in perspective and gave me a sense of gratitude, because no one was taking Maddy and Jonah away from me. I was more determined than ever to stay in their lives, despite the fact that they refused to set foot in my "stupid apartment."

My apartment. There are some dumpy-looking apartment buildings on Venice Boulevard in West L.A., but mine was OK. A well-kept, new two-story in Mar Vista, it had a contemporary white stucco Spanish look, tall trees in the front, and a small waterfall in the courtyard. And it was exactly fourteen minutes door-to-door to the kids.

When coming "home" to my new place, I would often pull into my parking space, turn off the engine, and sit there.

Sitting in my car was something I did a lot in those early days. It was an attempt to decompress from all the challenges of my life now that reaching for my stash was no longer an option. I also sat there because I didn't want to face the emptiness of my two-bedroom apartment sparsely furnished by the Swedes. After six months of sleeping on an air mattress, I had finally acquired a Badruka bed, a Laderlappen couch, and a Skogstokig dining set. Then came the Faktiskt twin beds for the kids' bedroom complete with Vabba bedding—pink for Maddy, blue for Jonah—all of which went unused.

"How did I get here?" I would ask myself as I sat in the car.

Then again, I knew exactly how I got there: thirty years of pot-smoking, the disintegration of my marriage, and the crash and burn of a once promising directing career due in no small part to my pot problem and some character defects.

"They never complain about the work, just the attitude," my agent used to say. The work was usually good, but my bad attitude led me to just enough trouble that my services were no longer required and *poof!* Career number two gone.

I felt stuck in the belly of the whale, hitting my bottom just like that poor schmuck in the Book of Jonah sinking to the bottom of the sea. I knew I needed to leave my marriage and to get sober for myself and for my kids, but I didn't know it was going to be this excruciating. I tried to explain everything to Maddy and Jonah, to reassure them that I still loved them and would always be close by, but none of that seemed to matter; they just wanted me back. There *was* friction between the kids and Nancy after I left, but I was the one who made the move, so they were much angrier with me. Sometimes I couldn't stand the loneliness without them, and late at night I'd sneak back into the house on Clarkson Road just to watch them sleep. Just to sit and watch them.

Jonah was twelve when I moved out, Maddy fourteen. She could be sweet and loving one minute, full of rage the next. "Piss and vinegar," Nancy liked to say. I could tell when she was upset because she would send me little signals, like the email that read, "I hate you, I hate you, I HATE YOU!"

On days when she was calm and sad, I would come visit her and sit with my arms around her while she cried, begging me to tell her we could still be a family. "Please don't tell me it's over, Dad, please say it's not over, please, Dad, please."

I just sat there holding her, telling her that everything would be OK, hoping that the day would come when things would, in fact, be OK.

There were also ups and downs with Jonah. We'd be at the beach together having a nice time when suddenly he'd start pleading with me, telling me that if I really loved him, I would come home. We'd get out of the water and I'd be drying him off as he stood with his long, wet hair, his big rosy cheeks and colorful board shorts, when suddenly he'd start crying. "Why did you leave, Dad? We had such a good family and then you just left. Why did you leave me with Mom and Maddy? Just tell me."

I couldn't tell him. How could I tell him everything that happened? "There are a lot of reasons, Jonah. Too many to try and explain right now. But I am so sorry. And I miss you too. And I want to be with you."

"And you promised you would be at the house every day. You promised me and sometimes I don't see you and what am I supposed to do?"

I tried to hold him like I did with Maddy, but he wouldn't let me. It got to a point where after all that turmoil with the kids I actually considered going back, if just for them. Just to make them feel better and to stop them from hating me. But when things calmed down and I was alone, I'd pull into my parking space at my apartment, turn off the engine, and think it all through, trying to figure out if I could do it, what it would be like to go back to Clarkson Road. Then I'd replay the film in my mind, all the messed-up things that happened in my marriage that led me to a life of isolation where I just wanted to be high and numb all the time. I hated leaving them and the fallout was miserable. But I couldn't go back.

"Adam, in a year's time your life will be totally different," a woman friend in recovery told me. I had no idea what that meant or what my life would look like. All I knew was that I sometimes felt like Spock when he mind-melded with the Horta, the rock monster who had lost her children. All Spock could feel from her was pain, pure unfiltered agony.

"I hate feeling my feelings," I heard someone say at an AA meeting. Yeah, sometimes feelings can suck, and now that I wasn't drinking or using, it was like I was feeling everything all the freaking time. Why did I have so many feelings? How was a program of recovery going to help me deal with them? How was I going to help my kids with their feelings?

It was destiny that gave me some insight into the connection between feelings and recovery. Happy Destiny—a tiny bookstore in the Westside neighborhood of Venice crammed with pamphlets, posters, and medallions all related to various twelve-step programs. I was looking for a book called *Living Sober*, which was required reading at one of my meetings, when a woman came out from the back and asked if I needed help.

Yeah, can you tell me why recovery is so freaking painful?

I told her I lived nearby but hadn't noticed the bookstore before. She said she'd been running the place for almost ten years to give back to the community and to the program that saved her life. "My name is Krystal, by the way."

"Hi, Krystal, I'm Adam."

The deep lines in her face indicated a life of hard living. Krystal was welcoming and kind in an I've-been-there sort of way, so it wasn't long before I was telling her my sob story about putting down the weed and the booze, and how I was struggling to move on from a loveless marriage while trying to stay connected to my kids. Krystal told me that putting down had forced me to deal with the challenges of "life on life's terms." She said I was growing all sorts of new feelings that had been in arrested development since my teen years, when I started using every day. Because of that, everything that was happening to me was going to seem overwhelming and intense.

I was growing new feelings. Like a potted plant.

All my life, whenever I had bad feelings about something, Mary Jane was there to numb me and take away the pain. During those teen years, when I started having trouble with my dad, I always ran to Mary Jane. Now I was going to have to learn to stop running and to deal with things on my own.

"And don't think you're going to think yourself out of the situation you're in," Krystal continued. "The mind that created the problem of addiction is not equipped to solve it. Just put your mind and your feelings aside for the moment. Put aside any grand plan you may have come up with and just concentrate on working the program." (How did she know about my Master Plan?) "And stay clear of new emotional entanglements—at least for a while."

"Emotional entanglements? Are you saying I can't date?"

"A new relationship is not going to bring you happiness, not now. It's the thirteenth step: newcomers should not be dating. You have way too much work to do on yourself before getting involved with someone else." As I was about to interrupt, she said, "You don't have to listen to me. You can take what you want from the program . . . but if you don't focus on yourself and do the work of recovery, you're just asking for trouble. You need to learn how to deal with your character defects, especially resentments. Without doing the work, you're never going to be mature enough for the real deal."

Listening to Krystal made me think of the Oracle of Delphi—like maybe I was getting some important information from a Greek priestess and I should just shut my mouth and open my ears. Happy Destiny did have the feeling of a sacred space. There was AA stuff everywhere— the cards, the books, the posters high up on the wall: Put Down the Magnifying Glass and Pick Up the Mirror; Work the Program from the Waist Up; and AA Has a Wrench for Every Nut Who Walks Through the Door.

"Remember, honey, you stopped growing when you started using, and now you're reacting to things the same way you did when you were a teenager. You need to give yourself some time to grow up."

Honey? This all seemed a little presumptuous. I mean, I had just met Krystal. How did she know what I needed?

"It's true for every alcoholic and addict," the Oracle continued. "You might also want to pay attention to uncomfortable situations with people who try your patience, especially family members, because those are the best times to let go of resentments. The people who challenge you the most offer the best opportunity for you to experience some personal growth."

Resentments, I would soon learn, are major obstacles to recovery. Anger, bitterness, and run-of-the-mill grudges arise out of wrongs committed against us, whether real or imagined. Clinging to resentments creates such havoc in recovery it's often described in AA as "drinking poison and waiting for the other person to die." It would take me just about four years of recovery before I was finally able to find resolution with the family figure against whom I had held my greatest resentments.

6

THE EL GRECO

When I moved back to L.A. in 1980 to attend law school, I quickly realized that living at my parents' house was not a good idea. I tried to stay out of Dad's way, I tried to make myself invisible, but issues kept cropping up like his missing tools and his confrontational attitude about John Lennon. And then there was my mother, who would use any pretext to knock on my door when I was deep into the law school casebooks or otherwise preoccupied.

"Adam, dinner's on the table."

"Adam, please lock up everything before you go to bed."

"Adam, is there a girl in there with you?"

I found an apartment at the El Greco. The two-story building was like a jewel in the crown of the Spanish architectural revival that was so much a part of Los Angeles. Built in 1929, the El Greco was named for the Spanish painter and modeled after his home in Toledo, Spain. It was one of the first apartment buildings in the Westwood Village, which was developed as a business district to support the new UCLA campus. When I first went to look at a vacant apartment, it looked like one of those buildings you could walk by a thousand times and never notice. Back then, the two-story facade was totally covered in green vines. Once it caught your eye and you took a closer look, you realized it was something special—definitely one of those portals into the past. The building had twelve units, a clay terra-cotta tile roof, a brick courtyard with koi pond, wood floors, and high-beamed ceilings. The apartment I rented on the second floor had a fireplace, a breakfast nook,

41

a view of the Plaza Theatre, and an astounding view of sunsets behind the Santa Monica Mountains.

After three glorious years there, some of that time with Nancy just before we were married, the El Greco was slated for demolition to make way for condos. One of the tenants had already started the process of designating the building a cultural historical landmark, which gave us some leverage in negotiating with the developer. We also organized all the tenants and simply refused to move out until something could be done about the building. The developer was more than happy to literally give us the building for free—provided we moved it off the lot. L.A. city officials then introduced us to Alternative Living for the Aging (ALA), a nonprofit organization that provided low-cost housing for seniors. Janet Witkin, ALA's executive director, managed to raise enough cash to buy an open lot in the Beverly Fairfax district of L.A., as well as hire an architect and a contractor to relocate and restore the building.

And so, in the middle of a fall night in 1985, Janet and I watched as a roofless El Greco, which had been cut into four separate sections each sitting on a series of dollies, rolled down Tiverton Avenue, made a left turn onto Wilshire Boulevard, and then continued its historic journey four miles east. (It was from my apartment at the El Greco, and with Janet's blessing, that I acquired the Gaffers and Sattler vintage stove that I brought to our new home on Clarkson Road.)

The following year, with the renovation complete and the El Greco ready to house low-income seniors, there was going to be a grand reopening celebration. I asked Dad if he would be willing to contribute to the event by underwriting the appetizers and drinks that would otherwise come out of ALA's budget. This seemed like a logical request, as Dad had previously agreed to lend his name to a fundraiser to save the El Greco, an idea that became moot once we found Janet and ALA.

His answer was no.

"What? Why?" I asked.

"I don't feel comfortable contributing to this event. The only reason you're involved is so that the organizers can use you to get to me, and I don't want to encourage that kind of behavior."

His response was devastating, and I was extremely angry with him. I expressed my disappointment but kept myself from throwing a fit as much as I wanted to. That was too dangerous. Once I was able to recover and think about it, I felt strongly that this was another instance in which I should stand up for myself, to stand up to Abraham. In an attempt to keep things from spiraling out of control, I approached Dad and asked him if we could discuss this situation with a family therapist. Surprisingly, he agreed, even suggesting we go see Dr. Robert Kampman—an odd choice, as Dr. Kampman was, at the time, my mother's Beverly Hills psychiatrist. (Perhaps even odder that Kampman agreed to see us.)

Days later, on a weekday afternoon, we found ourselves sitting in the doctor's office on Lasky Drive. I explained my side of it, about my role in helping to save the building and Dad's belief that I was being manipulated to get him to donate. Dr. Kampman then turned to Dad, who looked very confident, as if he had thought this through and knew exactly what to say.

"The problem is, if I do this for Adam, then I have to do it for every other charity that comes to me off the street looking for money."

The room went silent as Dr. Kampman's eyes went wide.

The doctor seemed like a nice guy, but his office was a dump. The entire two-story building needed an upgrade—it smelled like old Beverly Hills. Kampman's office furniture was ancient. The chairs were wood framed with green Naugahyde seats. The wood was nicked and the seats creaked every time one of us moved. The place had a schmutzy feel to it—you could see dust particles floating around, lit up by the sunlight coming through unwashed windows.

Kampman's mouth began to move. "But, Leonard, all you have to say is that you did it for your son."

Dad responded immediately. "Yeah, OK, I get it," he said. "I get it."

My father looked as if he'd been hit by a sucker punch anyone else could have seen coming. He sat with his head bowed, like he had just been shamed. He seemed to be trying to figure his way out of this predicament, trying to come up with some other response, some way to save himself. I felt a tremendous sense of vindication when Dr. Kampman came to my defense. But watching my dad was like watching a cornered animal—I was soon overcome by a wave of sympathy for him. I was old enough to realize he simply did not have the tools to cope with this kind of thing.

I had seen this again and again. I knew he never had a close relationship with his own dad—that he always dealt with his mother, and she could be tough and withholding. (This was a woman who, as a young girl, had to hide in a hay cart to get the hell out of Ukraine during the pogroms, when the Cossacks were riding into town and killing Jews.) Dad didn't know how things between fathers and sons were supposed to work. He had no idea what to do when there was a difference of opinion. To make matters worse, this all took place at the end of 1986, which had been a roller-coaster year for my father. Although *Star Trek IV* opened to critical and commercial success, that year also saw his split from my mother and the beginning of their messy divorce. My parents' marriage had been on the rocks for years. It's interesting that just like me years later, for whatever reason Dad waited to leave the marriage while proceeding to drink his way through to the bitter end.

As we sat there all I could feel was sympathy for my father. Then I felt this urgent need to help him, but before I could say anything, he stood up and walked right out the door. Kampman and I looked at each other in shock. I went after him.

"Dad, I'm sorry. Dad, wait."

He kept walking, down the smelly carpeted staircase to the shabby lobby and out the glass doors onto Lasky Drive.

I followed him to his car.

"Dad, wait, I'm sorry about all this. You don't have to do it. Really. Dad. You don't have to. It's going to be OK. Dad."

On this occasion, I had no problem being the one to say "I'm sorry." I hated it when he was angry with me.

"Dad, please. It's OK. Really."

Without looking at me, he slid into his maroon Mercedes, backed out of the parking space, and drove away.

7

PAUSE WHEN AGITATED

THE CANVAS AWNINGS WE'D INSTALLED held up well over the years. The purple bougainvillea was in full bloom. The olive tree I planted out front when we moved in now reached the second story. Everything looked idyllic outside the white stucco house on Clarkson Road that Sunday morning. Inside was a different story.

Nancy and I were getting into it. Nancy, my soon-to-be ex. It had been six months since I moved out and went into recovery. Six months since she helped me pack my suitcase, a clear sign that on this, at least, we agreed—after more than eighteen years of marriage, it was time for me to leave. Nancy was cool about letting me come to see the kids until we worked out a custody arrangement. I always went over with the intention of keeping things low key, but on that Sunday I needed to give her some pointers on housekeeping.

"The house is a mess."

"Says who?"

"Is the vacuum broken?" I asked. "I'm just curious. The cat litter is gross, and you might want to think about calling the exterminators to get rid of that beehive in the backyard."

"You don't live here anymore, so you have no right to tell me how to run my house. And for your information, the vacuum works just fine and nobody cares about the cat litter *or* the bees."

She was right—it wasn't my place to tell her what to do. I hated myself for opening my mouth and jeopardizing a visit with my kids by complaining about stuff that didn't matter, but I couldn't help it. Then again, it wasn't really about the vacuum or the litter or the bees. It was about the whole messed-up situation, because there was no shared custody and the kids still refused to even come over and hang out with me. It was still my "stupid apartment." Thanks to me, everything was spiraling out of control, and the only thing left to do was leave.

I bolted out the front door followed by Nancy, who was wielding a spatula as she was in the middle of making pancakes. Right behind her was a barefoot Maddy wearing the extra-large Mickey Mouse T-shirt she liked to sleep in. Jonah followed in a T-shirt and boxers, playing an unplugged Fender Stratocaster.

"Oh yeah, that's right," Nancy yelled from the porch as I walked down the driveway. "Now that you're 'Mr. Sobriety,' this is your answer for everything—just walk away. Go back to your apartment where you can be *by yourself.* What kind of example is that for the kids?"

The "Mr. Sobriety" jab hit a nerve, as I was finally learning how to get through my day without even thinking about a bong hit or two or three. Being sober for the first time in thirty years made me hypersensitive (feelings, anyone?). I was also agitated much of the time, a symptom of withdrawal. No pot meant more dreaming and less sleep, so I often felt "restless, irritable, and discontent," as AA's Big Book puts it. The result was an argument with Nancy that was now spilling out onto the street. When was I going to learn how to use the tools of recovery to avoid this kind of thing? When were the words of Krystal, the Oracle of Delphi, going to really sink in? When was I going to grow up and learn to let go of some of my resentments?

Along with Krystal, just the week before this altercation I was getting similar pointers from Justin as we waited for the Wednesday-night meeting to start.

"I can't tell you what to do, because you're going to have to find your own path, grasshopper," he explained. "But what I *can* tell you is that when I'm in highly charged situations, recovery tools such as 'Pause when agitated' and 'Restraint of pen and tongue' have saved me from myself repeatedly."

That seemed to make sense, but because I was more of your typical run-of-the-mill pothead than an alcoholic, I still wasn't sure all the other AA mumbo jumbo applied to me. "Let Go and Let God," "Easy Does It," "One Day at a Time." What the hell did all that mean? I had been seriously thinking of bailing on the meetings when I met Justin.

As with the Oracle, finding Justin was like finding the Rosetta Stone, the key to translating the Egyptian hieroglyphics of the program into advice that made sense to me.

"Sometimes it's a struggle and sometimes I totally blow it," he said. "That's when I have to take the time to forgive myself. Trust me, homie, once you begin to practice these principles, life gets a helluva lot easier. Ya dig?"

Even though Justin was twelve years younger than me, his years in the program led me to believe that he might know what the hell he was talking about. There was this low-key confidence about him that made me *want* to believe. That and the fact that he played a badass bass, wore a chic selection of secondhand clothes, and was popular among the recovery crowd. His arrival was perfect timing, because "pause when agitated" and "restraint of pen and tongue" were recovery tools I badly needed. Although sometimes I forgot to use them.

To Nancy's credit, she was the one who suggested that our divorce should be a modern one—that we should be civil toward each other and get along for the benefit of the kids. Sometimes the combination of my recovery principles and Nancy's enlightened point of view worked just fine. Sometimes we would both have these little relapses and the wheels would fall right off the bus.

"Answer me. What kind of example is that for the kids?" she yelled from the front porch as I stood on the sidewalk below.

"And what's with the furniture?" I yelled back. "You moved the dining room into the family room and the family room into the study. It doesn't make any sense."

"You came here to help Maddy with her homework, not comment on my housekeeping. I can put the dining room in the family room and the family room in the bathroom if I want to!"

The situation was hopeless, so I reached for some recovery principles—I got a grip on my mouth and walked toward my car.

That's when Maddy called out to me: "*Dad!* Don't leave!" Maddy was my skinny string bean, but she knew how to yell.

"I'm so sorry, honey, I can't stay."

Jonah chimed in: "Dad, listen to this riff."

He started playing a lick from AC/DC's "Back in Black." Normally I loved watching Jonah play. He had big shiny cheeks and long hair, and when he was shredding, it was like watching a short, twelve-year-old guitar god. In retrospect, his timing was brilliant. In the moment, it seemed ridiculous.

"Jonah, honey, can't you see we're a little busy here?"

"Don't stifle his creativity!" Nancy yelled.

It just so happened that there were two police officers down the street taking a burglary report from one of our neighbors. After hearing the commotion, they decided to walk over and see what was up. One headed toward Nancy, the other to me.

"What seems to be the trouble?" the first cop asked Nancy.

"Oh, there's no trouble. Just a little difference of opinion with a soon-to-be ex-husband who still thinks he runs the show even though he doesn't live here anymore!"

"Ma'am, I'm going to have to ask you to drop the spatula and calm yourself down."

She ignored him and started to walk down the driveway. The cop got in her way and said, "Stop right there."

"Why should I?"

"Because you look like you're trying to escalate things."

The second cop turned to me. "Sir, what is your name?"

"Adam. Adam Nimoy."

"Is this your home, Adam?"

"Well . . . I pay the mortgage and the property tax and the insurance while my ex treats it like a frat house and—"

"Adam, *do you live here?*"

"Ahhh, no, I don't."

"Then I suggest you get into your car and drive away."

The officer was younger than me, which made me feel stupid, like I should act more like an adult. I took a breath and focused on the cop's name badge. What at first looked like "LAPD" was actually the word "LADY." Officer Lady.

I called back to the kids. "Maddy and Jonah, don't worry, everything's going to be OK. I'll pick you guys up for school in the morning."

"Dad!" pleaded Maddy.

I felt terrible leaving them. I felt embarrassed in front of the cops. I felt resentful that once again, Nancy got to stay and I had to walk away from our beautiful house on Clarkson Road. I forced myself into my car and drove off, under the watchful eye of a cop named Lady.

8

YOU'LL LOVE MY MOTHER

My phone started ringing. It was my mother. I wasn't in the mood, so I let it go to voicemail. A minute later she sent her usual follow-up text message: "Adam, I left you a voice message. Will you listen to it please?"

"Adam, honey, hello. I thought you said you were coming over to get your boxes out of the back. I need that space to store some things to make room for the new furniture I bought. Are you still coming over? It would be nice to see you. You know how I count on it when you say you're going to be here. I know you're very busy, but it shouldn't be such a problem for you to take a few minutes to come over and see me. I did go through six hours of labor to bring you into the world. Well, OK, goodbye dear. This is your mother in case you didn't know."

My mother still lived on Cashmere Street in Westwood, in the house we moved into in 1968. It's the house that *Star Trek* bought—a major part of our transition from a struggling one-bathroom family to a much more comfortable lifestyle. Westwood is an upscale neighborhood, developed, much like the Westwood Village (and the El Greco Apartments), when the nearby UCLA campus opened in 1929. I was twelve when we moved, old enough to appreciate the difference between where we came from and where we ended up. I vividly remember the excitement I felt the day I moved into my new bedroom with my own small, yellow-tiled bathroom and my own exit out to our beautiful backyard. It was like winning the lottery.

Over the years not much had changed at the house on Cashmere Street. The front yard with its white picket fence and rosebushes. There was a lush green lawn and a jacaranda tree, and olive tree on either side of the walkway that led to the front door. The house was deceptive. From the front it looked like a typical California ranch style, with its stone facade and covered porch. When you walked inside, you realized it was built on a hill and was split-level—you had to walk downstairs, through the family room, to get even farther below to the pool and a cozy backyard filled with trees, potted plants, and flowers.

The interior was woodsy and welcoming, but by now everything was outdated and worn. The paint colors were straight from Monet: pink, yellow, and green walls, blue and purple trim, all of which had become scuffed and chipped and faded. The dining room and kitchen were wallpapered with images of yellow and orange flowers, but the paper was yellowing and peeling. Knickknacks and mementos were crammed everywhere: pottery mom made in the '70s, paperweights and ashtrays, baskets filled with dried flowers. Except for the living room couches, most of the furniture was some form of wicker.

There were two pictures of my parents still up on the wall, taken when dad was acting in the miniseries *Marco Polo* in China in the early '80s. They were at the Forbidden City palace in Beijing. Mom was standing in front of a dozen palace guards, smiling with her head thrown back and her arms outstretched as if to say, *Look at my glorious life!* In Dad's photo, he was dressed in full costume with his robes and long wig and Fu Manchu mustache, in character as Achmet, the scheming court counselor. All other evidence of my father had vanished—including my favorite artifact: the Spock ears encased in plastic that sat for years on the living room mantel.

I tiptoed past the kitchen, where Santiago, my mother's housekeeper, was cleaning. He was only in his sixties, but his stooped posture and lined face made him look much older. He was wearing pink dishwashing gloves as he polished a silver platter. I put my finger to my lips, determined to get my stuff out of the back of the house, out of what used to be the darkroom, and then make a clean getaway. Santiago nodded.

Just as I was walking through the downstairs family room headed for the back door, Mom called from her bedroom on the second floor: "Santiago! Is that you?"

I was so close.

"No, Mother, it's me. I'm going out back to get some of my boxes."

"Could you come up here, please?"

"Ma, I'm kinda in a hurry here."

"I need to talk to you."

I climbed the faded blue-and-pink stairs to Mom's suite. She was in her late seventies and in relatively good health but spent most of her time in bed. Her platinum hair had recently been coiffed courtesy of Joe Veltri, the hustler/hairdresser who sold me the Clarkson Road house all those years ago. She was wearing the pajamas I bought her for Mother's Day: white flannel with pink roses. The bed was littered with books, newspapers, magazines, and a white wicker tray with an espresso cup, a dish of caramels and chocolates, and a pill organizer.

Next to her bed sat Helen, the fiftyish Filipino woman who took care of my mother. Helen was working her knitting needles.

"It's nice to see you, stranger," Mom said, a stock line used to elicit guilt by Jewish mothers everywhere.

"Mother, I was just here last weekend," I said, leaning in to give her a kiss. "Hello, Helen. How's the patient doing?"

"She's fine. Still complaining about her eyes, but she'll be fine."

"I have double vision," my mother insisted.

"You see very well, Mrs. Nimoy."

"But I have to strain to do it!"

"Mother."

Helen packed up her knitting. "We have an appointment in two weeks with the eye doctor. I'll leave you to talk. I'll be downstairs."

As soon as Helen was out the door, I turned to my mother. "Why can't you be nicer to her? She's only here to help you."

"I like my privacy."

"But you can't take care of yourself."

"Yes I can. And whatever I can't do, Santiago can do for me."

"Santiago has enough to do, and he can barely handle that."

As if on cue, a crash came from the kitchen—the sound of a silver platter hitting the floor.

"It's all right, Mrs. Nimoy," Santiago called from below. "Nothing is broken. It's not broken, it's all right."

"Nothing is broken," I repeated to my mother.

The wallpaper behind her bed was completely stripped off. The old layers of paper and paint were exposed in a way that made the wall look like some sort of mixed media artwork. Six wallpaper samples were pinned up, all of them curled with age.

"Mother, when the hell are you going to cover this wall? It looks ridiculous."

"I haven't decided which pattern I want."

"Those samples have been up there for months. And the whole house needs repainting. You can't keep living like this—maintaining this house is way too much for you. You should have sold it after the divorce and moved into something smaller."

"The only way I'm leaving this house is on a gurney with a sheet over my face."

"That sounds a little melodramatic, don't you think?"

"Don't start with me."

"Fine."

"Can I get you some more coffee?" I asked, trying to defuse the situation. "Maybe something to eat besides chocolates and caramels? You know they constipate you."

I reached over to take the dish of candy, but she grabbed a chocolate and popped it in her mouth. "No, I'm fine, thank you. Listen, I know you're upset because you and Nancy got into it today."

"Who told you that?"

"Nancy. She called and gave me an earful about your behavior, which caused someone to call the police on you."

"Mother, no one called the police on me. Anyway, please stay out of it and stop talking to her."

"I love Nancy, but I know she can be tough. I think it's important to stay connected to her for the sake of the kids. That's also why I think the two of you should try to get along."

"Oh, you mean like you and Dad?" A cheap shot I immediately regretted.

"You and your sister were well into your twenties when your father left . . . on my birthday . . . when I was sick with the flu."

"Mother—"

"I just worry about those kids. Listen, did you get my check for Maddy's cello lessons?"

"Yes, Mom, I got the check. That was very kind of you. I appreciate it."

"Do you need one for Jonah's guitar lessons?"

"No, it's fine, really. But thank you."

"What's new? How's the dating going?"

"The dating? Oh, just wonderfully."

Despite Krystal's advice about avoiding emotional entanglements, I'd had a date with a woman I met at Junior's Deli on Westwood Boulevard. I couldn't help it. We were standing at the bakery section when she started chatting me up about the slow service. While we were talking, I was checking things off the list: attractive, age appropriate, and, as it turned out, Jewish. She also had grown kids, something I thought was essential so that prospective soulmates could relate to my challenges staying connected to Maddy and Jonah. All of that and she was hitting on me . . . at least I think she was hitting on me.

When I picked her up for our dinner date, she looked incredible in her faded jeans, leather jacket, and white blouse. Heads turned as we walked into a trendy restaurant in Venice, like we were a celebrity couple. After we ordered, I asked her where she grew up, which led her to a series of unflattering remarks about her mother, her father, and her ex-husband who'd been dead for six years. I couldn't wait to take her home.

"You should find a nice Jewish girl," my mother announced.

"I did. I married her. We grew apart. I self-medicated with marijuana. We're getting divorced."

"There must be plenty of Jewish women out there looking for a guy like you. You're a terrific catch."

"Maybe there are, Mom. I mean, who would pass up a divorced, middle-aged man who's in recovery struggling to get out of the ditch he's dug for himself?"

"A little melodramatic, don't you think?" Mom said with a smile as she popped a caramel into her mouth. "I think the real problem is you're too picky. Have you thought about the singles get-together at the shul after Friday-night services?"

"Ahh, no, Mom, I haven't. Friday nights are bad."

"Why? What else are you doing?"

"I have to groom my parrot. His feathers are molting. It's that time of the year."

"You don't have a parrot."

"I know, but it is molting season."

"All I'm saying is that when you're ready, I think you should look for someone who's, I don't know, well read and intelligent. A woman who graduated college. A woman who's in touch with what's going on in the world."

"You mean, like you, Mom?"

"Hey, I'm an intelligent person who's read fiction and nonfiction and can talk about what they've read. I don't want you to think of me as this, you know, this Jewish mother who cooks and cleans and whines."

"Cooks and cleans?"

My mother was in fact intelligent and kind, a woman with a big heart. She took very good care of me when I was a kid. After we moved to Cashmere Street, she had an open house policy—always said yes to having friends over to hang out, yes to sleepovers at a moment's notice. When my sister's friend Rainey had parents who were going through a contentious divorce, Mom said yes to having her stay with us until her parents could figure out the custody situation. She was the cool mom, a flower power priestess. She wore colorful summer dresses, loved all things paisley, and wore heart-shaped rose-colored glasses, and what used to be called a "fall"—a full-length wig that I absolutely adored. Mom always made sure there were dried, colorful flowers disbursed all over our house.

When my father left her after thirty-two years of marriage, she was devastated. Now, almost twenty years later, she was lying in bed medicating herself with prescriptions of Ambien, Klonopin, and Prozac. Sometimes she'd OD and we'd be out somewhere, at brunch with my kids for Mother's Day, and I'd notice her slurring her words and she'd have trouble standing. "I needed to take something. I couldn't sleep last night," she'd say. She'd be incoherent while I drove her home. Santiago and I would have to drag her into the house and put her to bed.

I loved her, I always loved her. But sometimes I wished she would snap out of it and stop playing the victim when she had her health, no money worries, and grandkids who adored her. Resentments were forming.

"Your mother is exactly who she's supposed to be," Justin would later tell me. "Your job is to accept her and be of service to her not to try and change her."

"Wait a minute," I said, "you talk trash about your mother all the time."

"My mother was a stripper, a hooker, an alcoholic, and a junkie. She's been that way all my life. But you're right, 'It Works If You Work It,' as we say in the program. When I shit-talk my mom, I'm not working it."

As I attended more meetings and heard more stories of recovery, **for** the sake of my mother and my own sanity, I was pretty much convinced I wanted to work it.

9

MY HIGHER POWER

SUNLIGHT BLAZED THROUGH the French-door windows into the family room, the family room we'd built when we added on to the house a decade earlier. The adjacent wood floors were beginning to buckle from the heat. The sun came through because the blinds were missing, Nancy having thrown them out when they became tattered and broken. I kept mentioning that the blinds needed to be replaced and the floors were going to buckle and the cat was going to have kittens, but there didn't seem to be any urgency to replace the blinds or fix the cat. It wasn't my business anyway.

Jonah was having trouble seeing the TV (because of all the aforementioned light streaming in). He was with his friend Yakie, and the two of them were sitting on the couch in their T-shirts and boxers, hair unbrushed. I had come over to walk the dogs and to remind Jonah that we had to go to shul for Shabbat services that morning. It was a required part of his bar mitzvah training—to see how services worked and how other people got bar mitzvahed. I'd been reminding him all week and all week he kept saying, "Yeah, no problem." I showed up at the house early to remind him again.

"I'll be back in an hour. You have to be dressed and ready to go. We'll drop Yakie off on the way. You have to be ready in an hour."

They stared at the TV as SpongeBob continued to annoy Squidward.

"Hello, Jonah. Did you hear me?"

"Yes, Dad, I heard you!"

"What did I just say?"

56

"I have to be ready in an hour."

"What time will it be in an hour? Jonah, look at the clock and tell me what time it will be in an hour."

He finally tore himself away from the TV. "Ten fifteen. I got it, Dad. Please let us watch."

I raced back to my place, took a shower, put on a shirt and tie, inhaled two scrambled eggs, then got back in my car and drove to the house. I was glad to be doing this with Jonah, to be taking him to shul so that we could see how everything worked, to be on top of it when it came to his turn. It was something I had been looking forward to. When I was younger, I actually liked sitting in shul with my father during the High Holy Days. There was something calming and meditative about it, and I loved picking up the Pentateuch, the five books of Moses, and reading the Bible stories as we sat there. I never really knew my father's thoughts about God or Judaism. Even so, it was nice to be sitting with him. It felt like we were carrying on a tradition—a small moment of connection to him. I was looking forward to having a similar experience with Jonah.

When I got back to the house, the boys had moved into Jonah's room and they were playing video games . . . in their T-shirts and boxers.

"What are you doing?" I asked.

"Mom said I didn't have to go."

"You just told me you'd be ready when I came back."

"I really don't want to go. I have Yakie here, and why would you think of taking me on a Saturday? It just ruins my weekend. Why can't we go during the week?"

"Because they don't have bar mitzvahs during the week," I said, trying to keep a grip.

Nancy came down from the master bedroom in her bathrobe, the master bedroom we built when we added on to the house.

"It's ridiculous that he has to go," she said. "It's too much for him to have to do." She was standing in the doorway of his room in her thick pink bathrobe and furry Garfield slippers.

I had recently heard a woman share at a meeting that she was responsible for her second thought and her first action. When things weren't going her way, her first thought was always *F you.* She said because she's an addict in recovery, she simply had to accept that about herself and hold on until that first thought and feeling passed so she could get to her second, more reasonable, more mature thought, which in turn would inform her action. That it's all about creating some space between the negative stimulus, your *F you* thought, and your first reaction. This was exactly what Justin was talking about when he advised me to "pause when agitated" in highly charged situations. "Count to ten, count to twenty" and "Don't just do something, sit there" were other AA-isms I had learned that seemed to fall into the same category.

Instead of opening my mouth and getting all pissed off and telling Jonah he was going whether he liked it or not, I decided to stop and breathe and think about all the work I had done up to that point. I took a moment to think about all the things I learned from Krystal and Justin and from the meetings and AA's Big Book and the shares. Because the New Me, the recovering pothead Adam, could then take the time to think about what was happening and what part Adam played in it and that maybe Adam should just say the Serenity Prayer and accept the things he cannot change and just keep his side of the street clean and let Nancy run the show and let Jonah deal with his own consequences. Let Jonah explain to the rabbi why he didn't show up to the service. That was all part of my second thought. Then I came across a third thought in which my mind said, *No, this is my twelve-year-old son, and he still needs a little direction from his dad. He needs some help. I'm his father and he needs my help and it would be perfectly in keeping with the program if I walked over to his side of the street and showed him how to put on a clean shirt and a sport coat so that he could fulfill his commitment.*

I turned to Nancy. "I've been reminding him about this all week."

"Well, you didn't remind me."

And I had to stop again. I needed to stop and get to my second thought once again, because I really didn't want to say something that would cause Nancy to head for the kitchen and grab that spatula.

"Can I just have a minute to work this out with Jonah, just let me talk to Jonah for a minute. Please?"

"Fine," she said as she turned and headed for the coffeemaker.

I took a deep breath then calmly got down on one knee.

"Jonah, you know you're supposed to go today. You know you're required to go because your bar mitzvah's in two weeks and they want you to go to one service before yours. You need to see how it's done so you have some idea of what's going to happen when it's your turn. I've been reminding you about this all week and you promised me you would go. I really want you to go with me."

"But it's two more weeks until my bar mitzvah, so why can't we go next Saturday?"

"Because next Saturday I'm coaching Maddy's soccer game and you know that. OK, here's the deal. I'm going with or without you, and you can explain to the rabbi when we meet with her next week why you didn't show up. So I'll see you later."

I got up to go. I didn't storm out, I just turned to go, because I can't do everything. I'd been with him at every Hebrew lesson with the tutor so he could learn his parashah, his Torah portion. I helped him write his speech. I booked the disc jockey, the caterer, and the reception hall. I was in the process of making the video montage, but I couldn't do everything. So if the floors buckled and the cat had kittens and he didn't go to services then I was just going to have to use the tools of the program, to learn how to surrender, to, "Let Go and Let God."

I walked out of his room and headed for the front door.

"Dad!" he yelled as he came after me. "Dad, I really don't want to go."

"I realize that, Jonah, and I understand that it's more fun just to hang out here and play video games with Yakie. I get it, I do. But we have to go. Please come with me."

He was looking down at the floor; he was in his T-shirt and boxers looking sad and down at the floor.

"All right," he said.

"Whose bar mitzvah are we going to?" Jonah asked while we were driving up Overland Avenue.

"I have no idea, but we're about to find out."

I started to panic, because I realized I didn't check out who was being bar mitzvahed at Wilshire Boulevard Temple that weekend and whether it was in the chapel on the Westside or the main sanctuary downtown. And what if there was no bar mitzvah scheduled for that day? That would not be good. Actually, that would be a disaster, because all this would have been for nothing.

Jonah cranked up AC/DC's "You Shook Me All Night Long" which had just come on the radio.

"Why does Angus Young wear those short-short pants?" I asked.

"Because he gets hot playing guitar and it helps him stay cool," Jonah replied with a smirky smile.

We got to the temple parking lot, and thank God we could see a group of people dressed in their Sabbath finery walking toward the sanctuary.

"Hey there's Ethan," Jonah said. Ethan was a friend of Jonah's from soccer. It was a relief for both of us to see one of his friends there.

The designated rabbi from a large group of six or seven clergy was Karen Fox, who was also assigned to Jonah's bar mitzvah. This was another stroke of good luck, because now we could see exactly how Rabbi Fox ran the service. In entertainment industry parlance, we would call this "preproduction." It also felt like all this good fortune was a case of my Higher Power watching out for me, helping me, showing me the way. My HP: something greater than myself that could restore me to sanity, or as Merriam-Webster says, "a spirit or being (such as God) that has greater power, strength, knowledge, etc., and that affects nature and the lives of people."

The Westside Chapel of Wilshire Boulevard Temple is modern with ambient light coming from floor to ceiling windows on the south side and a skylight over the stage. It also has beautiful stained glass behind the bimah, is carpeted, and has comfortable upholstered bench seating— a definite step up in coziness and style compared to Adat Shalom back in the day.

The service that morning was celebrating the bat mitzvah of a girl who happened to be in Jonah's Hebrew school class. She was all aglow in her white lace dress and black patent shoes. She was impressive in the way she knew all the words to the prayers and all the hymns, even if she happened to sing way the hell off key. The whole service had a surprising impact on me: I became all choked up, because there I was standing next to Jonah, watching the Torah come out of the ark and seeing the sun break through the clouds and stream into the synagogue through the stained-glass windows. It felt like I was having some sort of spiritual experience. I started to think about all the things that had happened to me, about the incredible fallout with Nancy, about our marriage, which had started out with so much promise and ended so badly. About all the missteps and collisions with my father, all the times I wished we had bonded and found a way to get closer that seemed to always elude us. And here I was at a very difficult period in my life, and my dad and I were still having trouble connecting and communicating. I hadn't even called him when I moved out of my house, because I had no idea how he'd react and because he simply wasn't someone I would ever turn to for emotional support. My sister Julie told him well after the fact, and when he called me, he was nice enough to say he was sorry to hear about it. Other than that, he was typically detached.

I could feel the full impact of everything that was happening to me, all those crazy feelings, because I wasn't stoned all the time, and in that moment it just seemed that everything came crashing down. I was thinking about how I was trying so hard to get back to who I was, who I had been over thirty years ago, before I started using and drinking, back to the original me when *I* was a bar mitzvah boy. Before I became someone who needed to smoke weed on a daily basis to kill the pain, someone who couldn't stop using even if he wanted to. I wanted to go back to who I was before I became an addict. Of course I knew I could never be that person again; deep down I knew it was too late, the damage was done. At least I had made the decision to be an addict in recovery, but it was becoming clearer to me that the process of recovery was something that might continue for longer than I imagined. "How'd you stay sober for twenty-two years?" I heard someone ask an old-timer who was celebrating a sober birthday. "One day at a time."

I took a breath and finally came back to my body, back to the present moment, to live the experience I was having with Jonah. I started thinking about how great it was to be able to come to the synagogue with my boy—to stand next to Jonah as we watched the service. Just like I used to do with *my* dad. He looked up at me because he heard me sniffling and asked if I was crying. The old me, the drug addict who needed to control everything, would have looked down at him and furrowed my brow and said, "What are you talking about?" Instead, I just turned to him and smiled as I pulled out a tissue.

The Torah service was over, and we were into the musaf service, the concluding service. We'd been sitting in the back row—just how I like it. A couple of rows in front of us sat about eight girls, who were now talking and giggling more freely. Jonah had been looking at the girl on the end. She was wearing a little dark-red velour jacket over her white dress. When she turned around to see him, he smiled at her with his pudgy cheeks and long hair. Near the end of the service, she turned again, and he raised his eyebrows to let her know he was a little embarrassed for getting caught looking at her. A little embarrassed and a lot interested.

When the service was over, I was ready to get the hell out of there. I didn't want to stay for the kiddush, the reception where they have the blessing over the wine and the bread, because I didn't know anyone there and I'd had enough spirituality for the day. I wanted to get back in the car so I could talk to Jonah about the service, but he was still fixated on that girl sitting on the end.

"Let's get out of here," I said.

He turned to me and said, "Dad, can we stay for the blessing?"

"Oh, honey, I don't know."

"Please, Dad, just for the blessing? Please, Dad. Please."

Jonah's bar mitzvah took place just over a year after I moved out, yet everything went off without a hitch. Before the service, we took the most incredible pictures of us together as a family. Jonah's chanting of the prayers that morning was spot-on. We honored my dad that day with an aliya: he came up to the bimah to read the Hebrew prayer before and after the Torah reading. He knew the prayer by heart. Nancy and I sat together on the bimah in front of all our family and friends. We were of one mind, in harmony, and so proud of Jonah. No one ever got an inkling of the fights we were still having as we met with our mediator to finalize our divorce. When we were at odds it could be awful. When we were trying to be helpful to each other it was wonderful. The reception took place that night at the Hard Rock Cafe in West Hollywood. Jonah jammed on stage with all his buddies, including me. It was the perfect day.

10

BABYSITTING THE BABYSITTER

"THEY DON'T COMPLAIN ABOUT THE WORK, just the attitude." That's what my agent used to say. Repeatedly.

During the years I was directing television I would stop smoking pot while I was on the job. I wanted to clear my head and focus on the work. The only problem is that when you stop smoking, you're in a form of withdrawal. While sleeping I'd have these vivid dreams that led to fidgety nights, which meant I was sleep deprived. When I went to the studio in the morning I was often restless, irritable, and discontent and generally not able to effectively manage myself when problems arose during production, which they invariably do. I'd sometimes snap at people who challenged me. My first response was usually "F you." Hence my agent's favorite quote.

In my recovery, I was confronted with what I was going to do for work now that the law and directing were behind me. Teaching came immediately to mind.

All my life I've looked for mentors, men and women I looked up to, who inspired me. There were so many influential teachers during my college years, like William McKane, whose knowledge and enthusiasm when describing the esoteric political theories of Marx, Hegel and Nietzsche made a huge impression on me. Or Erich Gruen and his outstanding lectures on the last years of the Roman Republic. After describing Cicero's tireless efforts to save the republic from sliding into the hands of autocrats like Julius Caesar or Mark Antony, the class was all ears as Professor Gruen recounted how the tide turned against

Cicero, forcing him to flee Italy only to be intercepted and assassinated by Antony's henchmen. Professor Gruen's delivery was riveting and reminiscent of my father's mind-blowing monologues as the psychiatrist Martin Dysart in the Broadway production of *Equus*. (Interesting how I was experiencing all these things at about the same time in the 1970s.) The idea of having a class of students of my own was something I always aspired to, thinking it would probably happen in my later years. My HP, however, had other plans.

———————————

In 2004 I became certified as a substitute teacher for the Santa Monica–Malibu Unified School District. I figured this part-time work would give me a taste of what teaching was all about before I committed to the full credentialing process. For the next two years, I picked up assignments at John Adams Middle School when my kids were there and then, as they got older, Santa Monica High School. I never had Maddy or Jonah in any of my classes, but I taught plenty of their friends, and I was always there to take my kids home from school; it was a way for me to stay close to them. I also drove them to doctor's appointments, soccer practice, cello lessons, guitar lessons, math tutors, and surf club at 6:40 in the morning. There's no doubt that I wanted my kids to have a different experience than I had with my dad. But it wasn't really a conscious effort to make sure I treated them the opposite of how my father treated me, I just naturally wanted to do it for them, to be with them.

Usually the kids would appreciate it when I was present. Even if they didn't say anything, I could feel the love and gratitude. Because I was sober, I could feel everything, and sometimes it felt great. Then again there would be times when the kids would still be mad as hell, like the day Maddy's mood went sour and she kept yelling at me in the car that she was never coming to my stupid apartment. "Well, Dad? How's it going to feel living the rest of your life alone? Answer me. How's it going to feel?"

Yep, I could feel everything, the good and the bad. What was interesting to me was that running off to light up a bowl to make all the bad feelings go away was no longer an option. The thought never even entered my mind. What did enter my mind was what Maddy said about me living alone, the incredible emptiness I was experiencing being on my own. Not just because the kids never came to stay with me, but also because I didn't have a partner to share my life with. I knew it was good for me, being on my own, and I wasn't convinced it would be for the rest of my life as Maddy was predicting. Something Krystal at Happy Destiny said was stuck in the back of my head: that if I kept doing the work of recovery, if I kept growing from the arrested development I had been in since I started using as a teenager, that someday I would be ready for "the real deal."

One day I was given a teaching assignment at Santa Monica High for a special ed class. I was teaching a challenging group of students who were having trouble in regular classes, and some of them gave me the stink eye when I walked in. But it still felt like a step up from my previous assignments at the elementary levels. Teaching fourth graders had its own lessons for me, like a newfound sense of humility, but it was also a jolt, because just a few years earlier I had been directing television shows at every major studio on million-dollar budgets. Even so, I was learning how to be in my own skin in recovery, to be in the moment and see the opportunity for what it was. Connecting with some of the kids at McKinley Elementary had showed me that I was exactly where I was supposed to be.

In that high school special ed class, I experienced a rewarding morning with the students as we talked about the savagery and symbolism of *Lord of the Flies*. Enthusiasm is infectious. I had always felt that way when I was on my game directing episodic television, and I could feel it that morning as the students who at first seemed wary of me responded to my excitement about the rich material William Golding had provided us.

At lunch, I walked through the campus to get a piece of soggy pizza and a sugary grape soda. Thankfully, teachers can cut to the front of the line, even us lowly subs. I then made my way to a patch of grass up the hill in front of the administration building. The hill was high enough to see out over the rest of the school, clear out to the Santa Monica Bay, straight out to the end of the earth, where the sun made everything sparkle on the surface of the deep blue. That's the crazy thing about L.A.: the urban sprawl goes on forever to the east and the south, but the Santa Monica and San Gabriel Mountains limit northern development, and when it came to the westward expansion, it's as if the Pacific shoreline put up a sign that read, STOP RIGHT HERE.

Santa Monica High—or Samohi, as it's called—is a huge school with some three thousand students. I looked at all the kids out and about, panning left to right from the cafeteria and Barnum Hall past the main quad and up another hill toward the history building. I spotted Maddy and her clique standing in the distance. I could see her chatting away, confirming that she didn't eat enough during lunch, which is why I always had a cold pack of food in the car for the ride home. Otherwise, there was a fifty-fifty chance she was going to have a meltdown.

I knew Maddy saw me, but she ignored me, although one of her besties, Katie, waved and smiled: "Hi, Adam!"

Then the other kids turned and waved. The Parnell brothers, Chloe, Jana, and Claire. "Hi, Adam!!!!"

Maddy stood behind them and made an *L* sign with her right hand. *Loser.*

It was a Saturday night and Maddy was babysitting out near Pasadena. I was supposed to pick her up between ten thirty and eleven when the parents came home, because Nancy was going to a late-night movie. Maddy said she'd call me when I was supposed to come get her. I was at my apartment with Jonah and a couple of his buddies. Jonah agreed to a sleepover only because I had stupidly offered to take him and his friends surfing at Point Dume in Malibu at six o'clock in the morning. I figured if I picked up Maddy and got home by midnight I could get just enough sleep.

Maddy finally called at ten forty-five. "Dad, the parents aren't home and they haven't even called yet and I'm freaking out."

"Maddy, take it easy. I'm sure they'll be home soon."

"No, Dad. There's a big party going on up the street and I keep hearing noises right outside the house and I don't know what to do."

"OK, listen. Just calm down. I'm going to leave right now."

"But I don't know when the parents are coming home."

"It's OK. I'll wait there with you until they do. I can be there in about thirty minutes. Just put on the TV and watch something until I get there."

I grabbed my jacket and ran out into the living room. The boys were watching *Jackass* for like the tenth time.

"I have to go pick up Maddy. You guys are not to leave this apartment. If you need anything, call me. Lauren my next-door neighbor knows you guys are here and she's going to stay up late and check in on you in about an hour. Do you hear me, Jonah?"

"Yes, we've got it," he said without once tearing himself away from Johnny Knoxville getting his ass kicked by a bucking bronco.

I jumped in my car and drove over. There was indeed a big party going on a few doors down. And there was a lot of beer and a lot of weed being blown. I could smell it on the porch as I waited for Maddy to open the door. She was so happy to see me but felt she couldn't let me in because she thought it would be weird if the parents showed up and I was sitting in their living room.

"Who are you babysitting?"

"Her name is Erica. Her parents are friends with Chloe's parents, but Chloe was out of town. She's one year old and she is *sooo* cute. She wanted me to sing her favorite song with her that she calls 'EIEIO.' I've got to go back inside, Dad. Please wait for me in the car. And thank you *sooo* much. I love you, Daddy."

As I sat in the car, I couldn't help but think about how cute Maddy was at that age, the "EIEIO" age. I replayed the memory of the night three-year-old Maddy tried to put a diaper on her Madeline doll. We were in the living room when she cleared the coffee table, laid out the diaper, and put the doll on top. But the Madeline doll was too small for the diaper, and it was a struggle. With fierce determination, Maddy retaped the diaper every which way. I just sat there with a video camera and let her have at it. Her determination could be really funny, but it could also be incredibly difficult, such as her refusal to go to sleep unless there was someone sitting in her room with her. I can't count how many times I tried to crawl out of there thinking she was asleep. I'd crawl across the room without making a sound and get to the door, almost home free, when she'd say, "Daddy, don't leave."

Back in my car. Twenty-year-old boys coming and going from that party with beers and all that weed, which kept wafting into my car. It reminded me of my hotboxing days, when my buddies and I would fill up the car with smoke trying to get higher. It never really worked, and we reeked like hell when we got out. I refiled that memory and turned on the radio. I listened to a show about the history of the Fab Four, a subject of which I never tire, because those boys grabbed me by the heart and soul when I was eight years old and never let me go.

An hour and a half later, I was still sitting there. I had called my neighbor, who informed me that Jonah and his buddies had moved on from *Jackass* to *The Exorcist*. But now it was 12:45 AM and the parents hadn't shown or called, and what the fuck is up with that? I mean, Maddy was only fifteen. Then she came out and tapped on the window. I was driving my '76 Volvo and had to actually lean across and crank the handle.

"Thank you so much, Dad, for coming. Really, thank you so much for waiting for me. I'm so sorry you had to come all the way out here."

"It's OK, honey, but have you heard from the parents?"

"No, but you can go now, because Mom just got out of her movie and she's coming over to sit with me. I love you so much, Daddy, thank you for coming out. I'm so sorry for calling you out here, but I was so afraid."

"Maddy, it's OK, honey. I totally understand, because that party was in full swing, and I'd be nervous too. You did the right thing."

As I drove away, I wondered how long it would be before all those thanks-yous and I-love-you-Daddys would wear off and she'd start yelling at me again about my stupid apartment, that I'd be living alone for the rest of my life and what a loser I was.

11

THAT SPECIAL SOMEONE

"How's the dating going?" Justin asked.

"You sound like my mother."

Justin and I were walking to the local branch of his bank in Venice. He wanted to take me to lunch as payback for all the times I'd treated him, but first he had to cash what he called his "paltry paycheck." (His day gig was working at Stein on Vine, a legendary music store in Hollywood where jazz greats had been hanging out for decades. Despite the store's huge reputation, Justin's salary was . . . paltry.) He knew about some of the difficulty I was having finding someone to be with. I mistakenly thought dating would be easier than what I had experienced when I was in my twenties.

"I just don't get it," I told him. "Either I meet women who are not right for me or I find someone I'm interested in and they seem to feel the same way until something happens and suddenly I'm persona non grata."

"Persona non grata?"

"An unwelcome person. A leper."

"Hah! Dude, that's a good one. I've gotta remember that."

"I just don't know what I'm doing wrong," I admitted.

"What happened with you and Holly?" Justin asked. I'd met Holly at the Wednesday-night meeting Justin and I regularly attended in Santa Monica.

"She relapsed. She went on a business trip to Houston, was invited to a sports bar to watch football, and confessed to me that the minute she found out there was coke in the bathroom she was all in. She's back in recovery, which is great, but now we're back to the thirteenth step, and I have no intention of dating a newcomer."

"What about Bianca, the blind-date girl? You know, I forgot to mention to you my ex is named Bianca. Did she by any chance have long brown hair?"

"Yeah, but, dude, she's not your ex."

"Well wait a minute, wait a minute. Let me ask you this: Did she by any chance have two breasts?"

"You're a moron."

"OK, seriously, what happened? I thought you liked her."

"I did, she was awesome, and things seemed to be going well. We were together for two months, which in L.A. is like a long-term relationship. Then suddenly everything changed. It was like I said or did something to piss her off, or her ex came back in her life, or I don't know. I literally have no idea. She started forgetting plans we had made. She even invited me to her house to talk about our situation and she wasn't even there and wasn't answering her phone. I felt like a complete idiot standing on her porch."

"Persona non grata?" asked Justin.

"Yeah, non grata big time. And that's not the first time I've been dumped. What am I doing wrong?"

"Those women are exactly who they're supposed to be, and you're not supposed to be with them." Justin said. "You should consider yourself lucky you found out when you did. Lose any resentments you might have and just move on. As we say in the program, 'Rejection Is God's Protection.'"

"Yeah, well, that all sounds wonderful, but it sure would be nice to be with someone."

"A lot of us are looking for that special someone, and I promise you, she's looking for you too. Just stay sober and keep going to meetings and keep praying for me, because I need a new car. Patience, grasshopper. Patience."

Earlier that day we were at Beyond Baroque, a small theater space on Venice Boulevard where Justin and some of the other students from our writing class were going to read short pieces they'd written. When we met up in front of the building, he told me he'd decided not to read his story. He had read it to me the night before, and it gave me a whole different perspective on my self-confident buddy in recovery who wore black Dickies and silk shirts from Goodwill and could play a stand-up bass to jazz tunes and an electric bass to anything.

Justin had been my "Eskimo," commonly used in AA to denote a person who brings others in out of the cold, who takes them to meetings and shares what they know about the program. The story he was supposed to read that day showed me another side of him, some of the darkness he was carrying, maybe even some insight as to how he ended up a junkie. It described an episode with his mother—the stripper, part-time hooker, and drug addict/alcoholic who sexually abused him. It was the story of a sweet, innocent boy who had to walk home alone from elementary school every day, repeating the route in his head over and over so he didn't get lost. "Three blocks up, one block left, 1566 Reed Street." A kid who loved to sit on the floor of the tiny one-bedroom apartment he lived in with his single mother and watch reruns of *The Odd Couple* while his mother and her friends were getting high on acid or speed or coke. They'd sit behind him watching him from the couch as they did up lines of blow.

Justin liked to mimic the voiceover at the beginning of the show: "*The Odd Couple* was filmed in front of a live audience."

"Isn't he a trip!" his mom would say to her friends as they sat back, all fucked up.

I was standing out in front of Beyond Baroque waiting for him when he walked up to me and said he wasn't going to read it. "Are you kidding? Dude, that piece is so powerful and painful, you've got to read it."

"I can't. I know it would probably be good for me, but I can't do it."

"The class is going to freaking love it. It is without a doubt one of the best pieces I have heard this entire semester. What's the problem?"

"Every time I read it, it makes me angrier and more resentful toward both my parents, especially my mom, even though she's back in the hospital and hopefully this will be the end of it."

We walked into the bank and got in line behind half a dozen people. Justin immediately started checking out the tellers. "I think I'm going to go after a bank teller," he whispered. "They seem to have it together."

He definitely had a reputation with women. He would often show up to meetings with someone new.

There were several young, attractive Latina women working behind the windows. Every time a teller became available, a bell rang and a lightbulb glowed at their station.

"The thing I want to tell you," Justin continued, "the thing you need to know, is that there are plenty of hot women in this town, but what you really want is *una mujer de calidad.*"

"*Una mujer . . . ?*"

"*Una mujer de calidad.* A woman of quality. You want to find some-one who can get beyond herself, beyond any insecurities or self-esteem issues she might have so she can show she's clearly interested in *you.* But what's important is that even though you still need to work on your recovery, and even though this may take some time and you have to be patient, you want to find her relatively soon, while you're recovering from the economic wipeout from your divorce, while you're still living in an apartment, while you still have relatively nothing."

"Thank you for reminding me."

"No, that's the good news, because the thing is, since you have noth-ing, all she's going to want you for is *you.*"

The bell rang and it was Justin's turn at the window. "Wait for me, homie," he said before walking off.

When we got back on the street, Justin was pumped, having scored the teller's phone number. "I was lucky, because Mariana happens to be my favorite. I've wanted to ask for her number, but lately I've been getting the wrong teller. I still love *all* those women in there. Did you notice? They're always decked out in the latest Banana Republic, sexy, low-cut sweater vest over crispy white blouse with shirtsleeves rolled up. I think they have a hiring criteria: female, eighteen to twenty-five, Latina, attractive, single, responsible, good with numbers, friendly, open to new ideas. They must run the copy like a singles ad."

"That all sounds so superficial," I said.

"Yeah, but no, this is different. Whenever I go in there and I'm lucky enough to get Mariana, she always smiles at me, asks me how I am, if I need anything else, and she always hands me money right before I leave."

"Dude, it's your money!" I blurted out, laughing.

"Yeah, but you're missing the point. Mariana has to check my bank balance whenever I go in there, and she knows I have next to nothing. She *knows*. And still, she gave me her number."

"*Una mujer . . .*"

"*Una mujer de calidad.*"

A program of recovery, as it turns out, is a program of action. You have to do stuff to stay sober, like attend meetings, get a sponsor, read the Big Book, work the steps, take commitments, be of service, rinse, and repeat. Doing all this stuff is what finally got me out of my head so that I could lose the obsession I had with marijuana: how to get weed, what kind of weed, what's it going to cost, how to get high, should I roll it or bong it or vape it, where to get high, when to get high, how long it's going to last, when can I get high again.

Even though he was not officially my sponsor, I would occasionally take direction from Justin, who was determined to keep me in a program of action. On one occasion, he instructed me to do something for someone and not let them know I did it. "Anonymous giving" he called it.

"What if they find out?" I asked.

"Then it doesn't count."

I immediately started thinking about my mother. In bed all the time, depressed most of the time, lonely because she had lost so many of her friends who couldn't deal with her depression. Sometimes I felt sad for her and sometimes I felt that lingering resentment because my mother had no major health problems, was financially secure, and had a loving family. In AA, that would make for quite a "gratitude list."

To try to make up for some of the resentment, I called to see how she was doing.

"Jonah called me last night," she said.

"Oh really?" I replied. I knew he called her the previous night, because I made him do it.

We were in the car. It was July 2 and I was driving him and two of his friends to Inglewood to buy fireworks.

"Dad, not right now. I have all my friends here. I'll write her a note later."

"No you won't, you'll call Nonnie right now. She just gave you $400 for no apparent reason."

One of his buddies chimed in from the backseat: "Jonah, it's all right. My parents made me call my grandma when she sent me a check for my birthday last week."

I called my mother's ancient landline and handed him the phone.

"Well, he called me last night when he was on his way with some friends to buy fireworks, and he is so sweet. He is such a loving person to call me like that."

We were flying through Inglewood, looking for the fireworks stand that I knew was around there somewhere.

"Thank her for the card and the money and ask her how she's doing."

"He said how much he appreciated the card and the money I gave him, and he asked me how I was doing and when was he going to see me."

"Tell her you'll see her on Sunday."

"He told me he'll come see me on Sunday, and he is just the sweetest thing. It was so nice of him to just call me like that on his own."

It counts.

12

DOUBLE VISION

DURING THOSE FIRST YEARS of my recovery, I didn't have much interaction with my father. Old issues seemed to keep coming up between us, even though he had stopped drinking and I had stopped smoking. I started attending Al-Anon meetings—Al-Anon is a mutual support program for people whose lives have been affected by someone else's drinking or drug use—and was learning about "detaching with love." Dad had been married to his second wife, Susan, for over fifteen years by then, and they had built a nice life together. My dad seemed to be living a happier lifestyle with her in their new home in Bel Air. Even though I didn't visit with him, I was glad for him, and happy that he had found a new partner for life. I still attended events honoring him, and I did call him on special occasions, like his birthday and Father's Day.

I even called him on my fiftieth birthday to congratulate him on the news of his involvement in the revival of the *Star Trek* movie franchise, to be directed by J.J. Abrams, but he cut the conversation short. "What do you want from me?" he asked accusingly.

Thankfully, I was learning how to handle these situations. "Not a thing, Dad. I just want to have a decent relationship with you. That's all."

While I stayed detached from my father, the focus for me and my sister Julie during this period was our mother. She had been dating Pete, a jazz musician and a terrific guy. But Pete lived in San Diego, and for the most part it was up to me and Julie to make sure Mom was OK.

In the early days, when Dad was out hustling odd jobs in between his acting gigs, Mom took care of most things at home. When he was totally gone for *Star Trek* and *Mission: Impossible*, it was all on my mother. Sometimes she'd get overwhelmed, because my sister and I were a handful—especially Julie. (Years before *Star Trek*, when we were little kids living in our tiny house on Palms Boulevard, Julie led me on one of several trouble-seeking expeditions, this time through an open back door into our neighbor's house, where we made off with a bag of potato chips and a cherry pie.) We definitely drove Mom a little nuts, but she always seemed to know what we—what I—needed.

One of my earliest memories was when I was crying one night while sitting in a car seat in the back of my mother's powder-blue Fiat. I must have been three or four years old, and I couldn't stop crying. Mom was driving, and my aunt, her younger sister Frances, was sitting shotgun.

Aunt Frances was annoyed. "Why is he crying?" she asked.

My mother turned to her and said matter-of-factly, "He's tired."

My mother then parked the car and went inside the Akron, leaving me with my aunt. Located on the corner of National and Sepulveda, the Akron was an import mart where my parents regularly bought cheap furnishings like wrought-iron butterfly chairs and teak tables.

Mom soon returned with a pillow and handed it to me.

All better.

Now my mother was lying in bed all day, needing regular care and attention. It was beginning to wear on Julie and me. My sister was married with three kids and was herself trying to re-create her life by going to cooking school with an eye toward starting a catering business. With just a part-time job as a substitute teacher, I was beginning to feel like one of those guys who still lives at home, never finds his place in society, and spends his time looking after his aging mother. Sort of like Norman Bates in *Psycho*, who took care of his immobilized (i.e., dead) mother while running a mostly vacant motel on the side.

"I didn't know you were coming over," I said to Julie as she pulled up in front of the house on Cashmere Street. I had just arrived myself to check on Mom. Julie seemed irritated.

"What's going on?" I asked.

"I'll let Mom tell you."

Julie and I always had a close relationship. We could fight like hell sometimes, since we were very close in age, her being only seventeen months older. She could actually beat me up until I was fifteen. Then one day she dug her nails into me and I just stood there laughing. It was also a huge relief to have gone through the ups and downs of our family experiences with Julie, to have someone else there to enjoy the good times and power through the darker periods. She knew what I went through with Dad. Though we agreed she had a better relationship with him, there was still plenty of conflict between them as well.

After ascending the faded and chipped blue-and-pink staircase to my mother's room, I was confronted by some unwelcome news.

"You did what?" I said.

"I let Helen go," Mom said.

"Why?" I asked.

"She only reads *People* magazine, for chrissakes! She couldn't discuss anything about politics. Anyway, Santiago said he could take care of me. Santiago!"

Mom was in bed with her newspapers, magazines, chocolates, and pills. Julie jumped into the conversation: "Mother, Santiago is sixty-five and hasn't been feeling well."

"I already talked to him about it. Santiago!"

"Mother, will you please stop yelling?" I asked. "He has more than enough to do just to keep this house going. The cooking, the cleaning, the polishing. He can't take care of you."

"I can take care of myself. All he has to do is feed me and get me to my appointments."

We could hear the sound of Santiago coming up the steps. He finally appeared, carrying a tray of coffee and more chocolates. He was clearly rattled, because he had the shakes.

"I'm sorry, Mrs. Nimoy," he said as he laid the tray down on the bed. "I was waiting for the coffee."

"Tell them what you told me," my mother said.

"I'm very happy to take Mrs. Nimoy to her appointments. Now please excuse me." Santiago gave a little bow then shuffled out the door.

Julie went all sotto voce with a hint of rage. "He's had two car accidents in the last six months. You are not driving anywhere with him."

"Then you guys are just going to have to help out here a little more, because I am not letting another stranger into my house!"

Julie struggled to check her temper. The thought of taking her to an Al-Anon meeting had occasionally crossed my mind. Recovery meetings specifically designed for Adult Children of Alcoholics could be found all over this town, and I had started to go to meetings to help me deal with my two "qualifiers," my father and my mother. I felt that Julie might benefit as well, after her experiences with Dad and now a mother who was regularly dosing herself.

"I'm in cooking school all day, and then I come home to three kids who need to be taken care of. I've been driving you around and taking care of you for years."

The two of them then turned to me.

"No, I have a job," I said.

"Yeah, substitute teaching. I'm sure you can take a day off," Julie said.

"Do I have to remind you that I'm helping out with your kids' expenses?" my mother said.

There was no way I was going to go along with this.

"No. Absolutely not. No way," I said. "Santiago can take care of you. Santiago!"

———————————

The following week I was driving my mother through UCLA to the Eye Institute. Along the way we passed some medical buildings.

"Hey, Mom, isn't that where your foot doctor is?" My mother had been having some trouble walking. She'd gone to several foot specialists, but no one could find anything wrong.

"Yes, but I don't see him anymore."

"Why not?"

"Because he dismissed me."

"He *dismissed* you?"

"He told me there was nothing more he could do for me."

At the eye clinic, we were led into an exam room, where we waited for the doctor. She'd already seen this guy about her double-vision problem; he told me over the phone he was recommending surgery, which made my mother extremely happy. The doctor walked in. He must have been six foot five. Six foot five and as welcoming as a lox. To break the ice, I commented on his cool, colorful Looney Tunes tie.

"I love your tie," I said.

"It's for the kids I have as patients."

Before examining my mother with a penlight, the doctor handed me some "informed consent" papers listing all the possible side effects from the surgery. It was a long list, and I was still reading when he finished his examination and drew a long breath.

"Well, Mrs. Nimoy," he said, "the indications I had seen in your last visit are, for some reason, no longer present. I really can't recommend surgery at this time."

"What?" my mother said.

"There's no reason for the surgery. I know you're disappointed," he continued. "I can't really explain it, but you don't have the crossing of the eyes that I thought you had during your last exam."

Mom looked confused.

"It *is* possible that your double vision may be caused by some rare blood disorder."

Mom suddenly brightened.

The doctor sent us down the hall so that they could draw a blood sample, which in two days' time would come back negative.

I took my mother home and made sure she was comfortably back in bed.

"Adam, when you read that list of possible causes of my condition, was there anything dire on there?"

"Dire? Ah, no, mom. It wasn't a list of causes; it was a list of possible side effects from the surgery, and there were a whole bunch of them. I'm glad he called it off, because knowing you, the side effects would've outweighed the benefits and you'd be more miserable after the surgery then you are now. So, no boubie, sorry, nothing dire. You're probably not going to die from your double vision. Can I get you a cup of coffee? Some chocolates, perhaps?"

13

BEWARE THE RECEPTIONIST

SOMETIMES I FELT THE PULL of a career, that I should be out beating the pavement looking for new jobs, possibly trying to find a way back to directing television. Directing single-camera, one-hour dramas is a demanding and at the same time mind-blowing experience. Preproduction generally lasts eight days, during which you're breaking down the script, meeting with writers and producers, scouting locations, casting guest actors, and coordinating with department heads: special effects, visual effects, props, the art department, makeup/wardrobe, stunts, the assistant director, grip, lighting, and camera. Then there's actual production, when you're shooting the show, which also lasts about eight days, each one scheduled to last twelve hours, but they often go much longer.

My dad used to say that if you've done a good job prepping the show, if you've done all the homework during preproduction, then when you finally get to the set and say that magic word, "Action!" you should be able to relax, stay present in the moment, and watch great performances all day. And that is exactly what I did. It was during those moments, when we were cooking and there was a collective, collaborative energy and flow and enthusiasm on set and we'd be getting these fabulous performances on film, that I'd think to myself, *Wow, it just does not get much better than this.* Yet as hard as I tried, calling agents, calling producers, calling my contacts at the networks and the studios, getting back into the rotation of directing episodes did not seem to be in the cards. For now, I would just have to focus on my recovery while also working on *The Maddy and Jonah Show.*

When I wasn't teaching or attending AA meetings, I was happy to be with my kids, to be in the moment with them. Taking them to school or soccer, listening to Jonah's funny stories about his buddies or the girls at school, listening to Maddy tell me in one breath that I was a loser with no friends and in another that she appreciated it when I drove her to school or her appointments because I was always punctual and she knew she could count on me.

Sometimes we did extraordinary things together. Not long after I moved out, the three of us headed to Disneyland, having put aside the trauma and turmoil we had been experiencing as we adjusted to our new family situation. Jonah put on his old cast from when he broke his leg skateboarding and hobbled around so he and Maddy could go straight to the front of the line. Maddy played the devoted sister—holding his crutches as the ride operator in lederhosen helped him maneuver into the Matterhorn bobsled. Long before selfies, I held out my little Canon camera, pointed the lens at us, and took a crazy video of us yelling and screaming as we flew down the mountain.

Mostly we did ordinary, more mundane things, like the Tuesday afternoon when Maddy and I were at the orthodontist to get her braces tightened. It was no big deal—a regular appointment we'd been to many times before—so I sat in the waiting area while Maddy was in with the dentist. I was flipping through a tattered *Us* magazine when the young woman who took care of the billing and insurance claims walked up to the front desk and handed some papers to the receptionist.

"Oh, hi, Mr. Nimoy," she said with a smile.

This seemed odd, because I'd been in there a half-dozen times before and she barely acknowledged me. I just figured she wasn't the friendly type.

"Hello," I said.

Twenty minutes later Maddy appeared with the sore gums that come with tighter braces. We were checking out when that billing and insurance woman made a point of verifying all my information.

"And your home address is the same, Mr. Nimoy?"

"Yes."

"And your insurance is still Delta Dental through the Directors Guild?"

"Yes."

"OK. Let me just make sure I have your most current insurance card on file," she said with a smile.

I wasn't sure what was going on, as we'd just been there three weeks before and went over all this. Maybe she forgot. Maybe she was distracted. Whatever it was, she kept glancing over and smiling while she was at her computer pulling up my information. OK, maybe she didn't forget. I'm usually so slow to pick up on this kind of thing, especially when it doesn't make any sense. Why she was showing interest at that moment was a mystery. I'd been bringing Maddy to that office for months, but it was like all of a sudden she decided she had a crush. Normally I wouldn't mind the attention, but a little shrimp named Maddy was standing next to me and was picking up on what was going down. I could see her temperature rising.

"I've got to get Maddy to another appointment," I said. "Why don't I email you a scan of my card?"

"That would be fine," she said, still smiling. "Let me give you my personal email and my direct dial in case you have any questions."

You mean like, *How about you and me get dinner sometime?*

The second we stepped into an empty elevator, Maddy released the Kraken: "Do you know how fucking obvious you are?"

"I didn't do anything!" The elevator doors refused to shut, and I had to press the DOOR CLOSE button like six times while Maddy let it fly.

"That was totally disgusting. I'm never letting you take me there again. You make me sick."

In the summer of '06, after having been out of the house for a couple of years, everyone seemed to be more accepting of the new order of things. Maddy even came with me to pick out a nice, new two-bedroom apartment in Santa Monica not far from the kids' schools. Since she helped me find the place, I thought for sure she'd feel more comfortable staying over. Or at least coming to hang out after school with her friends. Nope. If I wanted to be with Maddy, it had to be on her turf. So when the fall arrived and soccer season was upon us, I was on the field watching her every Saturday morning.

It was the third game of the season, and the kids were playing at MacArthur Field at the VA, the Veterans Affairs complex in West L.A., which by this time consisted of hundreds of acres of open space and aging structures built in the last century to care for disabled veterans of

American wars. Much like UCLA, the Sawtelle Veterans Home, originally established in 1887, was an anchor for the explosion of development in the surrounding area. Now developers were salivating to get their hands on this prime still-undeveloped real estate so they could build expensive condos. I loved that soccer field, because you could look around and still see and feel a sense of old L.A. Right next to the field was an arroyo—an ancient dry streambed. There used to be arroyos all over West L.A., but many had been filled in. Looking at it I could easily imagine a prehistoric L.A. with saber-tooths and sloths and mammoths roaming around the neighborhood.

Maddy, as it turned out, was having a pretty good day on the field. My pint-sized daughter managed to get herself in the right position and kicked a field goal.

"Way to go, Maddy!" I yelled as I high-fived the other parents. It was satisfying to see her so proud of herself after being congratulated by her teammates. During the second half, little Maddy was dribbling the ball up the field, and it looked like she had a clear path to score again.

"Go, Maddy, go!"

She was so focused on the ball she didn't see the amazon barreling toward her. The other girl kicked the ball away, and Maddy immediately went down clutching her leg. The ref blew his whistle and went to check on poor Maddy. He then signaled for the coach. The coach ran out, checked on her, then signaled for me.

Maddy was crying. "She kicked my foot, Dad! She kicked my foot!"

I carried her off the field, got her in the car, then called Dr. Nolan's office to have him paged and find out what to do. He's the pediatric orthopedist in Santa Monica I had taken Jonah to for his broken leg two years prior.

"Dr. Nolan's office, this is Martha, how can I help you?"

"Hi, Martha, my name is Adam Nimoy, and my son is a former patient of Dr. Nolan's. I'm calling about my daughter Maddy, who just had an accident on the soccer field . . . but wait, are you guys in the office today?"

"Saturday mornings during soccer and football season," she said. "Bring Maddy in and we'll check her out."

Poor Maddy was in such pain she cried the whole way down to Twentieth Street. By the time I carried her into the office, she had started to calm down. Martha put us in Exam Room 1 right across from her desk and left the door open. Maddy sat on the exam table, and I sat in a chair facing out the door toward Martha's desk. I could just catch a glimpse of her behind her computer. Brunette, maybe in her early forties? She must have been new, because I definitely would have remembered her. I needed to stay focused on Maddy.

"Maddy, do you want me to elevate your leg? Maybe you'll feel more comfortable."

"No, Dad. I'm fine."

"Can I get you anything? A cup of water?"

"Dad, I'm fine!"

Martha had smile lines. *She could be forty-five*, I thought.

Dr. Nolan appeared and immediately sent us to the X-ray department down the hall. The tech took a few pictures, then sent us back to the exam room, door open, seat facing Martha. As we waited for the doctor, I kept trying to catch little glimpses while pretending to read a *National Geographic*.

Dr. Nolan returned and came right out with it: "Well, Maddy, you must have been doing quite a job on that soccer field, because you broke your foot. What color do you want for your cast?"

"Day-Glo."

As he was wrapping the cast, Dr. Nolan said he wanted her to walk on it as much as possible, because walking creates an electric current that helps it heal. He explained that sometimes orthopedists use devices to send low-level pulses of electromagnetic energy to the injury site. In Maddy's case, she just needed to walk on it.

While we checked out at Martha's desk, I could tell Maddy was feeling much better, because she glared at me as if she was holding a neon sign that read, *If you hit on her, I will fucking destroy you.*

"Can I give you a credit card?" I asked as I quickly pulled out my wallet.

Martha seemed to sense what was going on. "We're good," she said. "I'm going to bill your insurance, and then I'll bill you for the balance."

"Thanks. OK, then. Bye!"

14

EVENT HORIZON

Sometimes it's a struggle for us beginners to surf at Ocean Park in Santa Monica. It's a beach break, and the waves don't always form well, but on this Thursday morning there was a nice swell with several sets of decent waves. Thirteen-year-old Jonah and I caught some crazy good long rides. Normally I'm not too keen about getting into the water at six thirty in the morning. Then again, there's almost no one out there at that hour, and on clear, sunny mornings when it's calm and glassy between sets and a pod of dolphins happen by, I'll look out on the horizon and get this feeling that I really am at the edge of eternity. I suddenly become aware that I'm not just sitting on my board in the water at Ocean Park, I'm sitting in water that covers over 70 percent of planet Earth.

I didn't want to take Jonah surfing that day. Not at first. He had a D in history, and it was impossible to get him to produce some schoolwork, any work. But it was the last day of surf club with his friends from middle school, so I gave in as long as he agreed to get out of the water on time so that he could avoid another tardy.

Maddy was a conscientious student. Jonah was a disaster. We probably should have sent him to a school for the performing arts, because he was obsessed with drums and guitars and simply couldn't understand the need for eighth grade science or history. When he was eleven, he was shredding on his mini electric guitar, surpassing my own guitar skills, which was amazing as well as incredibly annoying. Now two years later, he was playing my '68 Fender Telecaster (which, like my Stratocaster, was on permanent loan to him) like a pro, imitating Jimmy Page solos note for note. It was astounding to sit in his bedroom and watch him. He was so comfortable with that guitar, it seemed as if it had become a part of him. And when he got behind his drum kit, he was mesmerizing. A little literacy, however, would also have been nice.

I looked at my waterproof watch. "OK, mister, it's 7:15. We gotta go."

"I'll follow you out, Dad. I just want to catch one more wave."

"One more and that's it."

I waited for him on the beach. Of course, the water went flat, and the boys were waiting for another set. By 7:20 I was calling to him and waving him in. He ignored me. I yelled even louder. When he finally got out of the water, he called me an asshole.

"Don't talk to me like that, it really hurts my feelings," I said as we walked across the sand to the outdoor showers.

He didn't say anything as we rinsed off. I was used to the fact that he could be OK one minute, angry and upset the next. I knew that even though considerable time had passed, deep down he was still sad that I had moved out of Clarkson Road. I knew that the fact we didn't live together anymore still weighed on his mind more than whatever it was that seemed to be bothering him in the moment. So I always tried to cut him some slack.

When we got back to the car he started in on me: "I can't believe you made me get out of the water when everyone else is still surfing."

"I happen to know that those guys don't have the problems you've been having in school. You agreed to get out at 7:15, so please stop talking and take a minute to think about what I'm saying."

I struggled to keep a grip on my temper as I continued to load the car. I wanted to give him the speech about how lucky he was to have a father who not only respected but encouraged his talents. If he decided that college wasn't right for him, he could pursue music with the full support of his parents—the kind of backing my father didn't have.

"Don't be like your dad," Jonah said as he watched me bag the surfboards. "Do you want us to have a relationship like you and your dad?"

Jonah knew my dad and I were still plodding through our low point. Dad was no longer drinking, but he was also not working a program—that is, I happened to know through my sister and through my few direct communications with him that he was not going to meetings anymore, nor was he otherwise engaged in the activities associated with twelve-step recovery. Johnnie Walker may have been gone, but not much else had changed. Whenever conflict arose, we'd be right back at where we started—hurt feelings, recriminations, miscommunications, no resolution, with the net result of Dad mad at me for extended periods and me holding on to my resentments toward him.

Even so, I continued to attend events honoring him, like his photography exhibits and screenings. He basically ignored me at those gatherings, so I just stayed out of his way, standing back in the shadows while he hobnobbed and signed autographs for his adoring fans.

This all seemed weirdly similar to what Spock experienced in the *Star Trek* episode "Journey to Babel," in which Sarek, Spock's father, boards the *Enterprise* but ignores Spock's greeting, because he disapproved of Spock's decision to join Starfleet rather than attend the Vulcan Science Academy. (They later sort of reconcile when Spock saves Sarek's life.) By this time I was still attending Al-Anon meetings and still trying to practice the art of detaching with love, because things had become too difficult between us. My kids were a casualty of all that, having very little contact with their grandfather.

Our estrangement was on full display just a few weeks before, when we were all at the opening of the Leonard Nimoy Event Horizon Theater at the Griffith Observatory. The kids went with me even though Nancy wasn't invited, which hurt them badly. No one had more reason to hold a resentment against Nancy than me, but my sponsor and the program forced me to keep the focus on myself, stay aware of my own contributions to our problems, and make an amends to Nancy for my part in it. Besides all that, Nancy and I continued to work hard to get along for the sake of the kids. The bottom line is that she should have been invited.

The three of us arrived at the observatory well after the rest of the family, because Maddy had a late soccer game. Everyone had already walked the red carpet for the fans and the press. The kids were all dressed up—Maddy in a white lace dress and faux leopard coat, Jonah in a white dress shirt and sport coat. I didn't want them to totally miss out, so I pulled out my little Canon PowerShot as they walked in front of the step-and-repeat backdrop. Using the camera flash, I shot away from different angles, yelling at them like Italian paparazzi.

"Maddy, Jonah, *per favore*, here, look here! *Prego*."

"Maddy, Jonah, to please look here! *Bellissimo*."

When we finally caught up with the rest of the family and we were all waiting in the crowded line to get into the theater named for my father, Dad kept his back to me.

Jonah knew the score of what was going on between me and his Poppi. That morning at the beach I was determined to handle the situation differently from the way it would normally go with my father. My thirteen-year-old boy was still short and pudgy in his black wet suit. His hair was long and wet.

"I'm nothing like my dad when it comes to you," I said. "His career always came first, and when we did stuff together, it was never that much fun. I would never think of calling him an asshole, because if I did, he wouldn't talk to me for months—which is what he's doing now, and I didn't even call him an asshole."

Jonah quieted down while I continued to dry him off and help him out of his wet suit. I put a towel around his waist and crouched down to pull that rubber suit off his legs, while he put his hand on my shoulder to keep his balance.

After I finally got him into his clothes he said, "I'm sorry, Dad. I didn't really mean it. I just didn't want to have to get out before everyone else. How about a hug?"

"Can I finish getting the boards in the car?"

"Yeah."

When I got everything in and closed the trunk, I went over and hugged him. "Please don't be mean to me," I whispered.

"OK," he said, and hugged me tighter.

15

IT COULD BE CANCER

My mother was complaining of shortness of breath. She went to see a pulmonary specialist, who took a chest X-ray. The next day, the doctor called to say they found something and wanted her to come in for a biopsy. I learned all this one Friday night when I brought her some dinner. She was up and about and met me at the front door, which was unusual.

"They found a spot on my lung," she said. "It could be cancer." She could barely hide her glee.

We were standing in the foyer of the house on Cashmere Street, with the dining room on one side and the living room opposite. The house that *Star Trek* bought. The house she should have sold years ago that felt like an aging mausoleum when it used to be so full of life. My mother seemed small, like she was shrinking, like she had capitulated and was ready to move on, ready for a diagnosis to put her out of her misery.

Family pictures of happier times were scattered all over my mother's house, pictures that made me wonder what the hell happened to her. She had a happy if unconventional childhood, growing up as Sonia Zoberblatt in Cordova, Alaska, a frontier fishing town. That's where her adventurous father ultimately ended up after he left Russia. She had pictures on the mantel showing her splashing in a pond during the short Alaskan summer and building a snowman during the long winter. On a side table in the living room was a collection of photos from the '60s and '70s, a time when she kept it all together as Sandi Nimoy, Hollywood housewife, who threw terrific parties with great food and interesting people.

Unlike her mother, cooking and cleaning didn't particularly interest her. Mom had other things on her mind, like working at her potter's wheel, traveling the world with my father, and attending rock and jazz concerts. Incredibly kindhearted, she could always be counted on for love and support in times of crisis.

I really admired how my mother handled *her* mother. My grandmother, Ann Zober, was an Orthodox Jew who walked to and from shul, as driving isn't permitted on Shabbat. She was very loving to my sister and me, but constantly berated my mother. Before Shabbat dinner, mom and I would be sitting at the dining table at my grandparents' house to stay out of grandma's way while she made her pot roast. All the while Grandma Ann would be ragging on my mother from the kitchen, complaining about how we didn't keep kosher and how we never went to shul. Mom would calmly say things like "Not everyone wants to keep two sets of dishes these days" or "We go to shul on the High Holidays, that's plenty."

I also admired how my mother handled herself in the beginning, when we had nothing and Dad was out hustling, how she managed to keep things going at the house. Then when *Star Trek* arrived, Mom was right there to help my father. It was the exact same pattern every night: Mom would have dinner ready for Dad, then, just before he went to sleep early for an early call, she'd sit on the bed next to him and run lines. Night after night, the sound of their voices was so specific and consistent I can still hear my mother feeding Dad dialogue cues from *Star Trek* script pages and him responding—not in character, just monotone to make sure he knew the words.

By the 1980s, when *Star Trek* hit the big screen, Dad was an established star and so much of their lives revolved exclusively around him. At some point along the way my mother began to lose herself, until finally she was just Mrs. Leonard Nimoy—all that mattered was Dad and his career. It was as if the *drip, drip, drip* of accommodation and surrender gradually took over, until the mother I knew and admired had disappeared. Their relationship was in decline for years, and in 1986 Dad finally moved out, putting an end to their thirty-two-year marriage. When my father left, Mom came crashing down.

Now here she was standing in the foyer with so much hope in her eyes.

"It could be cancer."

Dr. Kruger seemed like a nice man, with his lab coat and glasses and his South African accent. He was holding my mother's file with the results from her biopsy, the results she so desperately wanted to hear. He came right to the point.

"Mrs. Nimoy, I can't find anything wrong with you."

We were in a windowless exam room that suddenly felt like all the air had been sucked out of it. My sister Julie was also present so that she could hear the terrible (now happy) news straight from the doctor's mouth. Julie and I exchanged a look as our mother struggled to get over the shock.

"Ah . . . ah . . . are you *sure*?" mom asked, her face slightly contorted.

"Yes, all the tests came back negative."

"What about the spot on my lung?"

"That appears to be some harmless scar tissue surrounded by mucous."

Julie had always been extremely close with my mother—she was definitely the favorite, which never bothered me. By attending culinary school, she was exercising some newfound independence in an attempt to re-create her own life and get some distance. Still, she was very dedicated to Mom and tried to throw her a lifeline: "But I'm sure the hot weather and the smog are causing her to have trouble breathing."

"I don't think so," said the doctor. "There are simply no medical indications pointing in that direction."

Dr. Kruger turned back to my mother. "Mrs. Nimoy. Have you been under any extraordinary stress lately?"

"No. Nothing extraordinary. I mean, my husband left me twenty years ago."

Julie and I struggled to keep it together.

"Because I think your symptoms might actually be caused by anxiety."

"Anxiety?" my mother protested. "Oh, get me out of here!"

"Mrs. Nimoy, I think that perhaps seeing a psychiatrist might help relieve some of your symptoms."

"But I already see a psychiatrist. Two of them!"

Patience. Tolerance. Acceptance. Those were the words I repeated to myself on the ride home. I knew that if I let loose, I would invariably say something that would qualify as an "emotional relapse." An emotional relapse—when negative thoughts start to erode the healthy behaviors and coping strategies learned in recovery. If that happened, I'd have to tenth-step myself: *Continued to take personal inventory and when we were wrong promptly admitted it.* My personal inventory in this instance was that I could be judgmental and critical. I was still learning that about myself and still struggling to become more aware of what was coming out of my mouth. I was so fed up with my mother's constant complaining and victimhood, but with the help of the program and people like Justin, I was beginning to understand that she was entitled to live the life she had chosen for herself. If I ever said what I was thinking, if I ever opened my mouth and let it fly, then I'd have to make an amends to her. Continuing to take personal inventory is a bitch to get used to, and I didn't always practice it perfectly, but in this instance it saved me from myself.

Julie, on the other hand, was not in a program of recovery.

"You have never let go of what happened between you and Dad," she said. "Dad left you twenty years ago and you act as though it happened yesterday. You have never . . . let . . . go."

To which my mother replied, "And I never will."

16

ONE STEP FORWARD, TWO STEPS BACK

"Dad, I just met the coolest guy. His name is James and he is *so* cute. I just can't believe I met him and I think he likes me."

Maddy was fourteen when she told me this one winter night. It wasn't long after I moved out, when she was usually in full-on angry teen mode, so what a nice surprise to pick her up from a late-night skating-rink party and see her in such a good mood. Because he didn't go to Maddy's school, it would be months before I even heard about James again.

One summer day, Maddy had me drive her over to James's house, where she was going to hang out with him and two of her girlfriends. James lived on the Westside with Chris, his divorced dad. After dropping her off, I had this weird feeling that I should go back and check the place out, as I had never met James or his father. When Chris answered the door, it was like, *Holy shit.* James's dad was a Keith Richards look-alike: short gray hair, hard lines on his face, crooked teeth, thick hoop earrings. Just like Keef, this guy looked like he had done some heavy partying and was maybe still doing it. While we made small talk, I kept trying to think up a good excuse to get Maddy the hell out of there. Then I noticed there was something oddly familiar about Chris. It was those crooked teeth.

"Chris, what's your last name?" I asked.

"Kelton."

"Kelton? Chris Kelton? Oh my God, it's me, man, Adam Nimoy!"

His eyes went wide. He broke into a smile featuring those telltale teeth. "Adam Nimoy! No way!" He gave me a bear hug and invited me inside.

Chris was pals with my neighbor Matthew when we were all in junior high and high school, and these were the guys my father particularly disapproved of back when he started to take an unwelcome interest in my life. Chris and Matthew were a year older than me. I first became aware of them when I was in the eighth grade and they were in the ninth at Emerson Junior High. They scared the hell out of me, because they were bad boys and I wanted to be good. When Mr. Larzelere, the boys' vice principal, told me to tuck in my shirttails, you better believe I tucked in my shirttails. Chris and Matthew would just laugh at him. I used walk down the halls and see those guys sitting in detention all the time.

A few years later when I turned seventeen, I wanted to be just like them (except for the detention part). That's when the two of them, along with the other guys they hung with, their gang of Merry Pranksters, taught me everything I needed to know about drinking and using. I can still see Chris standing in my bedroom playing electric guitar. My parents were out of town and Chris brought over a huge Marshall amp and a Stratocaster. He was wailing away while smiling with those crooked teeth. He wore faded bell-bottom jeans and cowboy boots. His pile of thick, curly hair looked something like a Jew-fro. Though Chris and Matthew were bad boys, they were smart and clever. I was a good boy who always did his homework, but during the off hours I went looking for them.

Now I was sitting at Chris's dining table in his modest rental house, his guitars, mandolins, and ukuleles close at hand. He told me about his own experience in recovery, how he finally hit his bottom ten years before when heroin had beaten him again and again, forcing him to get on his knees and beg God to either kill him or make it better.

We started holding a meeting at Chris's house, and soon a dozen people were showing up every Thursday night, including Justin, who had met Chris years before, when Justin was beginning his own journey of recovery. That meeting was how Maddy discovered I was in AA.

"Why do you go over to Chris and James's every week?"

"Because we're having a meeting there, honey."

"What kind of a meeting?"

"An Alcoholics Anonymous meeting"

"You're in Alcoholics Anonymous?"

"Yes, honey, I am."

"I knew you used to smoke," she said. "Why do you go to AA if you just smoked pot?"

"Because it's all related."

"And you're never going to drink again?"

"I wouldn't say never. But I'm pretty sure I'm not going to be drinking today."

Jonah was thirteen and Maddy fifteen when we started talking about all this. It would become a bigger issue later, when I knew they were both experimenting with weed, which most of their friends were into. I was glad that at least they knew what I was up to and I didn't have to hide the fact that if I was unavailable to talk, it was because I was at an AA meeting. Now when they call, I love texting back, "In AA. Call u ltr."

Back then, all was well with me going to Chris's Thursday-night meeting until things went south for Maddy and James. She was heartbroken over that boy, and she'd want me to come over after the meeting to talk about him: "Was James there? Did he ask about me? Did you say anything to him about me?"

Sometimes she'd cry and it would just be so painful, and just plain awkward being in the middle. But I felt lucky I could be there with her, to be sober and available to work through the experience with her. I think she secretly liked the fact I could spy on the goings-on over there. Soon, Maddy and James managed to work things out and became friends again. Sometimes she'd go with me on a Thursday night, and she and James would hang out and watch *The O.C.*

It seemed as if things were settling down and Maddy and I were back on track again. It's so nice with Maddy when things are right. While we were driving home from their house one night, I reached over and squeezed her knee.

"You've got knees, Maddy! You've got the knees in the family!"

———

"You know nothing about me, Dad. You do nothing for me."

The therapy session was going straight to hell with Shayna, our family therapist. Maddy was letting it rip. Unfortunately, it was an emotional relapse situation, because I left my recovery tools at the door.

"What are you talking about? I just took you and your friends to Tahoe for a little ski trip."

"That's not what I'm talking about. That has to do with money."

"Money? I flew up there with you guys to chaperone. And what about the car I just leased for you?"

"Again, you're talking about buying me things. You know nothing about who I am."

"Maddy, I have been to every one of your soccer games, I pick you up every day after school, on time with food so that you don't have a meltdown. I know all your friends and I make sure you put your lotion on when you're stressed so your skin doesn't break out. I've seen you through Barney, the Spice Girls, and Blink-182. I think I know who you are."

Maddy turned to Shayna. "He just doesn't get it."

Shayna chimed in: "Adam, you're counting things off a list like this is a courtroom and you're making a legal argument. Maddy doesn't care about the list. Just listen to what she's feeling right now rather than trying to defend yourself."

"Yeah, fine, OK, I get it."

"It's like, my friend Rachel and her dad have a *real* relationship. She can say anything to him."

I really loved Shayna's office. It had a warm, homey feel to it. Floor-to-ceiling windows along one wall, wood paneling on the others. It was like being in someone's living room. Shayna was a nice Jewish therapist. Frizzy black hair with gray highlights and a New York accent—she was straight out of central casting: "Role: New York therapist, female. Physical Attributes: Semitic. Special Skills: Able to deal with pugnacious teenage daughters and desperate fathers."

The comment comparing our relationship unfavorably to Rachel and her dad was a bridge too far. Recovery principles on hold, the Kraken came forth. I knew my rage had something to do with my dad, how I had to stuff my feelings down all the time, how it wasn't safe to express negative feelings around him, how I sometimes had this kind of rage toward him when I couldn't get through and I just wanted to shake him and say, *Dad what planet are you on?* I knew all this—I knew it—yet still there were times when I just could not stop myself.

"Are you kidding? When Rachel had her birthday party and her perfect parents left to go out to dinner, guess what?" Dripping sarcasm here. "They *forgot* to buy their daughter a birthday cake. And then you called me and I immediately ran to Ralphs and picked up that kick-ass brownie cake that everyone raved about . . . not to mention the candles!"

Shayna: "Adam . . . "

"What?!"

17

BEING SEEN

FINDING A PLACE TO LIVE in Berkeley in January 1977 was ridiculous. I had transferred there from UC Santa Barbara, and it was like there were thirty thousand students but only twenty thousand beds. (Maybe some of us should have just "doubled up.") I finally interviewed with a guy living in a two-bedroom apartment on Northside whose roommate had just moved out. His name was Marc, a grad student in urban development. Marc told me he had already talked to several people who wanted that second bedroom. When he saw my last name and I confirmed the connection, he told me I could have the room on the condition that we immediately run over to the Federation Trading Post. I had no idea what he was talking about.

The store was located on Telegraph Avenue, and I was amazed to see that they had all things *Trek*: games, puzzles, posters, dolls, and postcards, including one of me in my Spock makeup standing on the *Enterprise* bridge with Dad. I had arrived in Berkeley four months before the release of *Star Wars*, and *Star Trek* was very much on people's minds. The original series was in syndication five nights a week. During the holidays, there were twenty-four-hour marathon weekends. I would be in these study groups at the dorms, and it always amazed me how at 5:00 PM the place would empty out and everyone would cram into the TV room to watch the crew of the *Enterprise* on their five-year mission.

Ever the Boston hustler, Dad would go on these college tours where he made personal appearances in front of die-hard fans on campuses all over the country. In the fall of 1978, Dad booked a date at Berkeley.

He had never come to visit me in college, and I was looking forward to seeing him. The plan was for us to go to dinner after his lecture. Having experienced a dismal freshman year at UCSB, due in no small part to drugs and alcohol, I finally got my footing as a sophomore, which enabled me to transfer to UC Berkeley. I was proud of the work I was producing at Cal, despite an unfortunate F in a rhetoric class.

It was a cold, dark night when I walked over to Wheeler Hall. I took a seat in the back row of the auditorium. There must have been two hundred people there who listened attentively as Dad talked about his alter ego Mr. Spock, his theater career, his recording career, his pursuit of photography. Dad was always charismatic in front of a crowd; I admired how he could just get up there and hold people's attention for ninety minutes. I thought back to the days when he was making personal appearances while he was on *Star Trek*. He would take this ten-dollar guitar we bought in Tijuana (I still have it!) and sing folk songs and tell stories. That took guts, but he was always confident, so sure of himself. He once told me that after a particular college appearance, some students were supposed to drive him back to the airport. He got in the car with these Trekkies and they immediately popped in a cassette of one of his albums. He said he started nervously laughing thinking, *Oh no, this is not going to be good.* Then they got lost on their way to the airport.

After Dad's Berkeley presentation, there was a Q&A and then time for photos and autographs. When the fans finally dispersed, I waved to him from the top of the aisle. He came up to me, gave me a quick hug, and said, "I can't go to dinner after all. I have a commitment in the morning. There's a car waiting for me, and I'm already late for my plane." Then he made his way up the aisle and out the door.

"I'm taking Japanese."

"Jonah, you're not taking Japanese, you're taking Spanish."

"I'm taking Japanese."

Jonah missed open enrollment for Santa Monica High School. No surprise there, as school was of no interest to him other than being a place to hang with his friends. He did show some interest in an English class taught by a great teacher who had inspired Maddy two years before. Other than that, not much else appealed to him. Meanwhile his drum and guitar work were just superb. Before he even got to high school, he'd been invited to perform the lead guitar solo to "Stairway to Heaven" with the Samohi Orchestra. I videotaped the rehearsals from various angles until the music teacher threw me off the stage.

Instead of a fine arts class his sophomore year, Jonah opted for a foreign language, which made no sense. (Nancy and I had pretty much accepted the idea that he would not be matriculating on to college.)

"I want to take Japanese," Jonah said when we arrived at the school for enrollment makeup day. He was no longer my little cherub with the big red cheeks and long hair. He was fifteen and had gone through a growth spurt and was as tall as me. He had cut his hair, but it was already growing long again. His face was lean and tan. He wasn't my little boy any longer and was doing just what I did when I was his age: challenging his dad.

Jonah was determined to take Japanese. (I say "take Japanese" instead of "study" which is a word that has no business being used in the same sentence as my son's name. On that score, at least, he would agree with me.) The idea may have had something to do with his recent obsession with Japanese manga in the form of Dragon Ball Z books. Jonah couldn't get enough of those graphic novels showcasing the adventures of Goku and his friends. The stories of friendship and coming of age in an action/adventure setting were exactly what fueled my own obsession with the earliest of Japanese anime: *Astro Boy*, an animated series about an android boy with human emotions that first appeared on American television in 1963, when I was seven. One of the many things about Astro Boy that spoke to me was that he was an outsider, having been rejected by his creator, whom he called "Father."

"You're not taking Japanese, you're taking Spanish," I said.

"Why?" he asked.

"Listen, I totally get your obsession with all things Japanese, I do, but we both know your study habits basically consist of learning the lead to [Megadeth's] "Hangar 18." Japanese is going to be very demanding. Please reconsider."

"I want to take Japanese," he repeated.

"We have an excellent Japanese teacher," a young, perky counselor said as she jumped into the conversation uninvited. She was sitting at the enrollment table waiting for us to make up our minds. We were the only ones there. It seems the rest of his class had registered on time.

"Mr. Hatori has a great reputation. The kids really like him," she continued.

Will you please shut up? I kept thinking silently to myself. She probably had some quota to fill, like the Spanish classes were overflowing and they didn't have enough people in Japanese.

"Great, sign me up for Mr. Hatori's class," Jonah said, looking me dead in the eye.

The results were predictably disastrous. Reading Dragon Ball Z in English apparently didn't help him with his Japanese.

His musical performance work, however, continued to improve. At this point, he had played dozens of gigs, both on guitar and drums. Plenty of people wanted him in their bands—he could learn songs quickly. When I watched him perform, my heart would just explode; it was so exciting to see what he could do. He was meticulous about the work, which drove the neighbors a little nuts when he was banging away in the garage/studio on Clarkson Road.

In the spring during lunch hour, Jonah played drums with some older students: one bass player and four guitarists. They were jamming on the hill in front of the administration building, and they drew a pretty good crowd. Their metal repertoire ranged from Metallica to Megadeth to Slayer. Jonah was so confident on drums. He was clearly the star of the show, the anchor that held all those guitarists together. I took plenty of videos, and even though metal is not my genre, watching those videos still blows my mind. Jonah so looked the part of West Coast teen rocker with his long hair, Vans tennis shoes, board shorts, and a T-shirt of an anime cartoon boy tearing an anime girl's heart out.

I was sitting in the Samohi parking lot waiting for Maddy to get out of a tutoring session. I had gladly agreed to chauffeur her to the Third Street Promenade to meet up with her friends. Things had improved since our therapy session. That's the way it was with her, a roller coaster ride of emotions. Shayna assured me that around the age of twenty-five, Maddy's brain would be fully formed and things would begin to settle down. Twenty-five. Only a decade to go.

Samohi sits on prime real estate just four blocks from the beach. In the afternoon, the sun is right there heading for the western horizon, and you can feel its warmth along with the ocean breeze.

Maddy jumped in the car.

"How was school today?"

"Good. I got an A in Mr. Harris's class. He even read some of my paper aloud."

"Wait, the one you wrote about that Margaret Atwood book?"

"Yup. Mr. Harris liked that I wrote about what women have to do to take care of themselves during a war."

"That was definitely the best part of your paper. It's so nice when you finally get a little recognition for your work."

"Yeah, but it was also a little embarrassing."

"Embarrassing?"

"It just got a little weird when everyone was looking at me while Mr. Harris was reading my paper. It's just kind of uncomfortable, because I'm not used to it. Jonah doesn't seem to have that problem," she said.

"No, he doesn't."

"Then again, he's a complete fuckup in school."

"Yeah, well, we're working on that. Just stay focused on how well you're doing."

Maddy always adored Jonah. Ever since we brought him home when she was two years old, he never stopped being *her* baby. I often see her hugging him and kissing him for no reason other than the fact that he's so cute and funny. They did have their moments when they'd get into fights and she felt the need to remind him who was boss. Like when it came to riding in the car, she always had to ride shotgun. Always. Sometimes as we'd be heading for the car, they'd race for the passenger door. He'd challenge her, and they'd both end up holding on to the door handle waiting for me to get in the car and unlock it so they could push their way into the front seat. Sometimes I'd stand outside the car watching them, laughing as they jostled each other from side to side. They'd also be laughing, even while she'd be yelling at him. But she always won. Or he let her win. Sometimes when we were on our way to the car and she wasn't looking, he'd motion for me to throw him the keys. Still, in the end, it was almost always Maddy in front. Sometimes they did get into serious arguments and she'd be swearing at him and calling him names. Then, sooner or later, she'd always end up hugging and kissing him.

"Thanks for taking me to the Promenade, Fasha," she said as we drove out of the parking lot.

Fasha. That's what my kids called me when they were happy with me.

"You're welcome, honey. Happy to do it."

The thing about teenagers (or anybody, for that matter) is that you've got to pick your moments. Bring up a sensitive issue at the wrong time and the Kraken comes out and it's over. Sometimes, though, they give you a little opening when you're pretty sure they're feeling good about you. And themselves.

"Maddy, I do want to talk to you a little about what happened at the concert, you know, when you confronted me while I was talking to that woman."

We were at a fundraiser at the Samohi amphitheater. Jonah was sitting on my right and Maddy was two rows behind with Nancy. To my left was a woman named Cynthia.

"Very exciting to see Jackson Browne in such a small, beautiful setting," she said, just before Jackson came on to headline the event. Cynthia was from the UK, age appropriate, interested, and interesting.

After a couple of minutes of small talk, Maddy appeared and stood right in front of us. "Dad, you and Jonah need to find new seats."

I couldn't get her to sit back down. It was an embarrassing standoff on an otherwise picture-perfect day. It felt like the receptionist nightmare all over again. I was at a total loss as to how to resolve the situation. I looked back at Nancy, who was smiling, as if she totally approved of Maddy's behavior. Finally, Jackson took the stage and Maddy went to sit down. Jackson Browne and my HP (Higher Power) were watching out for me.

Later, back in the car with my pip-squeak: "Well Dad, I just think you should wait."

Of course she did. Like until I was dead.

I had to watch myself here, because my social life had become a hot topic at a recent therapy session after Maddy found out I was dating Rebecca, a woman I met online. I tried to keep my social life quiet, but when Maddy found out about some of the people I was seeing, she trashed them.

Rebecca had two sons around Maddy's age, one of whom was at a rehab center out of state where he was dealing with a drug problem.

"What kind of a mother could she be if her son is so messed up he has to be sent to rehab? Well, Dad? Why would you even think of dating a person like that? How do you think it affects me? Can you explain that to me? Why won't you answer me?"

I kept my mouth shut and let her vent. This was not a case of being withholding or inscrutable like my father; this was a case of trying to keep a lid on it and practice some recovery principles. When I discussed all this one-on-one with Shayna, she said that although I had been in a loveless marriage and was entitled to move on with my life and find someone new, things were still feeling like they were moving too fast for Maddy.

When I met Rebecca, we had a lot in common and I liked hanging out with her. Over time it became clear there was not enough of a spark between us, that something was missing. In the end we both felt the need to move on. Maddy's "bad mom" argument had nothing to do with that, but her attitude brought up these horrible feelings of resentment, because it reminded me of how my dad used to cross-examine me about stuff like the location of his tools or the company I was keeping.

I didn't want to live in the past. I didn't want to bring any of the baggage from my relationship with my dad into what was going on with Maddy. No small order when she knew how to push my buttons . . . just like him. It was a question of holding on and staying in the moment and giving myself time to breathe and to count before reacting. It was a question of growing up enough to begin breaking the cycle of dysfunction. This idea of creating space for myself between a negative stimulus and my reaction was clearly a huge part of my recovery, something I would be given the opportunity to practice many times over. It's a fine line, because sometimes I felt the need to stand my ground as a parent, like trying to dissuade Jonah from taking Japanese. Other times I needed to just keep my mouth shut—like in therapy with Maddy.

But now, on the drive to the Promenade, I sensed an opportunity for her and me to talk through some things. I did feel a lot of empathy for her. Because I didn't live with her anymore, I could see how me spending any free time with someone else, particularly a woman, would be hard for her. It made her feel resentful and jealous and maybe nervous that if I found someone new, I might leave her and Jonah behind.

"Well Dad, I just think you should wait."

"Wait? Maddy, Mom and I are divorced. How much longer do you feel I should wait?"

She grinned. "Another year."

"I know Mom went out with someone while she was in New York last month and that's why you had that huge meltdown. I know you were calling her all night and then she called me to go pick you up from Katie's because you were so out of control."

"She said nothing happened."

"Oh, right."

"You don't believe her?"

"I don't know what to believe, but you were way out of line on that one."

"Well, doesn't it make you mad, the thought of Mom going out with someone else?"

I always believed Nancy should find happiness with someone new, and I told her so when we finally signed our divorce papers. It was a nice moment between us. I assured her that when she did find someone new, I would welcome him into the family by taking him skeet shooting, Nancy knowing full well that I had never touched a gun in my life.

"Well, Dad? Doesn't it make you mad that Mom's going out with other people?"

"No, honey, Mom's entitled to go out with other people. Usually when couples split up, they find other people."

"Did you leave Mom for another woman?"

"Yeah, I've been hiding someone in my closet the past three years. We only go out late at night when you're in bed asleep. Or actually we go out every weekend morning, because I know you'll be crashed until noon."

Maddy thought that was funny.

"No, honey. I did not leave Mom for another woman."

We arrived at the Promenade, and I pulled into the loading zone and tried to stay in my loving Dad mode, hoping Maddy would be receptive to the point I was trying to make. "I'm really happy to be talking to you about this stuff, really I am," I said. "This way when sensitive issues come up, maybe you'll be able to calm yourself before everything spirals out of control?"

"Yeah, whatever. I have to go. Emily and Anna are probably there by now. Don't worry, mom will pick us up. Thanks, Fasha."

And she was out the door and gone.

18

GOODBYE FOREVER

FOR FATHER'S DAY IN 2006, I gave Dad a photo I found of him in *Fiddler on the Roof*. It was an East Coast summer stock production he starred in back in 1971. The picture was of Dad as Tevye, the pious Jewish milkman who lived in Anatevka, a Ukrainian village that fell prey to Russian Cossacks. Dad was outstanding in the role, probably because it so closely mirrored his parents' experience when they lived in Zaslav and were forced to leave due to the constant threat of violence.

My father wasn't a shoo-in for the part. Zero Mostel, an actor with a big persona, had originated the role, and Leonard Nimoy, a thin actor best known for an emotionally restrained character, was likely not the first person who came to mind when casting Tevye. On top of that, Ben Shaktman, who was directing the production, knew nothing about *Star Trek*. Apparently the first audition didn't go well, and Dad had to call Ben and ask for a second chance.

Very recently Ben told me that he also got a call from my mother: "Ben, this is Sandi. I shouldn't be making this call, but I want you to know that Leonard was born to play this part, and he really wants to do it."

Ben said she wasn't pleading or fawning; it was more like Detective Joe Friday from *Dragnet*: dry and to the point. Although it wasn't the reason Dad got the part, Ben said "she certainly moved the ball down the field." That was my mother.

I have a terrific family photo from the *Fiddler* tour. There was a catered dinner after one of the performances when we were also celebrating my fifteenth birthday. Ben had given me a tennis racket, which

I was opening while he was sitting at the table finishing his dinner. My father had his hand on Ben's shoulder and was leaning down to tell him something, which made Ben smile. My mother was on the right side of the frame serving birthday cake. She was wearing her fall and a head scarf and a low-cut dark-blue summer dress with white polka dots. She was smiling as she handed someone the plate of cake. She was beautiful. That was my mother.

Star Trek fans showed up to help sell out the tour. The cast and the orchestra and the production were magnificent, garnering standing ovations throughout its run.

In the photo I'd found of Dad onstage as Tevye, he was sitting on his milk cart daydreaming and smiling, singing about what his life would be like if he were a rich man. I had it custom framed and sent to his house in Bel Air. This was during that seemingly endless period when our relationship was in serious trouble. "Detaching with love" essentially meant that we were completely estranged. In Genesis, after Abraham is stopped from sacrificing his son, he returns to his servants and sets off down the mountain, leaving Isaac behind. They are never mentioned interacting ever again. Even so, I still reached out to my dad on his birthday, on Father's Day, and on holidays. Those limited conversations continued to be strained and sometimes contentious.

When Dad received the framed photo of Tevye, he sent me an email thanking me and wishing me a happy Father's Day as well. He also mentioned that in his opinion, unconditional love was "a romantic notion." He said that it was clear to him we never had a relationship that was "meaningful and satisfying" and was sadly convinced we never would. He signed off by wishing me well.

It was at moments like this when the Akedah, the Binding of Isaac, would come back to me, and I could see Abraham reaching for his blade. I could see it. I could feel it.

Days later, when the shock of his email finally wore off, I realized I was not totally surprised by what he had written. He was a man from a distant generation (or planet) who simply did not have the tools to engage. As Justin put it, "People will challenge you, especially the ones who love you, because they think you'll always be there. That's why they believe even negative engagement is better than none."

Was that what Dad wanted, negative engagement? With our estrangement weighing heavily on him, was he looking for a fight because that was better than nothing at all? I had spent a lifetime trying to process our disagreements so that he might possibly see my point of view. I had struggled all this time trying to get him to be the father I wanted him to be. Now I was worried that responding to his email would just lead to another fight. Instead of responding and engaging and arguing, I opted to take "contrary action"—which meant doing nothing at all. In Al-Anon they say that making a decision *not* to act is in itself an action. I decided to let Dad have the last word, hoping that would be the end of it, praying that maybe someday things would calm down and we might find some safe common ground on which to build a relationship.

Some months later, he followed up by sending me a six-page letter. The letter listed all the things I had done that he took exception to, all the wrongs he felt I had committed over the years. He wrote about all my screwups and missed opportunities, about my lack of accomplishment despite his numerous efforts on my behalf. He wrote about all the stupid things I had said or done. The letter read like an account of a failed and wasted life. I was shaking as I turned each page.

Much of my adult life I have struggled with the father-son dysfunction among the Hebrew patriarchs; Abraham's attempted sacrifice of Isaac and the betrayal of Isaac by his younger son Jacob, who tricked his father into giving him the blessing and inheritance intended for Jacob's older brother, Esau. Jacob went on to have twelve sons of his own but didn't care much for those boys—except the two youngest, Joseph and Benjamin, because they were born of Rachel, Jacob's favorite wife. To show his favoritism, he gave Joseph a coat of many colors (the Technicolor Dreamcoat, for you musical theater fans). The question that had nagged me throughout my life was, what can be done about this cycle of dysfunctional behavior, so clearly delineated in Torah stories written thousands of years ago? Can I break the cycle with my own father or are we doomed to repeat it?

When it came to my dad's letter, my first reaction was to waver and let him crush me; I could feel myself being bound and blindfolded. After I calmed down and had a few days to reflect, I had to admit that much of what he had written, all the examples of my mishaps, miscalculations, and mistakes through the years, that a great deal of it was true. It wasn't long after that, however, before I finally arrived at what is normally my first thought, my *F you* thought—when the idea came into my head to respond to his letter with a letter of my own. I wanted to stick it back to Dad with a list of *his* defects, just to show him that he wasn't the only one keeping score, that I had my own inventory of all the things he had pulled on me over the years, all of his screwups, all of my resentments against *him*. After a day or two of that twisted thinking, my recovery finally kicked back in and I realized that writing him back in anger would constitute an emotional relapse for which I'd have to make an amends, and there was no way I was going to do that. Once again, nothing left to do except to do nothing.

I shared all of this at the AA meetings I had been attending, while always maintaining my anonymity (Most people didn't know that I was the son of a celebrity, and I liked to keep it that way.) My brothers and sisters in recovery were all like, "Yay, Adam. That's so great. You're really working the program—by not reacting, you're 'practicing these principles in all your affairs.' This is what recovery should look like." For me, that kind of support is what the fellowship of the program is all about.

Then I told Chris Kelton about the letter. After thinking about it for a couple of days, his response was quite unexpected. Chris came up with the insane idea that I should meet with my dad, go through his letter, and make a ninth-step amends to him for everything in it. "Making an amends for all of your father's grievances and resentments is the only way to set him free and, in the end, to free yourself."

"Chris, I've done this before. I've tried to patch things up, and it never changes anything. I just can't seem to get through to him. And him writing this letter was outrageous. The guy's been sober longer than I have, and here he is taking *my* inventory."

"Writing that letter was probably not great for your dad's recovery, but that's not your concern."

"My father has never made an amends to me for the decades of drinking, so why should I make an amends to him? That would totally validate some pretty bad behavior."

"The amends isn't really for him, it's for you. Although he's probably going to feel a lot better. Your resentment toward your dad is something you've carried your whole life, and it's a major stumbling block to your recovery. Now's your chance to do something about it."

All of this from Chris Kelton. Back in the day, my father had loathed Chris and Matthew and their band of Merry Pranksters. Now, here we were decades later, and it was Chris telling me how to finally make things right with Dad and with myself.

I needed some independent verification on all this.

"I totally disagree with doing that with your dad," said Justin.

"What? Why?"

"You're going to go through your entire list of grievances with your father?"

"No. Chris said I should let my dad go through *his* list with me from that letter he wrote and that I should make a sincere and honest amends for everything and anything he throws at me."

"Ohhh . . . interesting. . . . I totally agree with doing that with your dad."

"I'm not sure I can do it. I'm not sure I can take it," I said.

"Yes you can. You've come a long way, and I can honestly tell you, my friend, this is going to lift a huge weight off your shoulders."

I didn't want to do it. The resentment was mine. I didn't want to capitulate; I didn't want to surrender; I didn't want to Let Go and Let God. I'd carried it all my life, and it was a comfort to me. Whenever I felt bad about myself, I could always pull my father out of the closet in my mind and pummel him for all the things he had said and done over the years, when he brought out Abraham's blade and held it against me. The problem with that kind of thinking is that there's no serenity in it. Chris was right. My recovery—not necessarily the possibility of relapsing by drinking and using again but my *emotional* recovery—was at risk with my resentment always looming in the background. The truest form of "contrary action" for me in this case was to take the letter to my dad and make the amends.

"You might also want to pay attention to uncomfortable situations with people who try your patience, especially family members, because those are the best times to let go of resentments. The people who challenge you the most offer the best opportunity for you to experience some personal growth." Here was an opportunity for me to finally grow up, as Krystal had advised years before. The "patience, tolerance, acceptance" that are so much a part of the program of recovery now needed to be applied to the mother of all challenges—my father.

At the end of most twelve-step meetings we as a group often recite the Serenity Prayer:

God, grant me the serenity
To accept the things I cannot change,
The courage to change the things I can,
And the wisdom to know the difference.

A woman who was the guest speaker at a recent meeting translated what this prayer meant to her: "God, please show me how to accept them and then show me a way I can change myself. Accept them, change me."

In the end it was two recovering junkies who showed me that the letter presented me with a choice: I could be right and justified in my resentment toward my Dad, or . . . I could be happy. But if I wanted to be happy, if I wanted to "trudge the road of happy destiny," I had to make the amends.

So I took that letter and I went to my father's house in Bel Air.

———————

The house was originally built as a sprawling one-story Spanish hacienda. Dad and my stepmother, Susan, had managed to morph it into something akin to traditional Japanese. The red roof tiles were painted black, and the terra-cotta stone floors were replaced with wood and then stained black. A teahouse was constructed in the backyard. The furnishings and artwork were all meticulously placed. Their home was the height of taste and style.

Dad and I sat in a room with shelves that housed an impressive collection of art books. "I like your hair," I said. "It looks good long."

"I actually just had it cut. It was even longer. We're experimenting with it for my role in the new *Star Trek* movie."

I read right through his letter from beginning to end, apologizing for my mistakes and shortcomings and all the things I had said or done that he took offense to, while at the same time thanking him for all he had done for me. Dad seemed pleased by the experience. I was feeling a sense of numbness, a detachment from my body. I couldn't quite believe what I was doing.

When it was over, Dad walked me to the door. Just before I walked out he said, "Why don't you come over on Friday night for Shabbat dinner?"

Part II

THINGS CHANGE

19

THERE ARE NO ACCIDENTS
IN RECOVERY

"WHAT CAN HE TEACH?"

"Producing, directing, acting. He can teach anything." So said Janet, a producing instructor, as she reported back to Dan Mackler, the dean of the New York Film Academy (NYFA), where I was applying for a position. Although based in Manhattan, NYFA had a significant operation in Burbank. Substitute teaching had been a satisfying (and humbling) experience, but it was time to move on.

"Can you lecture for three hours?" Dan asked.

"Dan, I can lecture for three days."

Janet had just sat through an audition/presentation I gave to her producing students about the ins and outs of directing one-hour dramas. She wanted them to get a director's perspective. Having directed over forty hours of sometimes unwatchable television, I had just enough experience to fool the class into believing I knew what the hell I was talking about.

"Directing is also performance art, the audience being whom?" I'd asked the class.

"The cast and crew?" someone responded.

"Yes, the cast and the crew and you the producers, because we the directors want to do a good job so that you'll ask us back to direct another episode. In terms of actual production, the producers, cast, and crew look very closely at guys like me who come in as guest directors, because they want to know if we know what the hell we're doing—whether we can handle the workload and whether we can handle the sometimes strong personalities of talent who star in these shows."

I mentioned to the class a series I worked on for Warner Bros. where the show's star had a bad-boy reputation. He was known for fast cars, hard partying, and misunderstandings with the IRS, and I was a little worried about this guy. On the first day of shooting, he was late to set. As we waited, I tried to distract myself by thinking about the camera shots I had planned for that day. I wasn't aware I had been pacing until I looked up and saw the crew all standing there watching me, whispering. They must have thought I was losing my marbles. The star of the show finally arrived, and he walked right up to me.

"Hey, man," he said in this low husky voice. "I just want you to know I'm a big fan of your dad's." Then he shook my hand.

OK, I know Spock has a lot of fans, but I was still a little surprised by this. "Really?" I said.

"Yeah, I started watching *Star Trek* when I was a kid, and Spock was always my guy. He had a big impact on me. I saw a lot of myself in Spock."

"Wow," I said. "Well, thank you for telling me that." Then I put my arm around this guy's shoulders and began to lead him off the set as I said fairly loudly, "Do you remember the episode where Spock had to steal the *Enterprise* to help Christopher Pike get to Talos IV?" With that I turned back to the crew and said, "Take five, guys, we'll be right back." And ha-ha, the star of the show and the crew thought that was funny, and every single day for the next eight days of production we kicked ass. The series came and went very quickly, but I prepped the hell out of that episode, and there was this creative energy and sense of fun from that very first morning.

After the class, Dan hired me on the spot. In time I would be given the opportunity to teach classes with aspiring producers, directors, and actors. Along with my former directing career, it was one of the great experiences of my life.

It must have been a hundred degrees in the San Fernando Valley that morning. I was on my way to work at NYFA and had to get off the 101 southbound to take surface streets, because as usual the freeway looked like a parking lot. As I made my way down Ventura Boulevard, I was ranting to Justin over the hands-free speakerphone.

"I'm just so totally frustrated right now. That amends to my dad was not pleasant. And I've been dragging my mother all over town trying to find a doctor who'll tell her she's dying. Maddy can be sweet as pie one minute then go into full attack mode. I'm the only tenant in my entire apartment building who remembers to take the trash down to the curb on Thursday nights, and the water pump on my car went out again to the tune of $250, and did you know—"

"Quality problems," Justin said as he cut me off.

"Yeah, well, wait a minute I'm not done. We live in a town of like four million people and I have yet to find a decent date. Not one. I just don't get it. Can you explain any of this to me?"

"Have you written a gratitude list lately?"

"Yeah, you can take your gratitude list and stick it. I mean, come on, man, this is ridiculous."

I arrived at a red light at Ventura and Coldwater Canyon. As always, Justin listened patiently before responding.

"All I can say is that you have to let go, and it's going to happen. The universe is conspiring for your happiness, and I promise you, at this moment, someone worthy is looking for you. You have to give it up to your Higher Power, and when you least expect it, something's gonna happen. Look at it this way: God is like a badass Hollywood agent working to get you the best deal in town."

"Oh, that's comforting."

"And what happened to that girl you met on Match? I thought you liked her."

"She was terrific until I found out after weeks of dating that she's a freaking card-carrying member of the Anti-Sex League."

"Dude, that's hilarious, you gotta write that down."

"George Orwell already did. You know, I'm completely convinced that internet dating is total bullshit."

"Another Orwell quote?"

"Yeah, I'm pretty sure it's somewhere in *Animal Farm.*"

Sitting at a red light that went on forever, late for work, cross traffic whizzing by in front of me. A hundred degrees in the San Fernando Valley.

"What about the one you met at the bowling alley?"

"It was great for a few weeks, but all we really had in common was . . . like . . . bowling, and I'm not even a bowler. It just gets to be so infuriating, and I feel like . . ."

BAM! Somebody smashed into the back of my car and I lurched forward.

"WHAT THE FUCK?!" I yelled as I grabbed the steering wheel and pushed the brake pedal to the floor to keep from being pushed into the cars whizzing by in front of me. People were honking as they swerved to avoid me. It was scary as hell. I finally screeched to a stop.

"Dude! What just happened?"

"Some motherfucker just slammed into me! The light was still red, and the motherfucker drove right into me!"

"Are you OK?"

"Yeah, I'm fine, but what the fuck! I gotta call you back."

"Count to ten and get a grip," Justin warned me. "You don't know what's going on with the guy who hit you, I'm sure it was unintentional."

"Yeah, I'll count to fucking ten. I gotta call you back."

I jumped out of my car and tried to breathe. Justin was right: I needed to bring some recovery into this, because I didn't want to create a scene only to find out that the guy who hit me was six foot five and could kick my ass after he made up some bullshit story about how this was all my fault. Or maybe the poor schmuck had a health problem and lost control of his car.

The guy was young and skinny, and as he was getting out of his Subaru, the front end of which was sitting on the asphalt, I noticed he had a cell phone in his hand.

He had his cell phone.

In his hand.

His cell phone.

I walked up to him and said, "Are you all right?" while thinking, *You motherfucking son of a bitch, you were texting.*

He was all apologetic and sorry and said, "Are *you* all right?"

"Yeah, I'm fine," I said while thinking, *You were fucking texting.*

"I thought it turned green," he said.

My mind started racing. *Yeah, right, you mean while you were sexting your girlfriend at thirty-five miles an hour, you were assuming it would turn green because you obviously didn't bother to fucking look.*

No brakes, no horn, no skid marks, nothing. Just used my car to help keep you from getting killed when you were about to drive straight into the intersection.

That's what my mind was thinking, stuck on that first *F You* thought, while my mouth managed to say, "Lucky nobody was hurt."

I got his information. He was all sorry and whatnot and I was like, OK, whatever. My car was a mess. The trunk looked like an accordion. I tried to drive it, but no way—the rear axle was grinding, and all I could do was get to the curb. I called for a tow.

I found out later this guy told his insurance company the only damage to my car was the muffler. Two days after that infuriating lie, the insurance adjuster called to tell me my back axle was so bent he was declaring my car a total loss.

Over the next few days, I could barely move my neck. My orthopedist said it wasn't serious, that I had some torn ligaments. He wrote a prescription for physical therapy and gave me a neck brace, which he said I didn't have to wear if it was too uncomfortable. The thing felt way too big, like I was on "the rack," like my head was being pulled off my body.

Justin told me that all this meant something, that because there are no accidents in AA, that my Higher Power was trying to tell me something.

"Oh yeah? Like fucking what?"

20

PAUSE WHEN REALLY AGITATED

I WAS DRIVING HOME FROM WORK one evening looking like an ostrich in that neck brace, which was practically choking me, when I got a call from Maddy. She was crying.

"Dad?"

"Hi, honey. What's wrong?"

"I need you."

"What's going on?"

"I don't know, everything is screwed up. I miss that you're not here and my room is a mess and I have all this work for school."

"How can I help you?"

"Can you come over?"

"Is Mom there?"

"No. She went out for dinner."

Nancy and I had been getting along, but the weather could still change, which is why I preferred to go over when she wasn't around.

"I'll see you in fifteen minutes."

When I pulled up to the house, I took off the neck brace and left it in the car. I didn't want anyone to know I'd been in a car accident. No need to worry the kids. I walked through the front door and into the living room, which was a mess. I resisted the temptation to put some books back on the shelf, take an empty In-N-Out bag to the trash, and transfer the surfboard, guitars, and snare drum to Jonah's room.

Maddy's room was also out of sorts—clothes on her bed, on her chair, overflowing from her hamper. Oh, and Maddy's room, which was once a light, calm shade of pink was now entirely a purplish red. Maddy had decided she wanted a little more color, so she and her mother painted it magenta. In-your-face magenta. *You're-gonna-get-a-migraine* magenta.

I gave Maddy a big hug.

"Why did you leave us? We were such a good family, and now you're not here and I need you." By then it had been four years since I moved out, but sometimes it still felt like we were in painful transition mode.

"I know, honey, and I'm so sorry. I know it's been hard on you guys, but I'll always be around. You know you can always call me."

"Did you see the living room?" she asked. I knew it bugged her that it was in disarray.

"Yes, Maddy, but there's nothing we can do about that now."

"What about my room? It's such a mess, there's so much stuff I want to get rid of. And I have a paper due tomorrow."

"OK, let's spend just fifteen minutes putting stuff away. We'll make a giveaway pile and then we can work on your paper."

"Thank you, Fasha. I love you so much."

"I love you too, honey."

Much like me, Maddy had always been good at organizing stuff, which we referred to as "organazizing," because that's what she called it when she was little. I dumped her hamper in the laundry room to make space for more dirty clothes. I got to work folding sweaters, stacking them neatly on her shelves. Color coordinated. Maddy grabbed some shopping bags and started going through all her drawers pulling out stuff she didn't wear anymore. Within the time allotted she managed to put together five full bags of giveaway. We made her bed, then she printed out her paper for me to read while she finished some math homework.

I was sitting on the floor next to her bed reading her essay about Winston and Julia's illicit love affair in George Orwell's *1984*—a book I knew something about. She had a lot of interesting ideas—about the telescreens and about Newspeak and Big Brother—but they were scattered, and the paper made no sense.

"Maddy, this is really good, but your ideas are a little unfocused. What do you think Orwell is saying about Winston and Julia's relationship?"

"Mr. Harris said we had to pick a topic, and mine was about betrayal."

"OK, great. What does betrayal have to do with Winston and Julia?"

"I don't know. That they got caught being together?"

"Yeah, they were definitely betrayed by those guys who turned them in, and you have that here. But isn't there more?"

"What do you mean?"

"Well, I'll give you a clue. Imagine yourself trapped all alone in a room full of clowns, which I happen to know would terrify you."

"Wait, you mean when they send Winston to Room 101?"

"Yeah, what happens in that room?"

"He doesn't want to say anything about Julia, because he still loves her, but when they put the rat cage in front of him, he can't help it and tells them to do it to her. I guess that's how he betrays her?"

"Exactly! You should write that."

"Mr. Harris doesn't care about that, just that I read the book and have some thoughts."

"But this could be a really good paper if you—"

"Dad! I don't have any time to make big changes. Just please make sure it makes some sense."

"But Maddy, I—" As I was turning my head to argue with her, I went too far and felt this sharp pain in my neck.

Right on cue, Jonah came waltzing in strumming my '68 Telecaster. "Dad, listen to this." He played some of the insane solo from Megadeth's "Hangar 18." He was note-for-note perfect. Then again, I had heard him play that riff about a hundred times.

"That's nice, Jonah. Really," I said while rubbing my neck. "But do you think you can give it a rest and maybe do a little homework?"

"Sure thing," he said as he gave me one of his fake smiles and riffed his way out of the room.

"Dad," Maddy said. "Did you hear what I said? Please finish my paper and don't make any major changes."

I managed to slowly breathe through the pain I was experiencing while I kept the pause button on my mouth, allowing me to keep my cool. With a wonderfully fake smile, just like Jonah's, I said, "OK, boubie. Whatever you say."

The front door opened and closed. I heard footsteps. Nancy appeared.

"Oh, hi. I didn't know you were here," she said, looking down at me.

This time, I turned my entire body so I could look up and talk to her. "Maddy wanted me to come over to help her clean her room."

"What's wrong with your neck?" she asked.

"Oh, I threw it out when I was at the gym."

"Hurt yourself while trying to 'keep fit'?" she said with a smirk.

Patience, tolerance, acceptance. Pause button.

"It does look good in here," Nancy continued. She noticed the give-away bags and started rummaging through them.

"Maddy you can't give this dress away; I gave it to you when you were nine. And this sweater is so cute. Why are you getting rid of it?"

Maddy looked up from her math homework. "MOM!"

"What? I'm just saying you can't get rid of all this."

"Yes I can!"

"I just think it's a waste," Nancy said as she continued to rifle through the bags. Then she turned her attention back to me. "Listen, before I forget, my check was late again, and I would appreciate it if you would pay me on time. And please don't tell me 'Check's in the mail.' It's not funny anymore."

I wanted to remind her that the last time she thought my check was late, it was sitting under a pile of junk in what used to be the living room. Instead, I took a deep breath. "I will pay you on time. And I won't say 'Check's in the mail.' Even though it is."

Later, when I left the house, I was still feeling somewhat agitated from my encounter with Nancy and the realization that, yet again, I had to leave what used to be my home and return to my apartment alone.

I got in my car and put on my neck brace.

My phone kept beeping, because I had a voicemail from my mother. Plus her requisite follow-up text telling me to listen to her message: "Adam, I'm calling to remind you about my appointment with the endocrinologist on Tuesday. Please be here at 12:30 sharp, because I had to wait two weeks to get this appointment and I don't want to be late. It would be nice if you could get here on time for your mother. Dr. Flax's office is in Mid-Wilshire, so it's going to take us a half hour to get there and—"

I deleted the message before my mother finished talking because I just wasn't in the mood. That stupid neck brace was such a pain in the neck (hah) that I pulled it off, got out of my car, walked to a trash bin that was sitting on the street, and smashed that thing until it was completely bent out of shape. I threw what was left into the bin, slammed the lid shut, and walked back to my car.

Pause button off, feeling much better.

21

VLAD THE IMPALER

MY NECK AND MY BACK were totally screwed. Even though I'd had a prescription for physical therapy, I didn't think I needed it until it became clear that I did. I soon discovered there are physical therapists all over this town. When you suddenly need one, you'll be sitting at a random intersection and notice a sign or an awning telling you that you're just feet away from a physical therapist. My orthopedist told me the only guy to see was Jake, a therapist in Beverly Hills "who worked wonders." It took half an hour to get there, when usually a twenty-minute drive to a medical appointment is my limit. If it takes longer than twenty minutes, get another provider. I made an exception for Jake.

At the first session, Jake assigned me to one of his underlings, who gave me one of the weakest back massages in the history of mankind—the guy's hands were like sponges. Then he left me on the table forever until some clown came in and ran me through a series of phenomenally lame exercises using quarter-pound weights. I suffered through three more sessions before deciding that PT in BH simply wasn't OK.

There had to be plenty of therapists in Santa Monica, which was where I was living. I was determined to get some help but didn't want to go the Google or Yelp route; I wanted a referral. That's when Martha popped into my head. Martha, the receptionist at Dr. Nolan's office, where I took Maddy for her broken foot. So many kids go through that office, I figured if anyone could refer me to a miracle worker—a real miracle worker—it had to be her.

Two days later, I was in Dr. Nolan's waiting room to see Vladimir, a therapist Martha recommended, who was subleasing office space for his newly opened PT practice. Martha was very nice as she took my prescription, photocopied my insurance card, and asked me to fill out some health info. There was something different about her. She looked much more conservative than the last time I saw her. Her brunette hair was in a tight ponytail, and she was wearing dark-framed glasses and a brown sweater with a high-neck collar. She was all librarian, as if she was trying to dress down so that men coming through the office would have no problem getting the message: *Don't hit on me.*

That didn't seem to stop some jerk who was leaning on the front counter trying to make small talk. My Spidey sense told me she wasn't interested. And that moron was blocking my view. I finished the paperwork and handed it back to Martha so that she had to turn away from that dick, who happened to be wearing a wedding ring. She thanked me, then went straight to answering her phones. Casanova gave me a snarly look before walking out the door.

I returned to the waiting area, picked up a *National Geographic*, and flipped to an article about the mating habits of cuttlefish. Apparently males attempt to fool rivals by pretending to be females as they enter the harem. Then, when the alpha male moves off, the counterfeiter turns back into a male and all hell breaks loose. I was trying to figure out how this might be some sort of metaphor for human behavior when Vladimir appeared.

A stocky thirtysomething with bushy eyebrows and a thick Russian accent, Vlad looked strong—like KGB interrogation room strong. He led me into a small exam room that had an unobstructed view of Santa Monica from Twentieth Street straight down to the Pacific Ocean. He asked about my accident and the pain in my neck and back. Next thing I knew I was lying shirtless facedown on a massage table, my face in a doughnut hole. Vlad started massaging my upper back as I asked him about his background.

Turns out he was a Russian dissident who received political asylum in the United States. "I left Moscow convinced that changes or reforms were impossible so long as Putin remained in power. Without a 'putsch,' or violent overthrow of the government, Putin will not be going anywhere anytime soon. Many people still support him—they see him as a strong leader even though he has overseen massive corruption and human rights violations during his presidency." (This of course was long before the war in Ukraine.)

Vladimir went on to tell me about the jailing and oppression of any political opposition in Russia and the suppression and intimidation of independent media. As he dug deeper into my back, I felt comfortable enough to tell him he seemed way too smart for this job. He dug in even deeper, which got me to thinking I might've insulted him. "Hey! I'm sorry if I offended you."

"No, I'm quite flattered. But I'm too old for med school and I'm pretty sure I don't have the necessary temperament anyway. Lately I've been thinking of other, more creative things to do, like welding—that is, metal sculpture. I've been working with scrap metal as a hobby for years."

In order to dig ever deeper, he began using his elbows.

"*Ahhhh!* You know, you're killing me here!"

"Yes, but you will feel better later and then you will thank me. And when you leave, there will be so many endorphins released into your blood stream you will be naturally high, and you will thank me for that, too."

Vladimir. Vlad. Vlad the Impaler.

After he finished his handiwork, I pulled myself together and floated out to the front desk, totally inebriated from those crazy endorphins.

"How was your first visit?" asked Martha.

"With Vlad the Impaler? He's certainly true to his name. That was painful."

"You'll get used to it." She smiled. "The first time is always the hardest. Some patients say hydrating helps. Can I get you a cup of water?"

"That would be great."

She crossed over to the cooler and filled a cup. As she was walking back, I was reminded of the beautiful Claudia Cardinale offering mineral water to a recuperating Marcello Mastroiani in the Fellini classic *8½*. Or more like Esmeralda offering water to Quasimodo. Even with her glasses and ponytail and turtleneck sweater, Martha glowed with her cover girl smile. She seemed to be a kind and sensitive woman and I started to think that—

"Are you OK?" she asked snapping me out of my sunshine daydream.

"Oh . . . yeah . . . I'm fine. Thank you."

Two days later, while waiting for my second session with Vlad, I picked up a copy of *Highlights for Children*. I really love *Highlights* but didn't want anyone to see me reading it, so I inserted it into an *L.A. Style* magazine.

Martha looked completely different—the glasses were gone, and she was wearing a low-cut red blouse. Her thick brown hair fell long and loose on her shoulders. My Spidey sense was tingling. Our eyes locked while she was on the phone. I smiled awkwardly, then looked away.

I checked out her left hand.

No ring.

She was talking to Sarah, a coworker, about the fact that it was April Fool's Day. I strained to overhear the conversation.

"Did Jonathan try to pull any tricks on you this morning?" asked Sarah.

"No. He slept late, and I think he forgot and I'm glad, because he's always pulling pranks on me, and I don't need any more than what I already have to put up with."

Jonathan, Jonathan . . . a boyfriend? A fiancé? A husband and they don't wear rings?

"Thirteen-year-old boys are a handful," she said as she got back on the phone.

We again locked eyes and again I awkwardly looked away. I turned to the Hidden Pictures page in *Highlights* but couldn't concentrate on finding the flashlight, the rabbit, and the glasses. My mind wandered off into a fantasy where Martha put down the phone and in slow motion shook out her long, beautiful brunette hair. Then she turned to me and smiled. I confidently strolled over to the counter, leaned down on my elbows, and gazed into her eyes as we fell deeply, madly in love.

Vlad suddenly appeared and I was caught red handed by a member of the Thought Police who was ready to take me to George Orwell's Room 101.

I was back on the massage table, only this time there was very little warm up before he began digging in. A whole lotta pain rushed through my body, but good pain—this guy knew exactly what he was doing. Facedown in the doughnut, eyes closed, wincing as he dug deeper into the two muscle spasms he'd pinpointed on either side of my spine. In between my groaning, we managed to talk about my sobriety (Vlad had been thinking about giving up the bottle), teaching as my creative outlet (Vlad was still thinking about metalworking), and my dating mishaps

(Vlad was married but regaled me with stories of his dissolute youth in Moscow). I told him how hard it was to meet quality people. He asked what I was looking for.

"Well, to start with, she must be at least twenty-five. I won't date anyone younger than that. I have a moral compass, you know."

He chuckled. "Twenty-five. That must be nice."

"No, she has to be at least forty, preferably with children so that she knows what the hell I have to go through with two teenagers. It would be nice if she maybe had a job and an active lifestyle."

At that moment—at that very moment—Martha popped into my head. Her face just appeared in my mind's eye, and I could not stop thinking about her. I didn't want to put Vlad on the spot by mentioning her. I didn't know what the office politics were, and it was none of my business. During the rest of the conversation, while we were talking about women and dating and Vlad was digging away, I had to struggle to keep Martha's name from slipping out of my mouth. It was like Winston in that torture room with those rats, fighting so hard not to give up Julia. I didn't want to embarrass myself if she was with someone. She was probably out of my league anyway. I didn't want to seem crass or out of place or too forward or—

"What do you think of Martha?" Vlad asked.

If I were directing this as a scene in a TV show, I would cut to a low angle under that doughnut my face was stuck into, a close-up of my eyes popping wide open when Vlad mentioned Martha's name.

I thought carefully about how to respond. In the most casual, off-handed way I said, "What *about* Martha?"

"She's divorced and has a thirteen-year-old son. It's hard for a woman in her position to meet people. I hear her talking about this with the other girls in the office. Do you want me to say anything to her?"

"No. I appreciate that. I should probably ask her myself. But thank you for considering me a worthy candidate."

"She's a very nice person," Vlad continued, "always cheerful in the office. And she's a very good worker, always a step ahead anticipating what needs to be done in any situation. She helps me get patients in and out at a pretty good rate."

Just then, as if on cue, there was a knock on the door followed by Martha's muffled voice. Beautiful, sexy, fortysomething Martha.

"Vlad, your eleven o'clock is here."

22

MY HOLLYWOOD MOVIE SHOOT

LIFE AT THE NEW YORK FILM ACADEMY was going surprisingly well. The first-year directing students were shooting little films with no sound so that they could work on visual storytelling, and they were coming up with some amazing little vignettes. Then we moved up to dialogue scenes, which we would discuss in detail and they'd prep the scene, then we'd all go out on location and shoot it.

One of the students brought in a scene about a couple having an argument at a gas station. The two of them are already into it when they pull up to the gas pump. While he is filling up, she is standing there accusing him of spending too much time at the office. *He* is upset with *her* for letting some guy hit on her at a nightclub. Gas tank full, he tells her to get back in the car, but she repeatedly refuses. He finally gets in and drives off, leaving her stranded. Later, while she's sitting on a bus bench in front of the station, he drives up. She gets in and they drive off together as if nothing happened, as if they've been through this routine a dozen times before.

Like most first-time directors, the students were obsessed with where to put the camera. "Where does the camera go, where does the camera go?"—I would hear this repeatedly in my first-year directing classes, and I always had the same answer, which came straight from the Leonard Nimoy School of Directing when I asked him the same question: "The camera goes where the camera goes," my dad would say. "The question is what is the scene about? Once you dig deep and figure out what's really going on, then you have a better idea of how to block the actors in relation to each other. Once you figure all that out, it becomes pretty obvious where to put the camera." This was a credo I lived by throughout my directing career, and it served me well.

In my own words, I tried to explain this to my students from day one: "We teach three things here at the film school: story, story, story. It's story, people, and it's always been about story for thousands of years. We just happen to be storytellers working in a visual medium. If your story has problems, you're in big trouble. What we really teach here is story, performance, and technique, and by technique I mean the technical aspects of filmmaking, all the things you have to do to get your story and performances on film. I'm talking about locations and cinematography and production design and editing and color correction and scoring—all things you need to know, and as you're learning from your course curriculum, there is a helluva lot to know. But if your story has holes or your performances are weak, no one is going to care about your technique; no one is going to care how pretty your movie looks.

In helping them develop the gas station scene, I again channeled my father: "If this scene is simply about a couple arguing because of his work obsession or her flirtation, then you're going to run into trouble, because you're playing it on the nose—you're playing it exactly as written and it's going to get boring very quickly. What else could be going on between these two people? What's the real story here?"

"She's pregnant and hasn't told him, because she's testing him to see if he's long-term material."

"Perfect! Yes. What else? What about from his perspective?"

"He wants to see how much she really cares about him, because an old girlfriend called and wants to get back together, and after the incident at the nightclub, he's considering it."

"Right on. Now you have a potent backstory. Now the actors have something to play because their characters have real life wants and needs."

Then they rewrote the ending so that when he came back to pick her up, the minute she got in the car they simultaneously said "I'm pregnant" and "I'm sorry and I love you."

Then we broke the scene down and plotted out where the actors should be and what camera angles would work best. All wonderful, except that when we got to the location—an Arco station at the corner of Franklin and Gower in Hollywood—the rehearsal descended into total chaos. It was as if we had never discussed the scene and my students were back to square one trying to figure out how to stage and shoot it. Then we discovered that someone forgot to bring the camera cards—i.e., the film. I was so annoyed I walked off to sit in my camping chair next to a gas pump to let them figure it all out. I sat there thinking this was a far cry from my glory days when I was shooting TV shows on location.

I was also a little preoccupied thinking about Martha.

After I got out of that second torture session with Vlad, endorphins raging, I floated out to Martha's desk.

"How was it today?" she asked as she handed me a cup of water.

"As painful as always," I said. "That man's a maniac."

"He's our secret weapon. He knows how to get the job done but doesn't take prisoners," she said with a sly smile.

The light was perfect. Her hair was thick and beautiful. That low-cut red blouse. What a gorgeous woman. In my blissed-out state of mind, I started to think, *I could love this woman.* After all the dating mishaps I had been through, after all the weirdness and disappointments, this was the way my mind still worked.

I could love this woman.

It was just ridiculous. I didn't even know her.

But *Vlad* knew her. Vlad vouched for her.

I was simply not ready nor thinking clearly enough to do anything about it, so I made another appointment and floated out of the office. Then I called Justin.

"Dude! She asked the Impaler about you. They talked about you. She wants to go out with you. This is perfect!"

He seemed overly enthusiastic. "Dude, you're getting way ahead of yourself. I'm not convinced they were talking about me. Don't you think she gets hit on in that office like all the time?"

"Yeah, but she turns them down, because she's been waiting for someone, someone very special, someone worthy of her love and affection—and that someone is you! You need to call her up and say you want to schedule another appointment or reschedule the one you have. When that's done, you say you need to schedule a coffee date for the two of you. Tomorrow—it must happen tomorrow."

"But what if she's seeing someone that Vlad doesn't even know about?"

"Then ask her if she's seeing somebody. If she says no—and she will—ask her if she *wants* to see somebody, that somebody being you. Or, you can simply say, 'What's your favorite ice cream? We should go get some.'"

I made the call. At first, she seemed a little resistant to my invitation to meet for a coffee.

"Is there an office policy against dating patients?" I asked.

"No, there's no policy," she said. Then she said the best time for her to get together was after work over dinner, and she suggested we meet at a restaurant that was located close to her office. It was a very hip, upscale place that boasted a "seasonal kitchen," which is a euphemism for "expensive dining." It was one of those places with high prices and microscopic portions, but I loved the ambiance.

Soft lighting, nice décor. Martha in another low-cut blouse.

After we ordered I asked about her background, and she told me of her Catholic school upbringing but said she wasn't devout and would probably burn in hell for her sins. She told me about her careers in modeling and stunt driving, both cut short by her mother, who convinced her that neither was a real job. She told me about her years working for United Airlines in corporate reservations until she was let go due to major layoffs after 9/11. Then we talked about working at the doctor's office.

"What I really want to know, Martha, is don't you get hit on all the time in that office, just sitting there all day, looking so pretty?"

She blushed and smiled. "Most of the guys who come in are married dads, which doesn't always stop them. Anyway, I try not to put that kind of energy out there."

Yeah, except maybe the day you showed up in a low-cut red blouse. "What do you say to them when they ask you out and you're not interested?"

"I thank them and tell them I'm seeing someone."

"What if you are interested?"

She hesitated. "You're only the second guy who's come through the office that I've gone out with."

"Only the second? How long have you worked there?"

"Almost two years."

"Wow. I feel honored. You know, at first, I wasn't really sure you wanted to go out. You seemed a little hesitant for some reason, and I was worried that maybe I was out of line for asking you."

Or out of my league.

"I was in shock that you asked me. The last time you were in you seemed as if you were unhappy about something. You never chatted me up the way the other guys try to do, and I thought you had no interest in me."

"It must have been my endorphin-induced stupor that Vlad puts me in when he digs into my back. I was totally spaced out."

That and the fact that while we were making my follow-up appointment, I was trying to decide where in the South Pacific we might go for our honeymoon.

"What happened to the first guy you dated?"

"What do you mean?"

"You said I was the second person you dated from the office. What happened to the first?"

"Why do you want to know?"

"Just curious."

"Tell me about your legal career. You know, my uncle also went to Loyola Law School."

"Don't try to change the subject. What happened to the first guy?"

She hesitated.

I knew this wasn't really an appropriate line of inquiry, but sometimes enquiring minds want to know.

Martha continued. "He was a doctor from another office on our floor."

"Oh, wow. And?"

More hesitation. The restaurant was filling up by then.

"On our first date . . . he got drunk."

"And . . . "

"And what? Tell me about when you were directing TV shows. That must have been interesting."

"What happened?"

"You're very persistent."

"You have me at the edge of my seat."

Martha looked me in the eye and appeared to be making up her mind. "OK, you asked for it. He got drunk and then insisted we go back to his place because he said he wanted to fuck, and surprise, surprise, I'm not that kind of girl. I had to ditch him and get a cab home and so here we are."

All I could say to that was "Please don't come back to my place. It's a mess."

I liked Martha. She was easy to talk to and felt comfortable enough to share that little story with me. I liked her because she was clearly a woman with discriminating taste. She also told me she had parents who were politically conservative Fox News devotees. I try to be tolerant and respectful of all points of view, but I was worried she herself might be too far to the right—the antithesis of the way I was raised. In 1969 my parents took me and Julie to UCLA for a candle-lighting vigil to protest the war in Vietnam. Dad campaigned in thirty-five states when George McGovern ran against Richard Nixon in 1972. He flew his single-prop plane all over Massachusetts campaigning for George H. W. Bush's future opponent Mike Dukakis when he first ran for governor. Thanks to Dad's connections, I interned on Capitol Hill for House Speaker Tip O'Neill and Colorado senator Gary Hart, both Democrats. I was pretty much convinced that Martha was more than likely a fan of Ronald Reagan, that our perspectives were too far apart, that a relationship didn't make much sense and that I should probably end it right there after that first date.

On our second date, we drove up to a beach in Malibu, where we re-created that scene in *From Here to Eternity* where Deborah Kerr and Burt Lancaster make out in the Hawaiian surf. Well, it was almost like that. Malibu is not Oahu and I'm no Burt Lancaster, but we did kiss on the beach, and it was lovely. As the sun set, we walked back to my car arm in arm, which felt comfortable and easy—like we'd been together for months.

All of that was running through my head as I sat in my camping chair, next to a gas pump, at an Arco station. Daydreaming about Martha, wondering how she felt about me, debating when I should call her to set up our next date. That's when the sound of Spock's voice snapped me right out of it: "Negative, Captain. The *Enterprise* is now moving in a circular course."

I turned around and looked up to see a TV inside the Arco convenience store showing a clip from *Star Trek*.

Seeing Spock at the gas station gave me a sense of pride, a feeling I usually had when dad's alter ego suddenly appeared. The fact is, when times with Dad were good or bad, Spock was always everywhere. Since the very beginning, I've had this radar for Spock. When I was a kid, I was always on the lookout for him, leafing through *TV Guide* or fanzines looking for images of my father. Sometimes my Spidey sense would tingle and I'd immediately spot him at random in a newspaper or magazine, on a billboard or in graffiti art, on a bumper sticker, or on a TV hanging in an Arco station.

Justin recently told me that whenever I was having a positive thought about my dad, I should act on it immediately and call him. Lately I had been feeling good about Dad. Since my amends, things had definitely gotten better between us and I was regularly showing up to Shabbat dinners. I was also beginning to understand that if we were going to succeed, I simply needed to accept him for who he was, let go of my resentments from the past, which he seemed to be doing with me, and steer clear of conversations that could lead us back to our downward spiral. Sitting there at the station, I knew it was a good time to call, because he was at that moment acting in the new *Star Trek* movie, and apparently things had been going quite well. While my class continued to wait for the camera cards so that we could finally start shooting, I called Dad, thinking he might be on set (just like me!) and I'd leave him a message. Turned out he was in his trailer in between scenes.

"We've shot two days already in a warehouse in Tustin. Must have been a hundred extras with green screen to add in thousands more. Three cameras going, big, complicated production, one camera that sweeps around and ends up in a tight close-up for my line. J.J. seems to know what he's doing. I think it's going to be good."

Our conversation went well. I told him I was happy for him. After we hung up, I started thinking, *One hundred extras, three cameras, J.J. this, J.J. that. I used to be a director too—until my pot habit and attitude problem led me to the crash and burn.*

One episode in the crash and burn went something like this:

WRITER/PRODUCER: *This is the way I want you to direct the scene.*

ADAM: *So what you want is melodrama.*
WRITER/PRODUCER: *If that's what you want to call it, that's what I want.*
ADAM: *Well, if that's what you want, why don't you direct it?*
WRITER/PRODUCER: *I will. Have a seat and watch.*

And that is, in part, how I ended up sitting in a camping chair at an Arco gas station on the corner of Franklin and Gower.

I picked up a copy of *Daily Variety* one of the students had brought to the set. I hadn't read the trades in years, because I hated reading about how all my colleagues were succeeding in Hollywood. On page 1 there was an article about a guy I knew in law school who had just been appointed cochair of NBC Universal.

I couldn't take it anymore. I called Justin.

"Dude," he said, "compare and despair. It makes no sense to compare how you feel inside to other people's outsides, because for all you know your law school buddy might be more miserable than you are because, like everybody else, what he really wants to do is direct. And lastly, my friend, the thing is, you have clearly chosen to be a bodhisattva in this life."

"I know that's a killer Steely Dan song, but what the hell does it mean?"

"Someone who is satisfied with very little so that you might show others the way. You may not be consciously aware of it, but you have chosen a much smaller path than your dad and your law school classmate. Your job is to walk that path well. Who loves you, baby?"

And then he hung up.

OK, whatever, screw it. The camera cards had arrived. I got up from my camping chair and walked the smaller path over to my students.

23

A PAGE FROM MY BOOK

It was eleven thirty on a Sunday morning when I parked my car on Clarkson Road. I brought a turkey sandwich that I was going to eat while I hung out with the kids. I picked up the Sunday paper, which was still lying in the driveway of the pretty Spanish house on the hill. As I approached the front door, I could hear yelling coming from inside. Nancy and Maddy were going at it. I let myself in and walked to the kitchen, where sparks were flying.

Maddy's mouth was moving. "You always do what you want. You never take my feelings into consideration! I don't want him coming to the party!"

Nancy countered: "It's a dinner party! There will be lots of people here!! What is your problem?!"

"What's going on here?" I asked.

They finally stopped to notice me.

"Your daughter is completely out of control!"

"It's not me, it's you! You don't care about my feelings!"

The kitchen was small, basically a square room in the middle of the house with a counter above the sink that opened up to the family room we had built. Nancy had the original cabinets painted a light purple, the countertop was sort of a turquoise green, and across from the refrigerator sat the white classic Gaffers and Sattler stove I brought from the El Greco.

Nancy and Maddy were both glaring at me when I asked a very simple question. "Has anybody had any breakfast?"

Simultaneously—Nancy: "What?!" Maddy: "No!"

I turned to Maddy. "Maddy, it's a good thing I happen to have a turkey sandwich." I lifted the bag and shook it.

"I don't want the sandwich. I don't need a sandwich. I'm not hungry! You always think I'm hungry when I'm mad!" She stormed out into a hallway that led to her bedroom, slamming the door behind her.

Right on cue, Jonah walked in with his (my) Fender Stratocaster. "Dad, listen to this riff." It was from AC/DC's "Hell's Bells."

"Jonah, honey, can you give me and Mom a minute here?"

"Yeah, sure," as he walked out wailing away.

Nancy was in tears. "What am I going to do with her? She treats me like I'm her prisoner. All I want to do is have some people over for dinner including Mark Greenberg, and she's throwing a fit and I don't even see Mark anymore. If I show anyone else any attention, she throws a fit. She has me on a leash and she's terrorizing me."

I gave Nancy a hug and patted her on the back. "I have an appointment on Tuesday with Maddy and Shayna. Maybe the two of you should take it," I said.

Through the sobbing she said, "Thank you, that's very nice of you. I so appreciate it."

I really enjoyed these moments with Nancy when we could be friends again and helpful to each other and leave the acrimony behind, and quite often now we were able to do it. (I also enjoyed the fact that I wasn't the only one getting skewered by Maddy about seeing other people.)

As Nancy reached for a tissue to blow her nose, we could hear Maddy (read, Kraken) coming out of her bedroom. She stormed back into the kitchen.

"Where's that sandwich?!"

24

THE DICK CHENEY DESK SET

"TELL ME YOU LIKE MY ROOM," Martha said as she lit some candles.

We had just finished a nice Italian dinner at Pizzicoto in Brentwood when Martha invited me over to "watch a movie." She was living with her parents at the family two-story in Brentwood, having moved there after her divorce. Since she was working full time, it seemed like a good decision, as her parents were willing to help take care of her thirteen-year-old son.

I had already been to the house to meet her parents and her son the week before. I was worried that Jonathan might be the conservative, country club type of kid, but no, he had long hair and wore a black T-shirt and Vans tennis shoes—the spitting image of Jonah at that age.

When I met her parents, I brought over a bottle of wine and some chocolates. Martha warned me her mother could be tough. With three sons and four daughters, I guess you have to be. When I was introduced to Betty, Martha stood behind me as if she was taking a position to catch me in case her mother took a swing. Her parents were definitely ham on white with mayo. They were also sweet people with fascinating histories of "Old L.A."—her mother said she could trace her roots back to the Portolá expedition.

"Do you know about Portolá?" her mother asked.

"You mean the expedition of 1769?" I replied. "What's interesting is that those guys stopped for water at what is now University High, my alma mater. The Tongva natives had a village there, and the freshwater springs are still bubbling up on that campus."

He shoots. He scores.

Martha's father's family bought the tract of land they were currently living on; they had purchased it in the early 1900s when Brentwood was still referred to as "the country." I asked her dad, Don, what it was like living there back then.

"In 1931, when I was just a boy, we had to rent out our house and move into an apartment because of the Depression. We rented it to Mr. Alisini who was an 'importer.'"

"You mean a bootlegger," I said.

"We never used that word. He was a very nice man—always paid my father in cash and always invited him in to 'sample the goods.'"

We must have talked for an hour. When we left to go to dinner, Martha said, "Well, *that's* never happened before. What do I have to do to impress your mother? Convert?"

Martha and I had been dating for three weeks, but I had never been up to her room and she had never seen my apartment. I enjoyed her company. I enjoyed the dining out and the hikes we took through the Santa Monica Mountains. Although we were affectionate, I was in no hurry to "move things along," because I was still worried about her conservative background and wasn't convinced this relationship made any long-term sense. Still, I went with the flow when she invited me back to her house after informing me no one was home.

"Tell me you like my room," she said as she lit some votive candles.

It was summer and the last light of day was streaming through the windows opposite the bed. White curtains, a warm, washed-out turquois color on the walls. Nice big California king bed with a stuffed fabric headboard. Her cat lying on the bed next to a teddy bear. Small alcove sitting area with a desk and a loveseat.

"It's beautiful, really. The lighting is incredible. I do like your room."

Gorgeous eyes, beautiful hair, cream-colored blouse, tight jeans. She was in stocking feet, having kicked off her ankle boots. She came close and kissed me. Her cat started meowing in the most irritating way. I like cats, but sometimes their timing stinks.

"I've got to take her downstairs and feed her," she said. "I'll be right back. Make yourself comfortable."

I walked around the room looking at her stuff. Videotapes of romantic comedies like *You've Got Mail* and *Under the Tuscan Sun*. Framed pictures of Jonathan growing up. Her little white desk with all her bills stuffed into a letter holder. Her open closet with a stack of jeans, pretty blouses, her collection of low-cut ankle boots. For a split second I thought of peeking into her dresser. Her bedside table had a framed photo of Martha and her family on a Hawaiian vacation. There was also a cool-looking pen-and-pencil box set. I picked it up and opened it. It was an official Richard Cheney vice presidential signature set.

My mind went into overdrive: *A Dick Cheney pen-and-pencil set by her bedside. Dick Fucking Cheney. Puppeteer of President George W. Bush and architect of the Iraq War. Approval of waterboarding torture and the lies about WMDs and the baseless claims that Osama bin Laden was pals with Saddam Hussein. Outing CIA agent Valerie Plame because her husband revealed the lie about Saddam supposedly buying uranium from Africa. Offering up his own chief of staff to go to fucking prison for leaking Plame's name. Lies and lies and three thousand US troops dead and over thirty thousand wounded or suffering from PTSD and over a hundred thousand Iraqis dead and what a fucking sack of shit.*

I was sweating. A lump was forming in my throat. I could feel a headache coming on. Martha burst back in and quickly closed the door. "Cat's happy. I left her downstairs."

She noticed me holding the pen-and-pencil set.

"Isn't it cool?" She looked up at me. "Is something wrong?"

"Martha, could I trouble you for a cup of ice water?"

"Of course. Are you all right?"

"Yeah, no, I'm fine. Throat's a little dry, is all."

She bolted out the door giving me a minute to pull my shit together. When she came back, I sat down on her bed and gulped the entire glass.

"Where'd you get the desk set?" I stupidly asked.

"A friend of mine brought it back from the convention." She sat down next to me. "Do you wanna see the rest of my pen collection?"

"Martha, I—"

That's when she jumped me and started making out with me. We fell back on her bed, and miraculously, I started to feel a lot better. Things got totally nutty as we were rolling around on that California king, wrestling like a couple of teenagers. Fully clothed but kissing and rolling and grinding and knocking shit off the bedside table, including that Dick Cheney desk set. It was crazy, absolutely nuts, but I had to put a stop to this before it got totally out of hand. I couldn't go through with this with Cheney in the room.

"OK, let's hold on a second. Can you wait a minute?"

Martha wasn't listening or didn't hear me, and that woman was strong, because she wouldn't let go and the rolling and kissing continued. She had told me she worked out at the Y, and she meant it. She started to unbutton my shirt and I let her. She began to unbutton her blouse and I suddenly felt the need to put a stop to this. I started making out with her then proceeded to roll us right off the bed.

Landing on her carpet seemed to make an impression. "What the hell is wrong with you?!"

We got back on the bed. As we were lying there, breathing hard, looking at each other, she seemed to be trying to figure out what was going on, searching to see if she could understand what was happening. She had the most incredible brown eyes.

"What if your parents come home?" I asked.

"They're at their house in Arrowhead for the weekend."

"What if your boy comes home?"

"He's with his father. I told you all this."

Another pause of her trying to figure me out. Then she seemed to let it all go as she crawled over and rested her head on my chest. She gently swept her fingers up and down my arm.

"You have beautiful striations in your shoulder," she said, "but you probably can't even see them."

There was this calmness. A pause.

"Can we just wait a little longer?" I asked.

She lifted her head to look at me, searching me with those eyes.

"I can wait if you can," she said.

It was nighttime by then, and the candlelight made everything glow. So glad to be sober, so grateful to be able to feel everything and stay in the moment, to just be in the moment with her.

"It's kind of refreshing actually," she said as she folded back into my arms. "Most men don't act that way."

I guess most men don't know Dick like I do.

———————

The following night I was at Brennan's, an Irish bar in Marina del Rey. Justin had just finished the first set of his gig playing bass with a cover band called Dazed and Confused. They played '70s classic rock songs like "Radar Love" and "Sweet Emotion." The band was tight and hilarious to watch. They all wore long-haired wigs—like, really long. Justin was amazing on his Rickenbacker bass with his black wig and aviator glasses, shirtless with a Sonny Bono faux-fur vest and tight black-and-white striped pants. He was an absolute force of nature when he played. I loved his energy. Maddy told me she thought I was a total loser until I brought Justin to the Clarkson Road house to meet her and Jonah. They adored him.

After the set, a sweaty Justin and I grabbed our club sodas and sat at a corner table. Brennan's is not your typical bar. It's painted yellow and green on the outside—a freestanding building that advertises turtle races every first and third Thursday. It has a whole setup next to the bar for these races, though I've never been to one and have trouble imagining the allure unless you're shit faced.

"The doctor is in, dig? Lay it on me, my homie."

"I'm worried about Martha. I think she's falling for me, and that makes me nervous, because I may need to get out of this. I'm just not sure she's the right woman. I mean, she's gorgeous and sweet and kind, but what if I have to get out?"

"You're thinking way too far into the future. You might want to relax and take this one day at a time. A Dick Cheney pencil is not worth flipping out about."

"Yeah, it's not just that. Her parents are full-on Catholic conservative. They're, like, total Fox News people. I'm really worried about falling head over heels for her, because then I'd be taking her home to meet my mother, who would never, ever approve, and all hell would break loose, and I just don't think I could deal with it."

I was fifty-one years old—too old to let my mother enter into the question of whether or not to continue with a relationship. Martha did check off so many things on the list I kept in my head. It was the things that I couldn't check off that worried me.

Justin nodded. "Dude, I've been giving your situation a lot of thought. It's quite simple, really: a hottie is totally into you and doesn't seem to care about *your* politics, so what is your problem? *Una mujer de calidad*, baby. You've been on so many lame dates, there is no doubt in my mind that some of those chicks were leftists, liberals, pinkos, or commies, so what difference does it make? You're two adults recreating together. Stop overthinking it and enjoy yourself."

Justin would have made a great therapist, but opted instead for a career impersonating doctors to get pharmacies to fill bogus opiate prescriptions.

"Shouldn't I at least try to tell Martha who Dick Cheney really is and all the fucked-up shit that's gone down because of him?"

"You are not empowered to educate her, fix her, reform her, or rehabilitate her. That is not your job. You cannot change people, you can only change yourself—hence the Serenity Prayer. And besides all that, are you seriously going to let a dick like Dick Cheney ruin your love life?"

25

MY CINNAMON GIRL

"Dad, I've been taking some pages from your book when teaching the basics about filmmaking to my directing students. Things you taught me when I was starting out."

"Really? Like what?"

"Like the time you gave me an assignment to go out and shoot something without dialogue. I remember you telling me that if I couldn't find ways to dramatize scenes using visual cues, then I hadn't done my job as a director, and that's what I'm trying to get across to my students."

"Good advice," he said.

Those were the kinds of exchanges I was having with my dad. We seemed to be getting back on track, and it felt good to be regularly communicating with him. He was very interested in the classes I was teaching and even gave me all his files with lesson plans from the acting classes he used to teach in the early '60s.

Most of my classes at the New York Film Academy were made up of foreign students. In one of my first-year directing classes, I had Julian from Spain, Isabella from Italy, Karl from Australia, and Manuel from Venezuela. The group showed promise and often managed to fool me into believing they were actually listening to what I was trying to teach them.

"OK, you guys," I announced in class one day. "I've seen all your ten-week films, and for the most part your work is excellent. All the films have a beginning, middle, and end. They have clear narratives dramatizing strong themes, there's some kind of character arc, and most of the films showcase strong performances. I also want to point out that almost all your films rely heavily on dialogue, forcing me to remind you once again there's so much more you can and should be doing in terms of visual storytelling. This is why the first three short films we assign you in this class are all MOS, which means what?"

Karl chimed in: "Mic out of shot?"

"Close, but why the hell would you want the microphone *in* the shot?"

Karl again: "Mic offstage."

"Mic way the hell offstage. We don't let you record sound while you're shooting your shorts, because it forces you to tell your stories visually. The minute we give you guys a microphone, what do you do? You turn your movies into talking heads. All of you have way too many scenes of people standing around talking. Anyone can shoot those. Anyone can shoot a master two shot and some over the shoulders and some close-ups of people talking. Your grandmother could do it. That's why we keep looking at clips from *The Graduate* and *The Deer Hunter* and *American Beauty*: because those films rely heavily on a visual narrative—you don't need dialogue to know what the hell is going on."

"But doesn't dialogue reveal things we need to know about the character?" asked Julian.

I just loved these guys. The ones who asked questions and challenged me all sat in the front few rows. We were in a classroom that looked weirdly like the church rooms where we have our AA meetings: linoleum floors, overhead fluorescents, uncomfortable chairs. The only difference was that we were on the ninth floor of an office building that had a pretty view of Forest Lawn Memorial Park across the street.

"Sure, of course, dialogue is important, but people say shit all the time. Talk is cheap. It's what people *do* that really has an impact, because what they do tells us who they really are. Let me give you an example. . . ."

The next part of the lecture was all from recent personal experiences with a certain special someone and her family, but I never let on that this had anything to do with me.

"A boy and girl start dating and they're really into each other. How do you show it?"

"Walking hand in hand," says Karl.

"Yes. What else?"

"Looking into each other's eyes," said Isabella.

Yes. What else?

"In bed."

"Julian, I was betting you'd be the first to get them into bed. Yes, the bed, but there are so many other things they could be doing together: bike riding, walks on the beach on a moonlit night, sharing an ice cream, window shopping, dancing—the list goes on and on. But wait, there's more, because we come to a sequence where the girl is going off on a camping trip with her family, and the guy, our poor protagonist, wasn't invited and he's there to see them off. Right? How do we show that?"

"The camera watches them driving away and then ends up on him alone," says Manuel.

"Perfect. Simple. Then we see our poor slob at his apartment reading or watching TV or playing video games. You can have a montage of this, little edits that show us what?"

"He's trying to distract himself."

"Bingo. Then he turns off the TV and picks up a picture of him and his girlfriend. Then we cut to him rummaging through his storage unit where he's pulling out camping gear. What's he doing?"

Julian: "He's going to go camping on his own to clear his head."

"Julian, for a Spaniard, sometimes you are so unromantic."

Isabella: "He's going after the girl."

"He's going after the girl! Next we see him driving through the mountains and then maybe a time cut where he's pulling into a parking lot in front of a lodge. And who does he see through his windshield getting ready to go out on a group bike ride?"

Karl: "The girl and her family."

"The girl and her family. So they ride off and he gets out of his car and takes his mountain bike off his roof rack. Cut to the family all happily riding together—the girl, her mother and father, and her brother. They're having so much fun when who should ride up from behind them? Our poor slob the protagonist. What a surprise! And the girl is beaming she's so damn happy, but her parents are like, *What the fuck is this?* So how do we show all of that?"

Manuel: "Close ups."

"Yes, but what are we seeing in those close-ups? Remember that scene from *Braveheart* where the king's son is marrying the princess from France and she discovers he's clearly not into her, he'd much rather be marrying his boyfriend who's standing nearby. How did they convey all of that?"

Manuel again: "Looks."

"Looks! Looks can tell us everything and no one needs to say a word. Looks. The girl's parents want their daughter to know they're pissed, like *How dare this slob crash our family vacation?* Then, of course, while they're riding up a fire road the chain on her brother's bike breaks, but no problem! Our protagonist has a chain link repair kit! Then we cut to dinner that night at the lodge. Our protagonist regales everyone with stories, paying particular attention to the parents, who are enthralled. When the dad asks for the check, the waiter indicates our protagonist already took care of it. The parents are all impressed by this guy. Then we cut to the girlfriend, who's doing what?"

Isabella: "She is smiling at him and glowing."

"But wait, there's more!"

"Cut to the sun rising over the Yosemite Valley. Our protagonist is sleeping on the ground in his one-man tent. Suddenly, the girl appears, scaring the shit out of him. The next shot is them hiking up to the base of Yosemite Falls, but it's so early there's no one around. She leads him off the path and they climb some boulders until they find a secluded spot. She throws down a picnic blanket and looks at our now not-so-poor slob protagonist with a smile. You guys know the rest.

"The next cut could be a time cut of the Valley; the sun is now well above the horizon with El Capitan completely lit up. Cut to the couple lying on their backs looking up at the sky, all blissed out. Then their POV, their point of view, looking at the tops of the trees that are swaying in the morning breeze. And the last cut, a wide shot of the couple where they lie, but now there's a shaft of light shining down on their secluded spot.

"So, what are we saying with all these images? What simple truth are we specifically trying to convey about this couple without using a single word of dialogue?"

Isabella: "That it is impossible for them not to be together, that they have come together in the sight of God."

26

EVERYBODY SHOULD
JUST GET ALONG

BOTH MY MOTHER AND MY FATHER met Martha for the first time at a college graduation party for Alex, my sister Julie's oldest son. We were at Julie's house for a dinner celebration with extended family and friends. Dad came with my stepmother, Susan, and my mother was there as well, so . . . it was a little awkward for everyone. People kept going over to my dad and Susan's table to say hello. I sat down next to my mother.

"Everyone is going over to your father's table to say hello to the celebrity and his wife," she said. "You father and his wife—"

At that point I cut her off. "Mother, may I remind you that this is Alex's graduation party, and it would be really nice if you could let it go and try to enjoy yourself."

Mom settled down, but then Alex put on some dance music, and when Susan got up to dance with my kids and Julie's kids, that was a bridge too far: "If she thinks she can just waltz in here and start dancing around with *my* grandchildren, she's got another thing coming."

Mom started to get up from the table.

I grabbed her arm. "Mother, I'm going to give you two choices. I can either escort you right out the front door and stick you in a cab and send you home, or . . . you can sit down and I'll bring you a nice piece of chocolate cake for dessert. Now what's it going to be?"

Mom stood there considering her options. The parents of one of Alex's friends were sitting nearby, and their eyes went wide as they witnessed this exchange. It was an otherwise beautiful outdoor dinner party in Julie's backyard—white tablecloths, candles on the tables, and string lights overhead. It was a warm June night in the San Fernando Valley. There was no way I was going to let my mother ruin everything by taking this opportunity to tell off my stepmother—an urge Mom had entertained for years.

She seemed to come to her senses as she slowly sat back down. "I'll have some cake. With extra frosting."

"Great. I'm going to walk away now. Please don't get up from the table."

Just as I was leaving, Martha appeared, sat down next to my mother, and started chatting her up. All seemed well in the world.

"Martha is very sweet," my mother said the following week when I was over at her house. "Although I still don't understand why you feel the need to date a Catholic. You know what they did to us during the Holocaust."

"Mother, I'll have you know that Martha's father fought the Nazis at the Battle of the Bulge when he was a teenager. He was wounded and awarded the Purple Heart. So do not even go there."

"Fine. And I'll have *you* know that when Martha and I were talking, I never let the word 'Obama' slip out of my mouth."

Then came the day for Mom to meet Martha's parents. I was nervous about that one. We were to have lunch at the top of Hotel Angeleno, that round tower at Sunset and the 405. I would have picked something more low-key and on the ground floor, but Martha's parents made the rez. I was nervous about my mother and her left-wing WAR IS NOT HEALTHY FOR CHILDREN AND OTHER LIVING THINGS poster lifestyle meeting up with people from *The O'Reilly Factor*. Martha and her parents arrived early and were up in the tower while I waited in the lobby for my mother, who was being dropped off by Santiago. When she showed up, I could tell right away she was high. That was so me when I was using every day. I showed up to everything stoned. Except I think I was much better at hiding it. Or not.

"Do I need to get my car right now and take you home?" I asked.

"No, I'll be all right," she said.

It wasn't all right. It was totally weird and uncomfortable. After an excruciating ninety minutes, my mother and I excused ourselves and I took her home.

Later, when I met up with Martha, I was floored to hear her say the exact same thing about my mother as my mom had said about her: "Your mother's very sweet."

"You think so?" I asked.

"Of course. Why wouldn't I? She has a good heart."

"My mother was on a few too many pills when she showed up this morning. It was super uncomfortable. Did your parents say anything afterward?"

"No, and they wouldn't. It really wasn't that bad; you should give her a break. People do what they need to do to get through their day. Besides she raised you, didn't she?"

"Meaning?"

"Meaning I think she did a pretty good job."

"Really?"

"You know she did. There are plenty of boys all over this town. Men are hard to find."

"A hard man is good to find?" I couldn't help myself. Sometimes I felt like a blathering lovesick teenager around Martha.

"Ha-ha," she said.

"That's very nice of you to say."

"Besides you and my dad and my high school boyfriend, I don't think I've ever really met any other men."

"I just hope I don't do anything to disappoint you."

"You better not."

———

Jonah got along just fine with Martha's son, Jonathan, who was three years younger. Occasionally that would worry me, because they were both scholastically challenged. Sometimes they'd go off to have lunch together and come back blitzed. Maddy and Jonah knew about my journey in recovery—I had extensive conversations with Maddy about weed, because she had plenty of friends who were stoned all the time. In her case I was pretty sure it was a recreational thing; smoking pot was certainly not interfering with her schoolwork.

When I tried to talk with Jonah about whether pot was affecting *his* schoolwork, this is what he had to say: "Dad, I was a fuckup in school way before weed came into my life."

Jonah, Jonathan, and I were at breakfast one morning at Junior's Deli when the subject of Jonathan's problems in eleventh-grade social studies came up. I didn't say anything about the weed issue, just simply suggested that it would be nice if Jonathan finally finished a project in that class that was way overdue. I had talked to his teacher, who said he could still get half credit even though the project was three months late.

"Woah, it's been that long and you haven't handed it in?" Jonah said, acting like the concerned big brother. I turned to Jonah and in the nicest of tones said, "Jonah, boubie, Jonathan has done more schoolwork in the last six months than you have done in four years. Please do not say anything."

He gave me one of his funny little smiles. "You're right. I won't," he said.

Jonah even came to Martha's parents' house for dinner in honor of Jonathan's birthday. He was funny and polite and talked his head off. Betty, Martha's mother, seemed impressed with him, even though he showed up with a red paper clip hanging from his pierced left ear. Jonah started eating when everyone else had their heads bowed for grace. He put his burger down and bowed his head. He went right along with everything that evening, no problem, although he did ask me twice if there was cheese to go with the burgers, and twice I had to tell him no.

Because Martha sent Nancy a card for her birthday, Nancy informed me she was much too nice for me. Working with Maddy on the issue of my new relationship was a little more difficult. I was over at Clarkson Road helping her with her laundry problem when she first found out I was dating Martha.

"Dad, can you take me and Jonah to Gyu-Kaku for dinner on Friday night?"

"I'd love to, but I can't."

"Why not?"

"Because I have a date."

"With who?"

"Her name is Martha."

"Where did you meet her?"

"In a doctor's office."

"Which doctor?"

We were sorting through all the stuff we dumped out of her laundry basket. I had enough sense on the subject to know lights, darks, and delicates.

"Dad, which doctor?"

"Dr. Nolan."

"Wait, the doctor I went to see when I broke my foot and Jonah broke his leg?"

"Yes."

"Oh," she said as she continued sorting.

I started throwing stuff into the washer but kept my eye on her as the pieces started coming together.

"Wait a minute. Martha at reception in Dr. Nolan's office?"

"Yes."

"Oh. My. God."

She seemed OK with that revelation, but then days later, things went back to normal and she was complaining that I was clueless about what was going on in her life. One night on the phone, she was so pissed she really let it fly: "Screw you and your 'perfect' girlfriend, you don't even care I have so much work. You are so out of it because you're never around . . ." and on and on.

I didn't even fight with her when she got like that, because I learned all I had to do was pull a little Al-Anon ninja response and simply say, "What can I do to help you?"

"Bring some food and just come over."

And I did and everything was all better again. Of course, I couldn't always do it. Usually I'd tell Maddy and Jonah when I wasn't going to be available if I knew I was going to be with Martha so that there was no misunderstanding and I could draw a boundary.

"So, Dad, what did you do this last weekend?" This while I was sitting in Maddy's room reviewing her English paper while she was dealing with her assignment for statistics class. I didn't even think of mentioning all the lovely time I spent with Martha riding bikes at the beach and hiking in the hills. When I did finally tell her I was still seeing Martha, Maddy asked me what I liked about her. I told her she was nice and fun to be with and I was grateful to finally have someone to do things with after four years of mostly being alone.

Maddy smiled at me and said, "That's because basically . . . you're a loser."

Overall Maddy had trouble relating to Martha, because Martha simply did not look or act like Maddy's mother or any of her family or friends. Martha wasn't heimish (one of us). She wasn't a yenta (busybody). She was shiksa (a Gentile). For Maddy, that basically meant that Martha was an alien from outer space. Still, she was always willing to help me buy Martha gifts for any occasion. Sometimes she seemed good about all of it, like the time we sat on her bed and I said it would be nice if she showed a little more tolerance for people who were not like her.

"Are you including Martha in there? Because at the moment I'm not having a problem with Martha."

At the moment. There was a time when I thought everything would work out between the extended families. Martha and Jonathan would come to Shabbat dinners at my dad's, and Julie and her kids would be there and my kids would be there, and everyone seemed to be getting along. They also came to a dinner party for Jonah's birthday at Louise's Trattoria. Nancy and her mother were there, as was my mother, and everything seemed to be working. Polly, Nancy's mother, even welcomed Martha to the family.

Maddy still occasionally gave me trouble about dating, but she did the same to Nancy, who was by then dating Bob, a bass player. So it was kind of funny when, at Jonah's party, Maddy crumpled up some wrapping paper from one of his presents and threw it at me. Only she missed me and hit Martha. Martha laughed, and Maddy was so embarrassed. I gave Martha permission to throw it back at her, only Martha missed Maddy and hit my mother.

27

THE MIND VERSUS MOUTH AFFAIR

I STARTED SPENDING MORE TIME with my dad. Sometimes I'd call him up to check in on him and he'd say, "What are you doing for lunch, why don't you come over?" He loved hearing stories of what was happening with the film school classes I was teaching and what was going on with my kids. He even suggested we go to an AA meeting together, and we attended several in Brentwood.

There is a popular men's stag meeting that used to meet in Santa Monica on Saturday mornings called Bread and Roses. It was a meeting I had been to many times, although I had never seen any bread or roses. (There's an offshoot from that group called Bagels and Lox, and you can be damn sure they have lox and bagels and onions and tomatoes and capers and lemons.) Bread and Roses is a big group of roughly seventy guys, some who are in their first days of recovery struggling to stay sober and some who've been in the program for decades. The old-timers often share about how they practice the principles of recovery in their relationships and in dealing with "life on life's terms"—that is, the challenges of everyday living.

The usual format of a speaker's meeting is that a guest speaker will share for the first fifteen or twenty minutes about their experience, strength, and hope, then the meeting will open up to three-minute shares. Bread and Roses is a double share, meaning two guys sit up front, each of them speaking for fifteen minutes. The secretary of this meeting came up to me and asked if my dad and I would come in together as guest speakers.

155

On one Saturday morning, there we were, at the front of a room full of men staring us down. Some of them I knew I had nothing in common other than a desire to live a life without drugs or alcohol. For me that's part of the miracle of the program—the fellowship, the fact that people with such diverse backgrounds can come together for one purpose: to live better lives. To lighten things up, I brought along a Spock figurine that I picked up many years before at Burger King. (I don't eat at Burger King but I had to have that Spock doll.) It was a small, horrible likeness of Spock, but it had a button on the back, and when you pressed it you heard my father's voice loud and clear: "Live long and prosper."

Occasionally, when the timing seemed right, I'd randomly push the button.

We were sitting in a large community room belonging to a church— the usual nondescript low-tech linoleum floors, white walls, sliding glass doors, rows and rows of folding chairs.

Dad shared first. "Drinking started becoming a problem for me when I was in my thirties and I was working long hours. I used alcohol to help deal with the pressure. The minute I got off work I would fill a paper cup and take it with me for the drive home. When I got home, I was ready for that second drink, and before I knew it I was drinking more and more. I thought it was a temporary thing, that I would only be drinking like that when I was in stressful work situations. Pretty soon I found myself drinking on weekends and when I had significant downtime. It got to the point where I had no control over how much I was drinking. I would make myself promises that I couldn't keep. I'd promise myself, *I'm not going to have more than a beer or two this weekend*, and by eleven be on the beer and by four in the afternoon move on to something harder until I passed out.

"I always took great comfort and pride that it never interfered with my work and I wasn't a blackout drinker, but I did have a number of experiences where I'd be driving home and couldn't remember how I got there. I was not an obvious fall-down drunk, but I would become reclusive, distant, remote, quiet, not there. By the time I was sixty, I had found a real sense of happiness in my life and couldn't understand why I was still drinking. That's when I called a friend of mine whom I knew was in the program."

As soon as Dad wrapped up, I pushed the button: "Live long and prosper."

"Hello, my name is Adam and I'm an alcoholic."

"Hi Adam!"

"So about a year ago, I got a call from my dad and my stepmother, and Dad I don't think I ever told you this, but I think you'll appreciate it or at least I hope you will.

"Anyway, I got this call from my dad and stepmom, and they told me that they were just calling to say they were really happy about our relationship, because we had some issues in the past and things had gotten much better between us. They went on to say that my girlfriend, who I'm still with, that my girlfriend had been very good for me, and that I was clearly much happier since I started dating her. It basically felt like they were saying that our relationship had gotten much better because I was dating someone new.

"And when they said that, my mind immediately started racing out of control, because I'm your basic run-of-the-mill pothead, and I just want to react negatively to everything that even remotely pushes my buttons. So while they were talking, I was thinking to myself, *Wait a minute . . . this is ridiculous. The reason things have gotten better between us is because I'm working a program. I go to meetings. I take commitments. I read the literature. I work the steps. I have a sponsor. I try to be of service and I have a Higher Power and women are not my Higher Power. I'm a poster child for AA, dammit, and that's why I'm SUCH A FREAKING HAPPY GUY!*

"That is literally what was going through my mind while I was on the phone with them but where the hell is the serenity in all that? Where is the spiritual awakening?

"The good news is that I managed to keep my mouth shut while all this chatter was going through my mind. I didn't say a thing until I could get a grip on my brain. Using some recovery tools, I counted to twenty before I opened my mouth and screwed it all up. I am responsible for my second thought and my first action, because my first thought when my buttons get pushed is almost always to flip the bird. I'm an addict and that's the way I'm built and I just have to accept that about myself, so I have to force myself to get to that second thought by trying to take some time before I react to stuff. That second thought is usually more reasonable and more mature, and from there I can take the next indicated action, which flows from that. This is what 'Count to ten, count to twenty' and 'Pause when agitated" means to me."

At this point I glanced over at my father, who was nodding his head and raising one of his Spock eyebrows.

"So when it was finally my turn to talk in that conversation with my dad and stepmom, these are the words that came out of my mouth: 'That's really nice to hear. I'm happy with our relationship too. Thank you so much for calling me to tell me this. I really appreciate it.'"

My dad started smiling and there were some laughs around the room, which was a relief, because I knew I was taking a risk by sharing about all this. It was weird, because I had never said stuff like this directly to my dad before. Never expressed these kinds of feelings.

"Because of the work I've done in here, I'm finally learning how to disconnect what my warped mind is thinking from what is actually coming out of my mouth. Immediately reacting to things and then saying what's on my mind, giving people a piece of my mind . . . that's always gotten me into trouble. I don't always have control when my mind is spinning, and I don't always do it perfectly, and that's when I have an emotional relapse and have to tenth-step myself and make an amends asking for forgiveness, but equally important, I have to forgive myself so I can move on. Forgiving myself is sometimes the hardest part, because I just love to beat myself up when I'm not perfect.

"What's ironic is that after that phone call, I took a walk to kind of clear my head and I realized *they were right*: I was and am much happier with that woman, because she's flat-out awesome. She's my age, and like me, she's divorced with a kid. She's got a good job and she's just a sweet, gorgeous person. What's important is that I know now it was the work I did in this program that made me ready for someone like her. It was here, in these rooms, with the help of guys like you and other people I have met along the road of recovery. It was in recovery that I learned I was in some kind of arrested development all the years I was drinking and using and that I needed to grow up. It was here that I learned to let go of resentments, to let go of my fears and to be of service to others. It was here where I learned I didn't need to fix my girlfriend or change her, all I had to do was love her and try to be helpful to her. Thank you for letting me share."

"Live long and prosper."

28

COPD

THE PHONE RANG. It was my mother.

"I just spent four and a half hours at UCLA with an immunologist and he's one of the top doctors in his field. He thinks my immune system might be affected. You know COPD is killing a lot of women."

"COPD?"

"Chronic . . . chronic . . . wait a minute, I have it on this piece of paper." I heard rustling in the background as my mother looked for the paper among the pile of newspapers and magazines on her bed.

"Shit! Where is it! Here it is. Chronic obstructive pulmonary disease. He did a CAT scan of my sinuses and took some chest X-rays and drew a lot of blood. I want you to go with me when he gets the results back."

This was just a few months after I got another call from Mom because her internist thought it might be her heart. The heart specialist decided she needed an angiogram, an intrusive diagnostic procedure requiring a general anesthetic.

On the day of *that* procedure, I drove my mother to the hospital and checked her in. A nurse came in and handed me a clipboard with an admissions checklist. I quizzed my mother about her medical history.

"Arthritis?" I asked.

"Yes," she said.

"Asthma?"

"Yes."

"OK, yes. Anxiety/depression, that would be a yes, definitely. Cardiovascular?"

"No," she said.

"OK, no. Confusion with hospitalization, yes."

"No!"

"No, Mom?" I gave her one of my exaggerated quizzical looks.

"I wasn't confused when I came in here and I'm not confused now."

"OK, Ma, OK, all right. Just checking to see if you were listening. Let's see here, constipation? Yes."

"Yes," she agreed.

"Cholera, no. Eyes/glasses, yes. Dementia, yes."

"No!"

"All right, Mom, all right. That would be a no. At least as of today."

"That's not even funny," she said.

"Then why are you smiling?"

"You can be such a pill," she said.

"Imitation is the highest form of flattery. And speaking of flattery, flatulence?"

"Occasional."

"Occasional, OK . . . . Heart attack?

"No."

"No. Kidney failure. No. Thyroid?"

"Yes," she said.

"That's a yes. Liver?"

"No."

"That's a no. Venereal disease?"

"NO!"

"That . . . would be . . . a . . . definite . . . no."

While my mother was having the angiogram, my sister Julie and I sat in the waiting room. After an hour or so, the doctor appeared. Dr. Lee was young and seemed very confident.

"Your mother is in recovery. She did very well. There are no medical indications."

Julie jumped in:, "You mean there's nothing wrong with her?"

The doctor crossed his arms. "All I can tell you is she's got a very strong and healthy heart for a woman her age. Now, if you'll excuse me, I have to answer a page."

I turned to Julie. "Oh, she's going to fucking love this."

When I went back to the recovery room my mother was lying on a gurney. The minute I went over to her she started crying. "I know something's wrong with me, Adam. I know it. I'm not imagining it."

I took her hand. "I know, Mom, I believe you. And we're going to figure it out. Just hang in there. Julie and I are here for you."

The results came in, so I took my mother to see the immunologist. We were sitting in an exam room at UCLA, in a building right across the street from the doctor with the Looney Tunes tie who said her eyes were fine. The immunologist was in his fifties but seemed cool and hip with his wide-wale corduroys and silver wristband. He flipped through my mother's file. "Well, the blood work and the CAT scan all look pretty good. The X-ray is also clear, except for a small spot on the bottom of your right lung, but I don't think it's anything to be concerned about."

My mother jumped in. "But it could be cancer."

She looked up at the doctor with a glimmer of hope. I was sitting in a chair against the opposite wall and my mother was sitting on an exam table, the doctor standing next to her. The two of them were backlit by a bright window that looked out over the UCLA campus. I could see building cranes across the way. They're always building something at UCLA. It's been that way ever since I was a student at the University Elementary School. That was in the 1960s, and since then parking lots have disappeared, older buildings have been torn down, and new buildings, walkways, and plazas have popped up everywhere.

"But it could be cancer."

The doctor looked up from the file with a quizzical expression, as if he couldn't quite believe she was bringing up the C-word.

"No, judging from the other tests, it's very unlikely it's cancer. Probably some sort of mucous nodule or maybe scar tissue. We'd have to do a biopsy to be sure, but I wouldn't be too concerned. Have you talked to your internist about your symptoms?"

My mother tried to answer: "Well, I—"

I jumped in to help her out. "Oh, yes. Her internist, her cardiologist, her ophthalmologist, her podiatrist, her psychiatrist, her taxidermist. We've pretty much covered all the bases."

My mother waited until we were safely out of the office before she let me have it: "You son of a bitch!"

I pushed the button for the elevator. "What?"

"You made me look like a hypochondriac, for chrissakes! My pain is not imagined, it's real. I'm still seeing double!"

"I know, Mom. That's why I'm taking you to every doctor you want to see, because if there's something they can do for you, I want to know about it."

In recovery, we call this "backpedaling." At least I do.

The elevator arrived. It was filled with people. I helped my mother in. She was seething.

When we finally walked out of the building, she continued. "You act like you don't even remember the times I was there for you. When you came home from school, I was there for you every day. I took you for your allergy shots twice a week. And that gray jacket you wouldn't take off, I had to come get you at school because it was so hot and you refused to take off that jacket. And I let you have friends over whenever you wanted. And when you had trouble with your father, I tried to protect you."

By then I realized I had totally screwed up. An emotional relapse par excellence. I was thinking that the tenth step might be the way to go here: " . . . and when we were wrong promptly admitted it."

"I know, Mom, you're right, you were there for me. I'm sorry I said anything."

"I was never judgmental toward you or any of your friends. Even Matthew and Chris Kelton and that bunch. I was always nice to them when they came looking for you, even though I knew what they were up to. That was a big deal for me, because I had a mother who was always criticizing me. That's the kind of modeling I had, and I didn't want to be like her."

"I know, Mom. You're right. I'm so sorry."

"I tolerated all that pot-smoking and told you just to do it outside because I didn't want to get a contact high. It really hurts me in my heart that you don't seem to remember any of this about me."

I put my arm around her. "I do remember, Mom, I remember everything. The concerts you took us to, the sleepovers we were allowed to have on a moment's notice."

Yes, it was good to be reminded that my mother "got" me. She was always kind and understanding, always made sure that I was OK, that I had what I needed. Without her I would have been lost.

"I only want you to give me my due, that's all. While your father was out pursuing his career, I was taking care of you guys. I know I made mistakes, but I did the best I could. I was totally behind you when you made your career moves. And after you and Nancy split up, I always kept my relationship with her, because I thought it was best for your kids. And I do it for you and because I still love Nancy, even though she's no cupcake."

"I know, Mom. You've been there every step of the way."

"I don't think I'm asking for too much and I'm not a hypochondriac!"

"No, mom, you're not a hypochondriac."

(Beat.)

"But you have been to a lot of doctors."

"I'm entitled!"

29

MY FRIEND JUSTIN

"My mom died last night," Justin said the minute he got into my car. I picked him up because we were going to a meeting in Santa Monica, a meeting we hadn't been to before at Santa Monica Place.

"Oh my God. I'm so sorry," I said.

"No, no, no, it's OK, really, I'm happy, I'm happy about it. It's the greatest gift she could ever have given me. I've been praying for her to die for a couple of years. My mother was a promiscuous, schizophrenic, white-trash-slash-Hispanic speed freak and alcoholic who molested me when I was nine. Her favorite career during the '70s was stripper slash hooker."

"You told me she recovered from her last stay at the hospital, but you never said she went back in. What happened?

"She started getting sick again a couple of weeks ago, and I thought, *Oh, thank you, God, thank you, thank you, thank you. Prayer does work. Let this be her time, God. Please let this be it.* Her liver and kidneys finally shut down after drinking and taking pills every day since she was fifteen. I went to visit her in the hospital last week and she could barely talk. They were supposed to take a kidney from her that day, and I thought, *Great. There is no way she's going to survive that operation.* When my aunt called me later that night and told me the news, I was devastated. I couldn't believe she fucking made it right through the operation. *Jesus Christ, when is the fucking woman going to die? She's like Jason from* Friday the 13th. *She keeps coming back.*"

"I'm so sorry you feel that way, but is this really how you're working your program? What does your sponsor say about all this?"

"I didn't learn this bad attitude from AA, but I did learn how to share honestly, and I'm just telling you as my soul brother what I'm honestly going through right now."

"I don't know what to say except I'm sorry—I'm so sorry you're having such a hard time with this. Do you want me to try and help you find someone to talk to about all this? To process some of what you're going through? I'm worried about what might happen if you can't find a way to work through all this resentment you've been carrying around."

"No, I appreciate it. Knowing you has been a godsend. I feel you're always looking out for me. I know I'm going to be OK, it's just gonna take some time."

He turned to look out the window, completely lost in thought. We stopped at a red light at Colorado and Fourth in downtown Santa Monica. Next to us was a car with a young woman sitting behind the wheel. We could see she was crying. Justin and I were watching this poor girl sitting in her car at the stoplight. She was on her phone and she was sobbing.

"I wish we could do something for her," I said.

"There're a lot of people in this town driving around in pain," he said.

"Shouldn't we try to do something?"

"No, anything we do will be totally misinterpreted. There's nothing to be done. Her Higher Power will take care of her."

"You were supposed to take her to a meeting, not nail her."

I was on the phone with him the following week. When we were at that meeting at Santa Monica Place, Justin met someone. Stephanie was in her twenties and a newcomer. She had that whole goth thing going: ripped black jeans, black Converse, pale skin, long black hair. She was a gymnast and had trained full time for the Olympics until she hurt her foot and was out. That's when she first got hooked on pills. Justin offered to take her to another meeting that weekend. They never got there.

"I drove out to pick her up, and she said she was too tired to go and wanted me to just hang out with her and watch TV. Then she said she wanted to get more comfortable and started cuddling up to me. I told her I wasn't going to sleep with her. Then she started taking off her clothes and the next thing I knew, I was inside of her."

In the time that I'd known him, Justin had had six or seven women. I never thought much about it, just that he was sowing some oats or trying to work out something about his mother. I never judged him, but this one really bothered me.

"You *know* this is way off base and that you might be in some weird cycle trying to work through some stuff about your mom."

"I know, you're right, I know that. But she's like my type. She even said I was her type, she was so sure about wanting to do it."

"What does all that mean? What's your type?"

"My type is someone who shows they love and care for me by having sex with me, but they have to look like my aunt, who rescued me from my mother."

"What does your aunt look like?"

"Pale skin, dark hair, pointy nose, and small like a ballerina."

"Like Stephanie."

"Exactly like Stephanie."

It crashed and burned pretty quickly. He said some disparaging things about her that were really upsetting. I couldn't believe this stuff was coming from him, it was like I was talking to a complete stranger. I couldn't believe this was the guy who had been leading me through the program all this time, inspiring me. He used to say he liked to go in and out of relationships "like a gentleman," and advised me to do the same. I didn't see any of that here. He dumped her flat. She sent him a scathing email and then said she knew that, in keeping with the program, she would probably have to send him an amends to make up for it.

"No," he wrote back. "You don't have to make an amends. I deserved it."

30

GOODBYE CLARKSON ROAD

WHEN NANCY AND I were mediating our divorce, we worked out a plan by which we would hold off on selling the Clarkson Road house for seven years, so that Nancy and the kids could live there until Jonah finished high school. As sure as the grass grows and the wind blows, that deadline was approaching. Jonah was turning eighteen and would graduate in June. Maddy was turning twenty and was loving her academic career at Bard College in New York State. The time had finally come to sell the house. Time for everyone to move on.

On a Thursday night, during spring break when Maddy was back from school, I brought my real estate broker Herb over for a walk-through. Nancy answered the door.

"Where are the kids?" I asked. "I don't see Maddy's car."

"Maddy's at Rachel's, Jonah's at Michael's. What do you want?" She seemed annoyed.

"This is Herb, the real estate agent I told you about."

Herb extended his hand. "Hi, Nancy. Nice to finally meet you."

Nancy glared at him and said, "Herb, would you excuse us for a minute?"

"Yes, certainly."

I stepped inside and Nancy slammed the door in Herb's face. "What's this all about?" she asked.

Count to ten.

"I sent you an email on Monday and you said it was OK to come by. We're just doing a quick walk-through, then we'll be out of here."

I opened the door. "Herb, come on in."

Nancy slammed it. "You didn't confirm it, and it's not OK, because I'm making dinner."

"Now, Nancy, let's stay calm here. We need to get some idea of what the house is worth."

I opened the door. Nancy slammed it. "I don't have time for this," she said.

I felt for Nancy, I really did. She was nervous and scared about her future and had told me as much in the months leading up to this moment. When we signed our settlement agreement, she cried and asked me to assure her everything was going to be all right. I told her that we would always be a family, that we still had so much to look forward to, that I would never abandon her. This situation with the house necessitated coming on more forcefully than I would have liked in light of my never-ending attempt to *work my program* as well as *trudge the road of happy destiny*. For almost seven years Nancy and the kids had enjoyed the house on Clarkson Road while I lived in an apartment. The fact that this arrangement would be coming to an end is what helped me stay out of any resentment—or, more accurately, minimized my feelings of resentment.

"Nancy, if you look at our settlement agreement, you'll be reminded that you and the kids could stay here for seven years, which is now coming to an end. We need to start the process of selling the house, because we don't want to miss the listing season."

I opened the door.

That's when Bob walked out of the dining room and said, "Nancy, is there a problem?"

Although I knew Nancy had been dating Bob, the bass player, I had never met him before. We were all standing there, the four of us in this incredibly wonderful, awkward moment with Herb on the porch and Bob in the dining room.

Nancy turned to Bob. "I got this."

She turned back to me. "Just so you and 'Herb' know, I don't give a shit about the listing season!" She then pushed me out the front door, slammed it, and locked it.

I turned to Herb. "Have you eaten dinner?"

Nancy finally gave in to the reality of selling the house, but she had some conditions. One was that she said I owed her an amends for all the pot-smoking I did during our marriage. Nancy apparently knew enough about twelve-step recovery to know she was owed an amends. I had actually made an amends to her during a therapy session we had after our separation. It was in that session that she announced she liked me better when I was stoned, because I was easier to deal with. (So true!) I gladly made the second amends to her for my pot-smoking and my part in the failure of our relationship. (As it turned out, a couple of years later, when Nancy and I had a disagreement about something else, she once again said I owed her an amends. "How many times do I have to make an amends to her?" I asked Justin. "As many as she needs.")

Nancy's second condition had to do with my real estate agent, Herb. After meeting at length with Herb, she decided she hated him and insisted on bringing in another agent to represent her interests. She asked Darla, an agent who used to live in the neighborhood and whose kids went to school with our kids. Darla met me for a walk-through on a weekday when no one was home. It was a little reminiscent of my very first walk-through with Joe Veltri some twenty-five years before. The living room was cluttered with artwork, surfboards, books, and guitars. There were stains on the wood floor in the kitchen and in what used to be the family room addition, which Nancy had turned into a dining room / art studio. The closet toilet in the laundry room had a note taped to the door: DO NOT USE. OUT OF ORDER. Jonah had taken over the converted garage in the back, which became his bedroom, now a pigsty. (Nancy reminded me that I had approved of his move out back—i.e., that one was not her fault). There was yet another active beehive in the backyard. There was an overflowing trash can with beer bottles and several ashtrays with cigarette butts left over from a party the previous weekend.

Tour completed, Darla turned to me. "When did it turn into a frat house?"

I borrowed the money to fix up the place, as there was no way we were going to be selling our once-beautiful home the way we had bought it, as a distress sale. I brought in Miguel, my Secret Weapon, who had been an apprentice carpenter when we built the addition to the house fourteen years earlier. Miguel repaired the fences and the gates and replaced the entire retaining wall on the back side of the property, which previously looked like the Leaning Tower of Pisa. I brought in a floor refinisher and a painter.

Jonah was getting ready to graduate high school and we were looking to enroll him into a music school in Pasadena in the fall, so he didn't seem to care about all the preparation to put the house back in shape. "Jonah, I put in a lot of work to clean up your room in the back. So please don't mess it up too badly before we have an open house."

"I won't. Now that I see everything getting cleaned up, I do have to admit we pretty much destroyed the place."

While all my guys were working on the house, Maddy pleaded with me endlessly to change my mind about selling it. "Dad, please. How could you do this to us?"

"Maddy it's been seven years. It's time."

"Dad, please. Just do this one thing for me. Just this one thing."

"Maddy, you're away at college most of the year, Mom's moving in with Bob, and Jonah's going to music school in Pasadena. It doesn't make sense to keep it."

That's when the pleading turned into yelling and screaming and door-slamming and a super-duper angry text message in which she said that she had just ripped down the FOR SALE sign in front of the house and that she was scraping the floors and that there is something mentally wrong with me and everyone knows it.

I never felt safe expressing my feelings to my dad. Maddy didn't seem to have that problem. Sometimes it felt like Maddy came into my life not just for the hugs and kisses and the love but also to help me practice using every recovery tool I had at my disposal.

––––––––––––––

I had ignored Maddy's love note about my mental condition in the hopes that she'd cool down. I went surfing to see if I could find some peace of mind. Meditation and prayer had been a great help to me in stressful situations and were also a regular part of my recovery. When I got out of the water feeling refreshed, I checked my phone and found Maddy had texted me, asking if I was at my apartment. This worried me, because I thought it meant she wanted to go over there and trash the place. Then she *called* and asked if I was there.

"I'm not, but I'm going to be there in five minutes," I said, knowing it would take me fifteen.

"Could you meet me on Main Street to talk about things?" she asked.

"Yes, if you can control yourself."

We met at the bead shop on Main Street in Santa Monica, where she was doing some shopping therapy, because my dad and Susan had given her money to buy something for herself. She was buying a pretty necklace. She was surprisingly sweet and conciliatory. Even loving. We walked to Starbucks and when we sat down with our coffees, she told me something I will never forget:

"I hate hating you. I finally realized I hate hating you more than I actually hate you."

We were sitting in the Starbucks on Main Street, the old one near Hill Street before they moved it down into what used to be the Coffee Bean. It had a warm, woodsy feel to it. Maddy was wearing a white blouse with lace at the edges and a faded jean jacket. She had on her black leggings and leather boots, several necklaces, and bracelets of leather and gold. So cute, my daughter. Quite the fashionista.

I want to remember this. I need to remember this so I that I'll always have something to hold on to.

"It was just that I felt like I wasn't a priority and was being marginalized behind Martha and Jonathan. I mean, I really don't want to dislike Martha, but I can't help these feelings I'm having, and I know I have to work on all this."

"Why are you suddenly feeling this way now? You were so mad at me. What changed for you?"

"Because Eli"—her boyfriend—"is going through something similar. I mean, things are even worse for him, but he's trying hard to keep his relationship going with his dad. That made me think harder about what was happening with us, you know what I mean?"

"Yes, sweetie, I do, and I really appreciate you saying this."

"Also the fact that mom's been away in Orange County for Bubbie's procedure, so being alone in the house gave me a chance to think about all this."

"Does this mean you're going to be OK about the house? Because I have more work to do to get it into shape before we show it. Is that going to be OK?"

"Yeah, that's fine. I mean, about the house, I'm sorry I sent that text. I said a lot of things I didn't mean. I just think you should know how painful it's going to be for me to come back from Bard and not have the house to come home to. The feeling is so intense for me, it's like reliving the divorce all over again."

"I get it, honey, I totally understand."

"I mean, Mom's moving to Bob's, and the room they have for me is tiny. And I just have this incredible pain in my body, I can feel it. It's like when you moved out, I just felt this loss and abandonment and I'm starting to feel some of that all over again, and sometimes it just hurts so much. Do you know what I mean?"

"I totally get it and I am so sorry," I said as I leaned over and gave her a big hug.

That was the moment I made an amends to her.

"I know I've made mistakes. I know it. And I know that leaving you was really difficult, just before you were about to turn fourteen, which was a very tough year for you, and I'm so sorry for all that. Really I am. You should also know that I would do anything to make you feel important, which you are to me. You have to know I would do anything."

"I know, Dad," she said. "I actually do know that."

"I would even fly out to New York on my own to visit you at Bard, anything I can do while still taking Martha's feelings into consideration."

"I know, Dad, and I appreciate it."

"Please tell me if you have any ideas that might help keep us together. Sometimes I feel like I come up with things to do with you and you just dismiss them. I need your help, honey. I really do."

"I know, Dad. I'm going to try harder. We're going to get through this."

I felt so close to her. It was the best. I will never forget.

We walked to a shoe store to see what they had for me, and she told me which ones to buy. While I was trying them on, she said she had to go, because she was having dinner with some of her friends down the street at Wildflour Pizza. We hugged and it was really good. After months of her trashing me over the sale of the house, it felt so good to have her back.

It was about ten minutes later, after I had just paid for the shoes and was walking out of the store, that I got a call from her. She was sobbing hysterically.

"Dad! Bubbie just died!" Bubbie meaning Polly, Nancy's mother.

"What are you talking about? They said it was a routine procedure."

"Something went wrong and now she's dead. You need to pick me up."

I jumped in my car and drove down the street to get her. Luckily, Jonah was visiting some friends nearby in Ocean Park. We scooped him up, hopped on the 405, and headed south to Orange County.

The loss of Polly was devastating. She was a very sweet person. At the same time, it brought us closer together, because we went through it as a family. Maddy later told me this was an important moment for her, because it proved that we could still be together, that we would always be together. The whole event was surreal and put a pallor over everything, including the sale of Clarkson Road. The process of transition had become that much harder.

"When are you coming over? I need help finishing my room."

We sold our home to a nice young couple with two boys. Maddy was back from New York to pack up all her things. This was her last day, and she had a plane to catch.

"I'm going to jump in the shower, and I'll be there in about forty-five minutes."

"Just hurry. I'm starting to freak out that I'm never going to be done in time to make my plane."

I helped her sort everything into three piles: boxes going with her mother to Bob's house, boxes going into storage, boxes that would be sent to her at Bard.

"Will you send my stuff to me right away?"

"I'll send everything tomorrow. Promise."

"What about all my perfumes and my jewelry and my little containers? All the stuff going with Mom. I'm worried they're going to break."

"I have bubble wrap and I'll drive all of that over to Bob's myself to make sure it gets there OK. Where are your babies?"

"You mean Baby Hat and Baby Hair?" These were the Madeline dolls that Maddy had since she was little. She called them her babies. Baby Hat because the doll had lost her yellow hat, and Baby Hair because she had lost her yellow hat *and* her red hair. "I have them," she said.

Nancy was proud of the progress she was making in her bedroom, having managed to tackle her unfathomable wardrobe. (I swear I have never seen so many black sweaters in my life.) Nancy was also sad that we were all there for such a solemn occasion. Jonah had been out back with Eduvina, our housekeeper of fifteen years, trying to get whatever he had left out there packed up and ready for storage. There was a moment when we were all in the family room, the new one we built, the one in which the kids ran around and jumped on the couch as they watched the video of the Who at the Rock and Roll Circus.

Nancy started crying. "I'm just so sad about all this. And about my mother. And I'm worried about things working out with Bob. I mean, we're crashing his party over there," she said.

"Nancy, it's all going to work out. We're so lucky to have had so many great years here. Transitions are hard, but we're still together to help each other get through this."

Then we had a group hug. We were still a family, and nothing could take that feeling away from us. "Feelings aren't facts," I hear people sometimes say in the program, and oftentimes I have found that to be true, especially my fears about stuff that might happen in the future and usually doesn't. But the feelings I was having about us still being a family felt like a fact, and I intended to keep it that way as we moved on down the road.

When Maddy was packed up and ready to go, I made a point of walking with her through the entire house so she could take a good look at it for the last time. It started raining, which seemed to make perfect sense.

"God's crying too," Nancy said.

Maddy was crying the whole time as she took her last look. If we had been shooting this as a scene in one of my TV shows, I would have asked for the rain machines. Rain and poor Maddy crying and now Nancy crying and Eduvina so sad and me feeling bad and our home looking better than it had in years all cleaned up and ready for a new family.

Before we walked out the door, Maddy turned to me and said, "I know it's going to be all right. It's just sad for me to say goodbye. Mom said you can't have joy without experiencing the sadness."

"No, you can't, Maddy. She's so right."

Maddy was born into that house. Now she was saying goodbye to all the family gatherings, the parties, the memories. We had been a family there and now she was leaving everything behind. It was the end of an era and we both knew it. I was grateful to be sober to feel the sadness and the loss Maddy was also feeling. Now we all seemed to be on the same page dealing with life on life's terms, recognizing that we were in the cycle of life, that everything has an end, that transitions can be incredibly challenging. It was a growing experience for all of us.

Maddy and I walked out the front door and ran through the rain to my car. I put her suitcase in the trunk. Before starting the car, we just sat there for a moment looking at our charming little house on the hill with the white stucco, the clay tile roof, and the purple bougainvillea. We were taking it all in, living in the moment, feeling our feelings. And we were doing it together.

Then we drove to the airport.

31

JUST DO YOUR SPOCK THING

AT FIRST JONAH HADN'T SEEM FAZED by the selling of the family home, as he was eighteen and looking ahead to more independence. Then something happened that seemed to bring up deep feelings he had been harboring. It was back during his senior year in high school, when I drove him to Pasadena to look into enrolling him at LAMA, the Los Angeles Music Academy. Nancy and I were of one mind on this: it was either that or get a job. Jonah had no intention of going to college, and I told him I would only help support him if he was either working or enrolled in a music school. He reluctantly agreed to look at LAMA. The classrooms, the practice rooms, and the common areas all looked good; there was a cool vibe about the place. After we took the tour and filled out some paperwork, we got back into the car and Jonah suddenly started crying.

"I don't want to go, Dad. Please don't make me. Please."

"I thought you were liking what we were seeing. You seemed impressed with what they have going on in there."

"It's not for me, Dad. It's another school and I don't want to do it. Please don't make me. Please."

This seemed to come out of nowhere. Normally, I would have (nicely) read him the riot act, because this was just so frustrating. But I didn't want to push him; after all the trouble I'd had with him in grade school, I didn't want another argument. When he was a kid and balked at going to school or went to the main office and had them call me to pick him up, it just infuriated me. I didn't want to go down that road again. I didn't want to react the way I used to. I wanted to be supportive.

"It's OK, Jonah. I'm not going to make you go if you're so set against it. It's not worth it if you're not into it. We'll work something out, I promise you. We'll come up with a good 'B' plan."

He was still crying when he said something that totally floored me. "Why did you do it, Dad? Why did you leave me alone with Mom and Maddy? I can't believe you just left me."

It was a blazing hot day in Pasadena as we sat in my car in a nice ncw blacktop parking lot next to the music school, a parking lot that felt like a sizzling frying pan. Jonah was a young man now. He was tall, wearing a white T-shirt and a black baseball cap. He had a light complexion and had switched the colored paper clip in his ear from red to green. He seemed worlds away from the eleven-year-old boy who was with us at Clarkson Road when I had to move out. Then again, maybe he wasn't so far away from that boy, but it was still a shock that now was the time he needed to look back at the past. We hadn't talked about any of this for years. He always seemed more accepting of our situation than Maddy. There were definitely moments in those early days when he would break down and beg me to come home, saying that if I loved him I would come back. But for the most part after that, I didn't have as much conflict and discussion about what was happening as I did with Maddy. He seemed to find more things in his life to keep him distracted.

I wasn't naive enough to think that everything was OK with him. Sometimes his feelings about what happened would get triggered by something else that was going on. I always felt that when we had problems, underlying everything was some kind of unspoken struggle he was going through to accept the new world order caused by my leaving. Putting Clarkson Road on the market and his resistance and fear about enrolling in music school seemed to now bring up some of those deep feelings. I felt so bad for him all over again. All I could think to do was make an amends.

"I know and I'm so sorry. I think you had it the worst of all of us, and all I can say is that I'm sorry. I am so sorry. And if there's anything in the world I can do to make it up to you, please let me know. Let's keep talking about it—if not right at this moment, let's talk about it more later. When you're ready. For right now, don't worry at all about going to school. Let's think about it over the next few days and see what else we can come up with."

I put my arms around him and he began to settle down. My Higher Power must have been on high alert, because at that exact moment I noticed an animal shelter across the alley from the parking lot. Jonah loved animals.

"Hey, why don't we go to the animal shelter and see who's there?"

We got out of the car and walked across the alley and into the shelter through a back entrance. Jonah petted some dogs and said hi to the cats. He immediately began to feel better. Then we went to get something to eat.

"I'm feeling much better, thank you," he said as he chomped into his third chicken taco. "I'm OK with going to LAMA."

––––––––––––

Things were looking pretty good the first semester Jonah was enrolled at LAMA. He was studying drums and percussion with industry heavy-weights that he respected, he met some other students, two of whom would become friends for life, and they all moved into a decent apartment not far from the school.

The following semester was more problematic. I was waiting for Jonah at a storage facility on the Westside, where he was coming over to get one of his drum kits. The minute he pulled into the parking lot, he jumped out of his car and started ranting.

"I hate that school. They don't understand me and I'm wasting my time there. I'm into metal and they say I play drums too loud and no one wants to play with me and they won't even let me into the practice rooms. I hate it there and I am not going back." He was wearing a T-Shirt, short pants, white socks, and Adidas sandals. He looked all SoCal casual and just like that he was off and running, without so much as a *Hi, Dad*.

While he was busy pacing and trashing the school, I stood there thinking to myself, *There is no freaking way he is going to quit that school. I just paid tuition for another semester, I got him into a new apartment in Pasadena and dropped a bundle on Ikea. I almost broke my back helping him put all that furniture together. **There is no freaking way he's going to drop out of that school. No way.***

Those were my first thoughts. But instead of telling him what I was thinking, I let him continue to blow off steam as I paused while agitated, counted to ten, etc., etc.

When it was time for me to speak, this is what came out of my mouth: "Take it easy, Jonah, it's all going to be fine. I told you when we went to enroll you, I'm not going to make you go if you're dead set against it, and I'm not going to make you do it now. Together we're going to figure this out. We're just going to have to come up with another plan. Just take it easy."

That seemed to take the wind out of his sails. What's interesting about this particular incident is that my HP seemed to once again be in the vicinity, because while Jonah was ranting, his phone rang. And because he was on a such a tear, making his point like ten times over, he let the call go to voice mail. If *I* had been the one talking, he would have put me on pause and answered his phone. Once he calmed down, he noticed the call was from Gregg Bissonette.

"Talk about timing," he said.

Gregg was Jonah's private drum instructor, with whom he had been studying for years. Gregg's a heavyweight in the music industry, having played with a number of great artists and for many years having been the drummer in Ringo Starr and His All-Starr Band. In fact, it was Gregg who helped Jonah get into LAMA, because he knew the guys who ran the percussion department.

Jonah pushed the playback button: "Hey, Jonah, I just talked to those guys at the school and I told them *they need you* as much as *you need them.* They agreed to work things out with you and accommodate you. They're going to help you out, so don't quit, don't quit, don't quit!" And then he hung up.

Jonah looked up at me and said simply, "Fine, I'll stay."

Things seemed to settle down, and several months later on a Sunday afternoon, Jonah called to tell me he had played an incredible gig the night before at the Roxy Theatre on Sunset with Brutal Force, a metal band he had joined. He had also recorded some metal music with a new band called Legal Tender, and he was going to be recording more stuff with them later in the week. Things were looking up.

Two days later his mother called to tell me he was having some kind of breakdown. I couldn't believe it. She said that he'd gone through a period of partying hard with his friends and was now going through some kind of depression. I figured this might also have something to do with the fact that school finals were coming up.

I went over to see him. "Why don't we go get something to eat and then figure out a plan so that you can pull yourself together and maybe get through finals next week?"

"It's not that simple, Dad. My life is all messed up right now, and I can't go through with it, I'm not going to do it. I'm not feeling good and finals are the last thing on my mind. "

He went on to tell me that although he could be happy and upbeat when playing and recording, he also felt he was crashing emotionally and was generally going through a dark period. I was worried that once again we had stuck him into an educational environment where he might not be able to function. When canvassing Nancy, her boyfriend Bob, the bass player, and Jonah's drum teacher Gregg, the consensus was clear that he should finish music school. Sometimes it does take a village. This whole episode felt like a valuable lesson for all of us as we plotted out a strategy to move forward.

Valuable lesson. Those words came straight out of the Leonard Nimoy playbook when I myself was resistant to pursue an opportunity I was offered. It was years earlier, when I was in the middle of my television directing career. I received an offer from a low-budget sci-fi show to direct an episode, and I didn't want to do it.

"Do you have another job lined up during that period?" Dad asked.

"No, but this is not up to par with the other shows I've been directing. They shoot the show in a warehouse, and there's zero money for overtime. They literally pull the plug after twelve hours. It's really not my genre, and it feels like I would be taking a step backward in my career."

"You shouldn't worry about all that, just take the job. I promise you, you will either learn a valuable lesson that will improve your craft, or you'll meet someone who can help you with your career."

I took the job.

When Jonah started to feel better and things had once again calmed down, I thought this might be a good opportunity to bring my father into the equation.

"Dad, we're going to pull a little intervention with Jonah."

"Really? OK, what do you want me to do?"

"Jonah's coming over on Saturday morning. Please be here and let me do the talking and back me up and maybe just do your Spock thing. It would be great if you could nod occasionally and maybe, you know, like every so often, raise an eyebrow or something."

"I can do that."

Sometimes when Dad's "sensibility informed his character" (or vice versa), it worked to my advantage.

Jonah showed up and was surprised to see my dad. "Oh, wow. You brought out the big guns for this one."

As he sank down into the couch, I began: "First of all I want you to know that Poppi and I are sympathetic to some of the struggles you've been going through. Separate and apart from everything, we know you're going through a tough period and we want to be supportive. And we are both fully aware of the difficulty of being in music school and having to deal with the curriculum there when you really want to be out in the world gigging and recording. In fact, we both believe you're old enough to make your own decisions on that score and that you are absolutely entitled to drop out of school, smoke pot, and play heavy metal music on the Sunset Strip. Seriously, if that's what you want to do, you're one hundred percent entitled to do it. But if that's what you *choose* to do, you won't be receiving any money from either of us. Not a penny. Keeping you in music school has been a struggle, and if you want to go an alternative route that's fine, but we don't think we should have to be paying for it."

Dad was perfectly Spock-like with his nod, his eyebrow, and an occasional affirmative "Mmm-hmm."

Jonah sat uncomfortably on the couch looking contrite and embarrassed. "*Ohhhhhkay.* Do I have any other choices?"

"Or you can go back to school, pass all your classes, and graduate on time. You will also need to figure out a way to generate a thousand dollars a month to help keep yourself afloat."

By June, we would be watching him pick up his diploma.

32

I THINK I'LL GET MARRIED

"WHEN YOU KISS ME LIKE THAT, I don't know where I am in the world."

Martha was becoming a real problem. I mean, who says stuff like that?

It was a summer afternoon when we walked down to the beach from my apartment and found a secluded spot under the Santa Monica Pier. The waves were crashing. The sun was setting. I kissed her.

On the weekends we'd hike the Santa Monica Mountains. Martha had been on the trail all her life—she knew where she was going, she set the pace, I followed. Sometimes we'd find ourselves alone high on a bluff on a clear, sunny day overlooking the deep blue water of the Santa Monica Bay. It felt like we were the only two people on the planet.

While on the trail she would point out the deer hidden in the brush, the family of quail crossing up ahead, the hawk calling to its babies. Looking out on the bay, she would indicate where whales were breaching. If I couldn't see them, she'd put her hands on either side of my head and turn me in the right direction so I could see the sprays of water against the horizon. If Martha said we might see rabbits on the trail, there would be rabbits on the trail.

Most people in L.A. think that they're just stuck on the 405. Martha always seemed to know we were on the planet. Sometimes we'd be hiking and, in my mind's eye, I could see us in the future, two old people in their eighties still walking through the Santa Monica Mountains, me following behind her flowing gray hair.

One summer she dragged me through the Yosemite backcountry, where we backpacked from one tent camp to another. We were carrying all our gear on our backs, and being inexperienced, I overpacked. She said one of the best parts of the trip was that despite all that schlepping around, I never complained. On our last day while crossing through Tuolumne Meadows, we walked along a sandy path close to the river. I looked down and noticed all these strange plants popping up out of the ground. I had this out-of-body experience where it felt like we were astronauts and our bodies were our spacesuits. It was probably because of the altitude, and I was tired and hungry, but I had the distinct impression we were on a mission to explore a strange new planet and Martha was the expedition leader.

She could also be incredibly annoying. Sometimes at six o'clock in the morning, she would let herself into my apartment and I'd wake up to her slipping into my bed and spooning me. Just for twenty minutes, she'd lie there holding me before she had to go all the way back home to get ready for work. Or sometimes I would stay over at her place, but she'd wake me up at five thirty because I had to be gone before daybreak, as her parents wouldn't approve. Half asleep, I'd drag a comb across my head, brush my teeth, and get dressed. Martha would seat me in the chair next to her bed then kneel down to put on my shoes and tie my laces. She'd lead me downstairs to the service porch, where we'd kiss goodbye and I'd slip out the back door. One morning, before letting me go, she pulled me close and kissed me for the longest time—a deep, loving kiss that caused me to totally lose track of where we were and what we were supposed to be doing. Then she abruptly turned me around and pushed me out the door into the cold morning, as if to say that if she didn't kick me out right then and there, she would have never let me go. Sometimes she'd later joke that although we thought we were being clever, it was more likely her mother, an early riser, would spot me from her second-story window and think to herself, *There goes Adam—sneaking out again.*

And then of course there were the *real* problems in our relationship, like the fact that her parents were devout Catholics, her father was a Fox News junkie, my mother would never approve, our families had little in common, and my kids were still getting to know her.

It seemed clear the only solution was to marry her.

———————

"What do you think I should do with Martha?"

Julie and I were at Mom's house on Cashmere Street. We were sitting in the backyard out by the pool, catching up while our mother finished her phone therapy with one of her psychiatrists. I figured now was a good time to test the waters.

Julie didn't hesitate. "If I were a guy, I would marry her right away."

"Seriously?"

"Right away."

"Why?"

"'Cause she's sweet and she adores you. You guys seem really happy together, and she fits right in at family functions."

"Sometimes I'm not sure," I said, though I was sure. I just needed independent verification.

I had already started the verification process by talking to Justin. "Dude," he began, "you've been with enough women to know who's out there. You don't have to be a serial dater, like me, trying to fill some endless black hole, like me, or fix some sexual abuse problem, like me. You, my friend, are truly blessed."

Justin may have been my guru through much of my recovery, but on matters of the heart his opinion was perhaps a tad suspect. Which was why I needed to hear from Julie.

"She's perfect," she went on. "She doesn't talk loudly, she doesn't try to draw attention to herself, she's a good listener. She always asks me how I'm doing and makes me feel like she really wants to know."

"What about my kids?"

"What about them? It's going to take some time no matter what, but they're eighteen and twenty. It's not like she's going to be raising them. And Maddy's going to give you trouble no matter who you're with, because that's just the way girls are. I'm talking from experience here. You've been with Martha long enough. You should marry her."

"I'm glad you think so, because I bought her a ring. Now all we need to do is tell Mom."

"Whaddya mean 'we'?"

My mother cried about the news. They were not tears of joy. "She's Catholic, Adam. She's Catholic!" Then she went on about what the Catholics did to the Jews during the Spanish Inquisition and the Holocaust.

Julie let her have it.

I could tell what was going on; I could read the subtext. It was as if my mother couldn't fathom that I had found happiness with someone new and that she might be left behind in her loneliness and misery. Because of that, I just felt sorry for her as I stood there counting.

Then came Maddy. I knew she still had a fear of losing me, a fear that once married, Martha would take me away and I wouldn't be there for Maddy when she needed me. I also knew that Maddy could be down on my relationship with Martha when there was other, unrelated turmoil in her life. Like the time she was invited to lunch at my dad and Susan's to see if they could resolve some of the problems they'd been having. There seemed to be some animosity between them, some kind of communication breakdown, and I suspected it had to do with their distance from Nancy, which made Maddy sad and uncomfortable.

At this time in my father's life, he wasn't the detached patriarch always wedded to life on set, the guy thinking about the next job when he was at the dinner table. "My life has become much, much more about family," he said in an interview. "The way I describe it now, I used to major in career and minor in family, and now I've turned it around."

He seemed determined not just to become a good father but a good grandfather too. I thought it great that Dad and Susan and Maddy were willing to sit down and hash it all out together.

It was Thanksgiving weekend and Maddy was home from her junior year at Bard College. She was pissed that I didn't call her on Thanksgiving Day. She and Jonah had decided to have dinner with Nancy and her side of the family instead of me and mine, a decision that I supported even though it had been years since we had Thanksgiving dinner together. I thought she'd be happy that I didn't make an issue about it. I was wrong.

"How can I make it up to you?" I asked.

"You can go with me to this lunch I'm having with Poppi and Susie to try and work out our problems."

I was driving her up to my dad and Susan's house when Maddy decided that was a good time to blurt out the following: "I'm not coming to your wedding. How does that make you feel?"

By then Martha and I had been engaged for eleven months with plans to marry the following January. I think Maddy and I were both a little nervous as we drove into Bel Air. Though I knew she had mixed feelings about me getting remarried, it felt like her announcement had more to do with what we were heading into.

She repeated the question: "How does that make you feel, that your daughter is not going to be there at your wedding?"

I reached for some Al-Anon tools. "Well, Maddy, it makes me feel sad, but I understand your feelings. In the end I'm sure you're going to make the right decision."

"Does that mean you might postpone the wedding?"

"No, sweetie, that's not what that means."

The lunch was delicious. We sat at the breakfast table in the kitchen eating Chinese chicken salad made by Lucretia, their cook who sometimes doubled as a housekeeper. Dad and Susan's kitchen was well lit, with a skylight and a large island in the middle where they typically served the meals we'd have when we were all over there for Shabbat dinners. The sink area looked out over their beautiful backyard and swimming pool and the teahouse pagoda.

Once we had eaten, the hard part of the conversation began. It started off on a positive note, and I was proud of my daughter. "I don't mind if you call me on my bullshit," she said. "I don't mind if you make an issue out of things when they come up instead of not saying anything to me and holding on to it. If I postpone a get-together or change a plan and that bothers you, I want to hear about it. I want to have a closer relationship with you guys, because I really appreciate what you've done for me. I think about it every day that I'm at Bard and how lucky I am to be there and how lucky I am to have grandparents who can help with the huge cost of going there."

Dad and Susan really appreciated hearing this. It was a sweet moment for all of us. Then somehow other issues crept into the conversation: boundary issues and personality conflicts, old grievances brought up for rehash. Some of it had to do with me, some of it pertained to Nancy—the kinds of issues I tried to steer clear of after I made my amends to my father. It was all getting mixed into their discussion with Maddy, and suddenly everything began to spiral out of control to the point where Maddy started crying.

I had intended to stay out of all this, to stand back hoping they could work through this stuff on their own. I had recently learned a new acronym in recovery: WAIT (Why Am I Talking). If no one asks your opinion, there's no reason to open your mouth. Then again, there are times when an intervention is called for.

I turned to my dad and Susan. "What you guys are saying has a lot of validity. There is no doubt a lot of mistakes were made; we've all made mistakes and I personally have to take some responsibility for some of the issues you've raised."

"Like what in particular?" my dad asked.

"I would ask if we could put a pin in some of that for right now and maybe discuss later, as this is Maddy's time with you guys. I think the question is, if you want to improve your relationship with her, we might want to focus on what we can do going forward rather than on all the things in the past that went wrong."

"But some of these issues are interrelated," said Dad.

"You're right, and I understand that, but it's just too much to deal with right now—which isn't to say that you're wrong or that you have no right to be upset about those things. What I'm asking is if you guys think it would be OK to maybe focus on what you think is the best way to move forward with Maddy so that we could try to avoid some of the mistakes of the past."

"That seems fair," Dad agreed. (Whew!)

Everything settled down after that. Dad and Susan just wanted their feelings validated. It felt like the amends I made to my dad at their house two years before—sometimes people just want to vent and be heard. We had Dad's favorite chocolate ice cream for dessert and left on good terms.

"That went pretty well considering," Maddy said as we got back in the car. "Thank you for coming with me, Dad. I love you so much for helping me."

"I love you too, honey. You should feel proud about the way you handled yourself."

"I was just so glad to have you there to help me. I don't know if I could've done it by myself."

"Thank you, sweetie. I'm so glad I could help you."

And then, as we were driving away from the house, she looked straight ahead and very matter-of-factly said, "I'm coming to your wedding."

33

ARE YOU MY MOTHER?

BESIDES EXCHANGING VOWS with Martha, the wedding was otherwise, thankfully, uneventful. Immediate family only at the Miramar Hotel in Santa Monica. It was supposed to be outdoors overlooking the bay, but it was January and, as luck would have it, it poured. Everything moved indoors to a cozy, elegant conference room that was carpeted and white. Martha's parents were kind enough to allow us to be married by a woman rabbi, with no parish priest in sight. We were wrapped in the tallis, the prayer shawl I wore when I was bar mitzvahed, as the rabbi gave us her blessing.

My father said a few kind and loving words, my mother ate plenty of cake, and the kids spent too much time at the bar. Martha and I fell over each other as we attempted to foxtrot to Frank Sinatra's "Witchcraft." It was a beautiful, positive experience. I felt so much gratitude to be on this journey with such a beautiful person, a beautiful soul. After a few days honeymooning right there in Santa Monica, things quickly went back to the mundane.

In the tradition of Poe's "The Fall of the House of Usher," the Cashmere house was falling apart. The most pressing problem was that the balcony outside my mother's second-story bedroom was about to collapse. My father had the balcony installed back in the 1970s. I can still see myself standing in the backyard looking up to see the carpenters cutting through the wall to make it all happen. Now the balcony was rotting, and when it rained, water leaked through and poured right into the family room below (where my dad and I had our disagreement all those years ago about John Lennon).

I called Miguel, my Secret Weapon, to see if he could fix the problem. Miguel climbed up to the balcony from an outside ladder. I walked quietly through Mom's bedroom to meet him. It was three in the afternoon. She was asleep and the blinds were closed. I tiptoed out the French doors. Miguel showed me there was water damage everywhere, meaning the entire balcony needed to be rebuilt. He proudly pointed out how they built it wrong, which he just loved to do, because he had gone to carpentry school to learn "how to do things right the first time." I OK'd him to get started right away.

Miguel smiled and shared one of his favorite refrains: "Your house is in good hands, Adam." Whenever I paid Miguel, he always said with a smile, "Your money is in good hands, Adam."

Miguel climbed back down the ladder and I quietly reentered the bedroom. As I tiptoed through, my mother woke up and called to me. I sat down next to her and petted her shoulder while she stayed curled up in bed.

"Is this my mommy? Is this my cute little mommy whom I love and adore?" I said.

"Yes it is," she said, smiling like a child.

It was as if I were saying it to Maddy or Jonah when they were little and in bed waking up. It all seemed to make sense. I had finally let go of any expectations for her, knowing my job was to simply love her and take care of her, just as she had once taken care of me.

"She's exactly who she's supposed to be," Justin used to say when I would complain that she was driving me nuts. In Al-Anon I discovered that my mother was entitled to live the life she chose. She had been trying to tell me this for years. I guess I just needed to hear it from another source. I could see everything differently now. When she was like this, when she was curled up in her bed, none of the other stuff she did that used to bother me mattered. She was simply my sweet, adorable mother.

The following Saturday night, April 2, 2011, Martha and I were attending a fundraiser for her son Jonathan's school. That's when I got the call that my mother had died at home from a sudden heart attack. Santiago was there with her, as was a new nurse we managed to hire. Mom always said the only way she was leaving that house would be on a gurney under a sheet.

Her funeral was the following Tuesday. Julie and I took a private moment next to her open casket. She looked surprisingly good. Her hair was perfect, as if she had just gone to see Joe. She had on makeup and was dressed in her favorite turquoise sweatshirt with the hummingbird on it. She had her reading glasses. I slipped in a Kurt Vonnegut paperback and some Hershey's Kisses. Julie and I cried. We hadn't just lost the woman who sat in bed complaining, waiting to die for the past seven years. We also lost the mom who watched out for us and took such good care of us all those years my father was hustling, the cool mom we had in the '70s when we were in high school and college—all the many things I admired about her before she began to slip away into my father's world. We lost the mom who knew us and saw us and loved us for who we were. We closed the casket, the curtains parted, and I stepped up to the lectern.

"My mother was born in Cordova, Alaska, a small town on the southern coast. Her father owned a clothing store where he sold suits. My grandfather sold suits in a fishing village. My mother's given name was Sonia, but by the time she moved to L.A. and met my father backstage at a theater in Hollywood, she was already Sandi. Mom worked hard to raise us while Dad worked hard to support us. Julie and I gave her a run for her money. Especially Julie. One of the many things I admired about my mom was that when times were tough, she stood by our dad. I was too young to really understand it then, but old friends and family members reminded me repeatedly that before *Star Trek*, when my parents were struggling and had nothing, my mother never wavered in supporting Dad and his acting career.

"In the mid-1960s, when *Star Trek* became a hit and a whole new world opened to us, Mom transitioned beautifully from '50s housewife to groovy '60s mom and wife of Mr. Spock. There were always flowers in our house—mostly dried, dead flowers and paper flowers and flower stickers that we put on the refrigerator. There were even cellophane flowers of yellow and green. Mom made sure there was lots of color in our home: the furnishings were in greens and oranges and yellows and blues. Mom wore cool clothes, tasteful jewelry, rose-colored heart-shaped glasses, and a long-haired wig called a 'fall.' She liked rock music and took us to see Eric Clapton and Cream during their farewell tour. My parents were colorful people and they attracted colorful people. Mom was like a second mother to many of our friends. Sleepovers were approved on a moment's notice. When one of Julie's friends needed a place to stay while her parents were getting divorced, Mom welcomed her in, no questions asked.

"Mom loved books, she was passionate about art, she generously supported many social causes, she was active in politics. She would have been thrilled to make Richard Nixon's White House Enemies List. She adored jazz and she absolutely loved her New York apartment. Sometimes she would fly from her bed in L.A. to her bed in New York just to hang out. In bed. Except for her lasagna, which was a hit, she otherwise took great pride in being a terrible cook. Mom was deeply devoted to her grandchildren, and they adored her.

"Despite some of the challenges Julie and I experienced with Mom, a Jewish mother, I believe our mother knew what was important in life. We were very fortunate to learn from her what it meant to be loved unconditionally. This, I think, is what was best about our mother: her generous heart and her capacity to love. It seems simple but is no small task when you have family conflicts and expectations and disappointments. I can't fully express to you the warmth and happiness, the pure joy I feel walking around on this crazy planet wrapped in the blanket of my mother's love. Mom, you will be missed."

When I got home, I replayed a voicemail my mother had left just after the last time I saw her: "Adam . . . I'm just calling to tell you I love you . . . and I'm proud of you . . . and the man you've become. You're much more tolerant and accepting than you used to be. OK? That's all. And thank you so much for bringing me dinner last night. I am so lucky. I just want you to know that. OK, goodbye dear. Goodbye."

34

DISTRESS SALE

"DISTRESS SALE." That's what Herb, my real estate agent, said without hesitation when he first came to look at my mother's house.

All the junk everywhere and the fading paint and the messed-up floors and the cracked tile in the bathrooms and the stripped wallpaper in the bedroom and the messed-up plaster in the pool. "Distress sale. Someone's going to buy it and flip it."

Over my dead body. Over mine and my Secret Weapon, Miguel's.

And so the work began. Just getting rid of the wicker furniture took three truckloads headed to various charities, not to mention the six sets of dishes, the broken TVs, the drecky artwork. We rewired the house, replumbed it, retrofitted it, replastered the pool, and painted the whole place white from top to bottom. Three months later, a complete transformation.

With a week and a half left before the first open house, Herb called. "We've got to show it this weekend."

"You told me next weekend. I still have dozens of details to take care of."

"People have been driving by and they've seen what you're doing. There is so much heat on that house right now, we need to show it this weekend."

Everything was perfect when we walked away—the refinished floors, the white walls, perfectly staged furniture in every room, the best artwork of the collection on every wall, flowers and orchids every-where. (We even found some places for the dead, dried flowers my mother loved so much.) The dining room was completely set for a dinner party with Mom's colorful china. In one corner of the living room, a chess game was in progress; on the window seat in the family room sat a tea service ready to pour. A comfort blanket was draped on the stuffed chair in the guest bedroom with an open book waiting to be picked up. It was karmic, it was payback, it was my way of saying thank you to an incredible house for being so good to us for so many years.

Herb told me the open house was like a garden party—there were drinks and appetizers, and everyone seemed to be enjoying themselves. A week later we had five offers—all of them over the asking price, two of them way the hell over. Ten days later, sold.

"What's the matter with you? You should be happy," Herb said. "What you did to that house was amazing."

Just like Clarkson Road, I was sad to see it go. I could still see my twelve-year-old self the day we moved in. We'd started out in our tiny home on Palms Boulevard, and when we moved to Comstock Avenue in '62, it was two bedrooms and one bath, still a little tight for a family of four. Four years later when *Star Trek* started, my parents had turned an enclosed flagstone patio into a master bedroom with a closet toilet and shower stall where the kitchen pantry used to be. By October 1968 we were living in a house with four bedrooms and four baths. It was all fresh and new and we had room and it was liberating and exciting.

Over forty years of memories there on Cashmere Street. The good and the bad. Mostly good. I'd learned how to play guitar in my room. (In 1970, after their breakup, my mother bought me the first complete book of Beatles music with diagrams on where to put your fingers for the chords.) All the friends I had over, all the sleepovers. All the incredible parties my parents threw. I had my bar mitzvah reception in the backyard in 1969, before we put in the pool. We lived there when Dad was in his last season of *Star Trek* and through all his seasons on *Mission* and *In Search of . . .* and all the plays and the *Trek* movies right up through *Star Trek IV*. Dad had a pair of original Spock ears mounted in a black box that sat on the mantel and then hung on a wall in the family room until he moved out in 1986, taking them with him. (Those ears are now on display in the Air and Space Museum at the Smithsonian.) All the cats and the dogs. All the pool parties and the late nights in the Jacuzzi. I was saying goodbye to so much history.

We threw a farewell party. I had Kinko's blow up a picture of the Nimoy family, the one from circa 1970 where we were all sitting in the living room and no one is smiling. They enlarged it and mounted it and I set it on the mantel.

We had arranged a jazz concert for my mom during her wake, while we were sitting shiva, the week of mourning. Pete, mom's boyfriend, put together a band, and they played a one-hour set of jazz standards while we served food. Now, for our Cashmere Street farewell party, it was time for the pop/rock performance. Jonah and I put a band together, and we played in the living room. Justin played bass and so did Nancy's boyfriend Bob, who had played professionally with many heavyweight rockers and for years had been in Jackson Browne's band. We played an eclectic set, from Chris Montez's "Call Me" to Neil Young's "Rockin' in the Free World."

Dad and Susan were there. Dad had attended the wake when my mother died in April—the first time he set foot in that house in twenty-five years. He came back for our farewell party, and he was with me in the living room, looking at all we had done to make the place pristine. In the living room where we took that picture of an iconic unhappy family in 1970. In the living room where, in 1974, Dad questioned why I was applying to UC Santa Barbara when I could live at home and walk right across the street to school at UCLA.

"Do you know how many students would kill to live here and walk to class?" he asked.

I thought to myself, *If I live here and go to UCLA, we're going to kill each other.*

And it was in that living room in 1985, when Johnnie Walker was also present, that we had one of our worst knock-down-drag-outs, the time Dad stood right in my face and I had to ask him to step away.

Dad was looking at the hardcover books all neatly lined up on the bookshelves he had built some forty years before. I walked over to him and said, "Alphabetized by author." He raised a Spock eyebrow and said, "Really."

"So what do you think, Dad?"

"You've certainly done a lot of work. It looks great."

"But how do you feel about it all? What does all of this bring up for you?"

"A lot of history here," he said. "A lot of history."

"Do you remember the time you had [Elton John lyricist] Bernie Taupin and [rock legend] Alice Cooper over for dinner?"

"Yes, I remember."

"How about the time [Swedish actress] Bibi Andersson was coming to one of our parties and you made sure the bar was stocked with akvavit?"

"Hah. I had forgotten that."

"Or how about the time you had the paint in the family room sandblasted off and you and I were using box cutters to get the last speckles off the moulding and I had to run you to the ER because you slipped and put a gash in your thumb?"

"*That* I remember. Lots of memories."

And that was it. That was all he had to say. So typical.

Sometimes I simply could not figure the guy out.

Right around this time, I had a dream about my mother. I was talking on the phone to my former agent, Richard, who had become a bigwig Hollywood player. While we were talking, I got a call from Mom. When I answered it, for some reason she immediately blurted out, "A million dollars," although I had no idea what she was talking about.

"Mom, I'm on the other line with my old agent and I gotta call you back," I said, forgetting that she was dead.

"All right," she said, and hung up.

Later in my dream, I was driving in my car and I called her back. When she answered, I said, "How is it on the other side?"

"It's all right," she said. "A little overrated."

Part III

THE DAD I NEEDED

35

IT'S GOOD TO SEE YOU

"There's no way my daughter is going to live two blocks from Venice Boulevard."

So declared Betty, Martha's mother, my new mother-in-law.

In addition to her lean toward right-wing politics (she was then reading an unflattering biography claiming to have uncovered "the truth" about Barack Obama), I at first thought Betty could also be a bit of a Brentwood snob. The lifestyle of the rich and famous is pretty comfy in West L.A. if, like Betty and Don, you happen to live north of Wilshire Boulevard and west of the 405, which is essentially Brentwood and the northern section of Santa Monica. The rest of us are doomed to live in less-than-exclusive neighborhoods farther south, close to the incredibly less-than-scenic Venice Boulevard. I was, however, wrong about Betty. One of Martha's sisters educated me on her extensive charity work for the poor and disadvantaged. Turns out she was simply concerned about the safety of her youngest daughter. She was also concerned about the run-down condition of the house we were looking to buy—just the way I like 'em.

The two-bedroom, two-bath house was in Mar Vista, two blocks north of Venice Boulevard, close to that first Ikea-furnished apartment I rented when I moved out of Clarkson Road. I used to jog through the neighborhood and always thought this particular street would be a nice place to live. And here we were. It was Herb, my real estate agent, who found the house. When I met him for a walk-through, I noticed a *Star Trek* commemorative plate prominently displayed on the mantel of the furnished living room. A closer look revealed the cheesy painted likenesses of Kirk, Spock, and the rest of the *Enterprise* crew.

Herb came up to me. "Oh my God," he said. "What are the chances of this? This is fate. You were destined to get this house. What could be a better sign?"

By then I had gotten to know Herb pretty well, including his twisted sense of humor. "Don't give me that crap. You planted this here."

The house also happened to be two blocks south of Palms Boulevard, close to the first house my father bought in 1956 shortly after I was born. Dad had been in the US Army Reserve and was able to qualify for a government loan for the $10,000 he needed to buy the place. That tiny two-bedroom where I have my first memories still stands but looks completely defeated, with its faded yellow paint, broken shutters, and neglected front-yard garden. I went to look at it during an open house when it was up for sale many years ago. It's amazing how your perspective changes when you go back to your childhood home. Everything was quite a bit smaller than I remembered. The patio Dad built on the side of the house had been enclosed to make more floor space, but it was all homemade and sad. The fish tank dad installed in the living room wall was gone, but the space he made for it was still there. As I left the open house, I could still see my mother and Julie and me running out the front door one morning, trying to get to school on time. When we got to the car, our '58 red Nash Rambler, Julie lifted her dress only to discover that she had forgotten to put on her underwear.

Through the years, whenever I walked or drove by, I would sometimes think that if I could just buy that little house and fix it up and sell it to a nice young couple, that somehow all the problems I had with my dad, which began with the distance I felt between us when we lived there, that somehow all of those problems could be put to rest.

The house Martha and I had chosen was made of weathered Spanish stucco painted pink. It had wood floors, a fireplace, and a big backyard, and thankfully the kitchen had been upgraded, although the appliances needed replacing. The place needed a lot of work, but I could immediately see the potential. I called in my Secret Weapon and Miguel tore out and replaced the termite-infested floors in the master bedroom and bath. He built a set of French doors leading to the backyard. We had the floors refinished and we painted everything. The gardener gave the yard a complete makeover, planting flowers everywhere.

"Oh, this is lovely," proclaimed Betty, as if having forgotten this was the same place she trashed six weeks before.

It had been seven years since Nancy and I split up, seven years of AA meetings and ups and downs with Maddy and Jonah. All that time, I just wanted some sense of balance and serenity in my life, a chance to start over with a satisfying career, a place to call home, and someone new to share my life with. Now by some stroke of incredible luck, I had it all.

Immediately after we were married, we moved in. Martha's big white bed fit perfectly, and she picked out the most beautiful material to make into bedroom curtains. It was so her—a cream-colored background with leafy vines, dragonflies, ladybugs, and butterflies. There was an in-law apartment out back where we set up a den and TV for Jonathan as a compromise to get him off the idea of painting his room black. Nancy had moved in with Bob and they were remodeling their kitchen, so that vintage stove I inherited from the El Greco now landed in *our* kitchen. We immediately fell into this routine in which Martha scrambled to get to work in the morning while I scrambled to drop Jonathan at the bus stop for school, after which I would head straight into the Valley and a day of teaching at the Film Academy. With Jonah at music school and Maddy in college, everything seemed to be falling into place.

On Valentines' Day a month after we moved in, Martha sent me an email from work.

> I just want you to know how beautiful this morning was for me. Waking up in our new home together. I woke up two minutes before you did. You turned my way and saw me. All these things, the light coming in from the window and it was quiet and peaceful no cars or planes and I could see your chest and your shoulders and your profile and your jawline it was just the way the light hit you. You were facing the ceiling and then you turned towards me and opened your eyes and it was like wow. Do you know what I mean? You got me. You got me good. And it's getting deeper; physically and emotionally and spiritually it's really deep for me right now and I'm having trouble breathing just thinking about it.

"I'm yelling at you because I'm afraid."

It was gray and rainy outside. Our bedroom was dark but we didn't like turning on the lights in the morning. We had a nine o'clock doctor's appointment. I wanted to leave at eight thirty, but Martha wasn't ready. She was yelling at me. I didn't think this was going to be anything serious. She had some back pain, that's all, and we were going to get the results of a scan. I had put on clothes that I was not comfortable in, but it was too late to change.

Heading up Doheny Drive, I was taking shortcuts to make some time and it was working, until we got caught at a red light. She was scared and it was beginning to affect me, although I still wasn't sure why we should be worried.

We screeched into the parking structure at Cedars-Sinai Medical Center and were four fucking levels down before I found a single space to squeeze into. Through the rain into the medical building, where we looked up Dr. Frankel's suite number. In the elevator she started crying, saying she was sorry because she made a mistake. We weren't seeing Dr. Frankel, we were seeing Dr. Reede, but she thought Dr. Reede might be on the same floor. I quickly looked him up on my phone and yes; he was on the fourteenth floor.

Miraculously checking in just after nine, Martha started to fill out the paperwork while I looked at the business card at the front desk and thought about Dr. Reede. Dr. Michael Reede. The name seemed so familiar. Through the powers of deduction, I managed to come up with Mike Reede.

The sign on the receptionist's window read, DO NOT TAP ON WINDOW. OPEN SLOWLY. I ever so slowly opened the window. "Is that slow enough?" I asked the receptionist.

She smiled. Martha laughed.

"Is Dr. Reede by any chance married to Shelly?" I asked.

"Yes he is," the receptionist replied.

"Wow. Thank you." I slowly closed the window and sat down next to Martha.

"I know this guy; I know Mike Reede. We used to hang out on the soccer field when Maddy and Mike's daughter played in AYSO."

Mike used to ask me what I made as a TV director, and I'd tell him and he'd explode and complain bitterly about how the insurance industry had ruined the medical profession, how he couldn't make the money he used to when he started his practice. He'd complain bitterly but he wasn't bitter, he was funny.

A nurse appeared at the door and called for Martha. We walked into an exam room, where she administered a breath test, took her temperature and her blood pressure, then left: "The doctor will be with you shortly."

To lighten the mood, I assumed a European accent and asked Martha about her medical history while pretending to take notes. "Vat vas your first sexual experience?"

Martha laughed. "I don't remember."

"Zen can you tell me, ven vas your first orgasm?"

"You're ridiculous."

"Pleeze can you tell me, ver you breast-fed as a child?"

The doctor came in, stinking of gin.

No, that's a line from Paul McCartney. The doctor came in, and it was Mike all right. He came right up to me and vigorously shook my hand. He was all gray with a stooped posture and a raspy voice. He seemed happy to see me. He told me about his daughter, the one who played soccer, that she was graduating from Bryn Mawr. I told him Maddy was graduating from Bard.

Gray day, gray light, gray doc.

Mike was very thorough, going through Martha's medical history, asking her all kinds of questions about her symptoms. When he finished writing everything down, he said, "Do you want to see the CAT scan?"

We followed him into his sparsely furnished office with piles of paperwork and files everywhere. We sat facing his desk as he closed the door. When he passed behind us, he briefly put his hand on my shoulder before making his way around his desk. Thinking this meant he was glad to see an old friend, I responded by asking about his wife, Shelly.

"She's fine," he said as he sat down and turned on his computer.

But that's not what he meant. When he put his hand on my shoulder, *It's good to see you* was not what he meant at all. It was his way of saying, *I'm so sorry to have to tell you this*. Then he pulled up Martha's scan and showed us the size of her tumor.

Martha never wanted to know her prognosis—she didn't want to hear anything about the likely outcome of her situation, a forecast of what might happen. She just wanted to get the treatment so that she could "get better." I couldn't live like that. I wanted to know what we were up against.

A week later, the rain had stopped and I was hoping that maybe better weather might bring better news, so I called Mike Reede. I didn't want Martha to know, so I called while I was out dropping my car off for repair. I was sitting in my car in a parking lot outside my mechanic's garage.

"Hi, Mike, thank you for taking my call. I'm alone now and want to know what the prognosis is for Martha."

"Well, we have to see how she responds to treatment."

"No, Mike, you said that before and we heard the same thing from the oncologist and the radiologist. I want to know what you really think."

He hesitated. I was in the parking lot at Precision Motors, which was basically a one-door garage in a warehouse complex where Andy, my mechanic, and his partner worked exclusively on European cars. I was lucky to find Andy, who happened to live in my first apartment building off Venice Boulevard. I'd sit in my car in the parking garage decompressing and he'd be at the other end of the garage working on his car. One day I walked over and introduced myself. There were plenty of Alphas and Mercedes and BMWs lined up for repair at Precision Motors. Sometimes they worked on old classic Ferraris and Maseratis in mint condition. Sometimes they let me sit in the driver's seat of those cars, and I would imagine myself driving the Amalfi Coast with the top down and Martha smiling next to me. She loved cars.

Mike Reede let out a sigh. "I'm sorry to be the one to tell you this, but I don't think she's going to make it. Her tumor is too big and her lymph nodes are involved, so it's spreading. You need to talk to the surgeon to get his opinion, but I think she's dealing with issues that are just too far along."

I thanked Mike before hanging up, then found myself crying, which was unusual for me. I mean, I'd cried for my mother just a month before all this. Other than that, I couldn't remember the last time I cried. I knew it had something to do with my dad, that all my life expressing my emotions was not safe with him, that he didn't know how to handle any of that, so I would stifle my feelings and keep them hidden. At least I think it had something to do with that. I can't be sure, and I'm certainly not blaming him. I just couldn't think of another explanation, and when I shared all of this with a therapist I was once seeing, she lit up like a lightbulb.

Back in my car it suddenly hit me that everything was about to change for us. I was crying for Martha, I was crying for myself. I was crying for everything we had and everything we were about to lose.

I had to pull myself back together, because I could see Andy coming toward me with his clipboard. I waved to him to give me one more minute, and he turned around and went back into the garage. Then I did something that would have been unthinkable just a few years before.

I called my father.

36

THERE'S MORE TO THE PICTURE

YOU ALWAYS HEAR STORIES about people who beat the odds. A good friend of mine had a glioblastoma, an aggressive and lethal brain tumor. The five-year survival rate for glioblastoma is 6.8 percent and the average survival time is eight months. His tumor was surgically removed over ten years ago, and miraculously he's still alive. You always hear stories about a relative or a friend who got into a clinical trial that saved their life. I didn't want to discourage Martha. I didn't want to throw in the towel or appear defeatist, so I always took her to treatment. And there was plenty to take her to: chemotherapy, radiation, scans, surgeries, blood tests, hydration. At her request, we even flew to New York so she could see a psychic healer.

This might look like "contrary action"—doing something you may not necessarily want to do, even going directly against your instincts. That wasn't the case here, because I *wanted* to take Martha to treatment. I wanted her to think I was willing to do anything for her to get better. I was determined not to let on in any way what several doctors had told me was inevitable. (It wasn't until late in the game, when the cancer had spread to her bones, that her oncologist felt obliged to inform Martha what was really happening.) Joe Nimoy, a cousin of mine who is a retired oncologist, called this the "duality of cancer," meaning that I could show Martha a facade of optimism while at the same time knowing this wasn't going to end well. The fact was, we could never get ahead of the cancer—we couldn't seem to stop it, as it had already spread to her lymph nodes and would later spread to her hip and her spine.

This idea of duality could also be applied to the doctors who gave us good advice and the doctors who gave us not-so-good advice. The surgeon at one hospital said he should go in and remove the tumor. The surgeon at another hospital said it made no sense to have surgery without systemic control of the cancer, that surgery would only make the situation worse, because while Martha was post-op, she couldn't receive the chemo she needed to stop the cancer from spreading. Then there was the pain management doc who didn't manage Martha's pain at all. I was given prescriptions for all kinds of opioids to get at CVS, which turned out to be the wrong place to go, as they simply didn't carry a lot of this stuff or kept the drugs under lock and key, where I could only get them if a manager happened to be available. When Martha was in serious pain one weekend, I called the doctor in a panic and her exchange neglected to tell me she was out of town and wouldn't be returning my call.

Then there was the infusion room where Martha received her chemotherapy. The room was a large open space run by nurses who were incredibly skilled and knowledgeable and patient and kind. These apparent angels of mercy moved throughout the room taking care of the sometimes twenty-plus patients sitting at stations. The irony is that this was before targeted therapy and immunotherapy and these women were basically administering poison.

Then there was the duality of Martha—beautiful, joyful Martha who looked exactly the same during her first ten months of treatment. She was diagnosed in May, and in November we took a break from the chemo and flew to Maui to finally take a real honeymoon. While swimming and sunbathing and taking excursions around the island, there was no way you could tell this vital woman had cancer spreading through her body. Things changed near the end of that trip, when she began to lose her hair due to her latest chemo protocol. We would swim and her hair would fall out. "It's like having spiders all over me," she said.

I took plenty of pictures before we shaved her. I shot some video of her walking along the beach. She was so incredibly beautiful. Finally she said we had to do it, that night. And so on a Wednesday night halfway through our trip, I shaved her head. I did a very professional job. A wigmaker had shown me how to do it—by taking a section at a time, rubber-banding it, then putting everything in a plastic bag so that he could make a fall for Martha when we got back to L.A. I did a really good job, but she was bald and we were in shock. I kept up our tradition of kissing in the elevator when the doors closed and we were alone. I didn't for a minute want her to feel that I loved her less. Many years later, Martha's sister said Martha told her she knew I really loved her because I agreed to shave her head.

Soon after we returned to the mainland, Martha had hip surgery, because the cancer was spreading to her bones. That's when everything completely changed—the vibrant, independent woman I had married just one year before was now a completely different person.

"You didn't sign up for this," she said. I never imagined it would come to this, and sometimes I wondered how and why this was happening to us. It was the principles of recovery and sharing at AA meetings that helped me see things from two perspectives—what we sometimes call "both/and"—*both* that we were in the middle of a tragedy unfolding day after day that was wearing us down *and* that I was also able to experience these feelings of gratitude for how incredibly lucky I was to have met Martha at all and how I considered it an honor to be the one to help her.

———————

I really needed all the help I could get during this period of my life, which is why I made the mistake of turning to Justin. Prior to Martha's diagnosis, Justin was set to go on tour with a certain hip-hop band from New York. These guys had a considerable following and his hope was that this was going to be the tour that broke him into the big time as a bassist. Then he could finally leave Stein on Vine and his "paltry paychecks." He told me that the spliffs and blunts that were constantly being passed around during rehearsals didn't bother him. He would always joke, "Time to *pah-tay*," but would not partake and told me he never felt the slightest urge to do so because reefer was not his drug of choice.

The tour turned out to be a disaster. He kept calling me from the road telling me it wasn't well publicized (this was before omnipresent social media) and no one was showing up to the performances—they were playing to empty nightclubs. By the time they got to New York, I called Maddy and asked her to please support him by taking her friends from Bard into the city to go to the show.

"How was the show?" I asked her the day after.

"They were good, but there was no one there. It was kind of pathetic," she said.

"Did you talk to Justin afterward?"

"Yeah, but it was really weird, because he was drinking. Did you know he was drinking?"

"No."

When he came back to L.A. I kept calling him, but he would never pick up or return my calls. I was going through so much with Martha that I needed my little Buddha to help me process some of it, to tell me I was going to be all right. I also wanted to be there for him to see what he needed to get back into recovery, but he never called me. So I went over to his house.

He was living in a converted garage. It was freestanding behind a small house on Tenth Street in Santa Monica, and it was actually a nice place. A studio apartment with its own kitchen and bath, and it was all white linoleum, new, and there was plenty of room for his musical gear. I walked right up to the window and looked in. He was sitting in a recliner chair with his back to me watching TV. I called his cell. He picked up his phone, looked at it, then put it back down. Then I had an emotional relapse and did something that felt totally un-Al-Anon and un-AA: I knocked on his door. He was shocked to see me.

"Where have you been? I've been trying to call you," I said.

"I know, I've been really busy." His eyes were glazed.

"You're high," I said. Then I got right in his face. "You're totally high! What the fuck is wrong with you?"

"Hey, man, chill out," he said as he pushed me away.

This was so unlike Justin, the guy I knew and loved. What a total letdown. I just wanted to grab him and shake him, shake some sense into him, get back the guy I knew. My bodhisattva.

I cooled down and put my recovery hat back on. "You should have called your sponsor," I said. "You should have called me."

"Yeah, I know. You don't need to quote the program to me."

"Yeah, whatever," I said as I turned to walk away. "I probably owe you an amends for losing my cool," I said as I made my way down the driveway.

"No you don't," he said. "I deserved it."

It was a Friday night and my father was taking me to a Shabbat service. I was so tired during that period because of all the things I had to do to take care of Martha—the doctors, the meds, the testing, the radiation, the chemo, the home care. It had been a nightmare, a nightmare in slow motion—which is exactly how I described it to Nancy, who was incredibly sympathetic and supportive this whole time while she was thankfully well settled and happily living with Bob.

In fact, it was during this period that Nancy made an amends to me. We were sitting at a table at the Mint on Pico Boulevard waiting for Jonah to perform as a guest bassist in somebody else's band. We were just sitting there, making small talk, waiting for the show to start, when out of the blue she apologized to me for her part in all the things that went wrong with our marriage. I couldn't believe it. It couldn't have come at a better time.

And then there was my dad. He just kept showing up. Every week he brought food that was prepared by Lucretia, Dad and Susan's housekeeper/cook. Roasted chicken, lasagna, enchiladas, salads—everything I needed for the week was there in the food packs he brought on Friday afternoons. Dad was the one I called about Martha and the doctors and the constant setbacks. And every other week or so on a Friday night to give me a break, he would pick me up and take me to a Shabbat service.

It was summer, so it was still light out as we drove east on Palms Boulevard past Mar Vista Park, where my dad tried to teach me how to fly a kite sometime around 1961. The west side of the park was an open dirt lot back then, and I remember him being frustrated with me because I refused to keep running around with him while he tried to get that kite up in the air.

Now, as he drove down Palms, I wanted to share something that had happened to me that morning. "I woke up and the bedroom was glowing. Dad, it was totally surreal—the sun was really strong and it was filtering in through the blinds and the whole room was lit up. I looked over to see Martha sitting on her side of the bed—she had her back to me. She was in silhouette with all that filtered light coming in. She was sitting in her pajamas on the side of the bed."

I had bought her the PJs years before from a store on Motor Avenue. They were similar to a pair I had given my mom, but Martha's had a white background with beautiful pink butterflies all over.

"Is this for a special occasion?" the saleswoman asked.

"No, just for love," I said.

Back with my dad in the car: "I got up out of bed and went over to sit next her. She was sitting there cradling a teddy bear someone had given her for comfort.

"I sat down and said, 'Are you holding your teddy?'

"She looked up at me with the most mournful eyes, and, Dad, it was the saddest thing to sit next to her and see her with her short hair and her face drawn and aged, and tired from all she's gone through. I felt so bad for her, so sad for her as I sat there. It felt unreal, like I was dreaming it, but I wasn't. It felt like we were somewhere else, like we were suspended in the air, and if I looked out the window it would be like looking out of an airplane—all I would see is blue sky and floating clouds.

"I put my arm around her and said, 'Are you holding your Teddy?'

And, Dad, she looked up to me and in the sweetest most innocent childlike voice said, 'Yes.'

"Do you understand what I'm trying to tell you?" I asked as I dug into my pocket for a tissue.

He pulled the car over and put his hand on my shoulder. "Yes, I understand. She's trying to hold on to her life and you're trying to hold on to her. All I can say is that I'm so sorry for you, Adam. I'm so sorry for both of you."

The Shabbat service was like nothing I had ever seen. This was my first introduction to Beit T'Shuvah, a congregation but also a residential addiction treatment center that my father and Susan had become involved with through their charitable foundation. They had helped establish a career counseling center for residents who had completed their stay and were ready to go back out into the world. Shabbat services took place on Venice Boulevard on the ground floor of a three-story building, but it looked like a basement—there were columns everywhere holding up the structure. The floor was made up of industrial cream-colored tile, some of it cracked, and the ceiling was low. It was as if they had converted the basement into a shul. The chairs were arranged in odd configurations to account for the strange shape of the room and to work around the columns that could block your view of the bimah and the stage. This was their sanctuary.

The place was packed. There was a carnival-like atmosphere, as if we were all attending one big party. It was noisy—there was so much chatter, and everything bounced off the walls and the tile floor like we were in an echo chamber. The service started at exactly 6:30, when the band began playing a rock 'n' roll version of the hymn "Shabbat Shalom." It seemed more like a revival meeting or a rock show—or an AA meeting, because the residents who lived upstairs in the building were sharing their experience, strength, and hope throughout the service. There was Harriet Rossetto, who originally founded the organization as a halfway house for Jewish ex-cons trying to assimilate back into society. Now it was a treatment center for anyone with an addiction issue no matter what their religious affiliation. There was Mark Borovitz, the rabbi, who had been an alcoholic and an ex-con. He showed up to that halfway house run by Harriet once he got out of prison, they married, and Mark became a rabbi. For over thirty years it was the Mark and Harriet show at Beit T'Shuvah, the House of Return.

During the service, Rabbi Mark walked around and shook everyone's hand. He was wearing a purple felt hat and a green velour jacket, under which was a T-shirt that read SPIRITUAL GANGSTER. *This is the rabbi?* I thought to myself. It was the craziest Shabbat service I had ever seen. The place was filled with addicts and alcoholics, people who had relapsed, those with years of sobriety, and those who looked like they had just been released from detox. All were welcomed. Those who shared expressed gratitude for Beit T'Shuvah, how it saved their lives, how they refused to be victims, all of which reinforced my own gratitude for the love I'd found with Martha and for being present to help her during what would be the last days of her life.

This is where my father knew to bring me on a Friday night. As the service continued, it felt comfortable to me. It felt like I was with people I could relate to. It felt like I was home.

37

WAITING FOR MARTHA

DID I SCREW UP THE APPOINTMENT? I wondered as I sat in my therapist's waiting room. *Probably.* I was driving when we rescheduled, so I couldn't write it down. I thought she said *tomorrow at ten*—tomorrow being today—but I might've been wrong. I must've been wrong. At that moment I needed less stress in my life. Sitting in a waiting room for a therapy appointment I possibly did not have was not less stress. Next time we add an extra session, she should text it to me. Live and learn, I guess. Live.

I had been preoccupied in the car that day with all kinds of things. With my kids. With my life. With Martha's life and what was left of it. Taking care of her the last fourteen months had been excruciating, and I wasn't sure how much longer I could keep it up. Her mother had been helping; Betty really showed up, although I was still the one responsible for getting Martha to her appointments and making sure she ate enough and that she took her meds—mostly pain killers, lots of pain killers. Sometimes I wished I knew the day she was going to die. The exact day and time. Then I could say to myself, *Well, I can make it till then. I can hang on for that long.*

If I knew the day, I would stay with her the whole week before. I would take off work and be with her all day, every day. I'd take her up to Pismo Beach so that she could finally see the monarchs, all those butterflies clustered together as they warm up and start to flutter in the winter sun. She loved butterflies, and we talked often about going to see them. Then I would drive her home down the coast with the Pacific

Ocean on our right and she would look out the window gazing far into the horizon until she died quietly in the car, happy at last that she got to see the monarchs. Then I'd drive straight to the ER at Cedars, the ER we'd been to so many times before, and park my car in their driveway. I'd walk inside and say, "My wife is a cancer patient here, she's in my car, I think she died."

Then it would be over.

Some orderlies would get her from the car while I was waiting there for her parents and my family, for her son, Jonathan. We would all go home, and it would be over. I would write the eulogy. We had already decided that she should be buried at Holy Cross Cemetery and not Hillside where I will someday be buried. Her parents agreed. There would be a memorial for her at her church, but we wouldn't have the Korean priest. I would ask that we please not have the Korean priest, because although he is a very nice man, I could never understand a single word he said, and I knew Martha's mother would agree.

We would notify all of Martha's friends and relatives and coworkers and they would all come and I would deliver the eulogy. It would be deep and heartfelt, and it would be funny too, because Martha liked it when I was funny. I would talk about the time I tried to teach her Yiddish and she thought *schlep* was a surfing term, because she always heard guys say they had to schlep their boards down to the beach or schlep them back to the car.

"No, not a surfing term," I told her. Not originally, anyway.

I would quote the Irish poets, because Martha was so much an Irish girl. I would quote from Joyce and Yeats and . . . U2. *It's a bitter pill, [we] swallow here, to be rent from one so dear.* And then we would go to the gravesite.

It would be winter in Los Angeles, but sunny and warm. Her closest friends and family members would gather 'round as we laid her to rest. To finally rest. Everyone would shovel dirt onto her casket below, but not me. I would take a handful of dirt and drop it down so that she knew I was still close, that I would always be close. But it would end up being the other way around, because when a butterfly happened by, I'd know that Martha was close. That she would always be close. I just had to watch out for the butterfly.

After the ceremony and the tears, after the priest said the final benediction and we all walked from the grave, I would post an album of photos on my Facebook page. That amazing portrait of her in her early twenties, the one her European boyfriend the photographer took of her. The one of the two of us in front of Yosemite Falls, because Martha was always at home when we were hiking on the trail. The picture of her on our delayed honeymoon on the beach in Maui, the one I took the day before I had to shave her head because her long brown hair was falling out. I wouldn't say anything about that on Facebook. I wouldn't write anything at all. I'd just post those pictures so people could see how vibrant my lovely wife was.

Then I would be done.

Thinking this all through was sickening. So was waiting for my therapist, who clearly wasn't coming. I couldn't believe I got the appointment wrong. I had to teach a class at one, so it had to be at ten o'clock. I was sure she said she was available.

Several nights before, I'd been reading to Martha from *Memoirs of a Geisha*, one of the many passages that spoke to us and our struggle with the cancer that kept appearing in different parts of her body. "We lead our lives like water flowing down a hill, going more or less in one direction until we splash into something that forces us to find a new course."

"Sweetie, are you awake?" I kept asking, because Martha was lying on her side with her back to me, when usually she sleeps sitting up because of the pain. Often she would nod off right away when I started reading, but it was important for me to read to her, because it was one of the few things we had left.

Martha didn't answer, so I assumed she was asleep and read on in silence. A few minutes later she started yelling at me. "Stop it! Stop it!" she cried. "Adam, can't you take me? I have to go to the bathroom! Didn't you hear me?"

"No, sweetheart, I'm sorry. I didn't hear you," I said as calmly as I could, putting my hand on her shoulder.

"I must have been daydreaming," she said, which is what she always said whether it was day or night and she woke up talking herself out of the dream she was having. I asked her if she had to go and she said no, so I just kept gently touching her shoulder, very gently, until she said it was nice but that I had to stop because of the pain.

She didn't look good yesterday when I left for work. Come to think of it, I got the time for that wrong too. Usually I'm meticulous about putting my work schedule into my calendar, but somehow I screwed up and found myself sitting in an empty classroom. Martha looked awful. She was weak and pale and defeated. She wouldn't eat the breakfast I made for her, the oatmeal and biscuits, because she had trouble swallowing—a common side effect of radiation. She was limping around the house with her walker because of the hip surgery, because lung cancer likes to move on to the bone. And the brain. Thankfully, her mother showed up to take care of her. By this time, she was coming every day to help take care of her.

I sat in my therapist's waiting room not sure about what to do or where to go. I started to think about what I had wanted to talk about, about how hard it had been to watch everything falling apart, our lives together disappearing right in front of us when it all started off so promising. I wanted to talk about how it all began with Martha, when our two divorces were long behind us and it felt like we were being given a second chance. It seemed that anything was possible then, that everything could work out between this conservative Catholic woman and this liberal Jewish man.

"What about religion?" Martha's mother had asked, before we were married.

"We don't see that as much of a problem," my brown-eyed girl had replied. "Anyway, Adam's never even taken me to shul."

"Shul?" Betty asked, "What is shul?"

"I don't know because he hasn't taken me."

I explained to Martha that shul was a temple, the synagogue. That's when I decided to teach her a little Yiddish. Just some words she could throw into the conversation when she met my mother. Martha was pretty good with the flash cards.

"*Schmaltz*," I said.

"Literally chicken fat, but *schmaltzy* is used to describe something overly sentimental."

"Very good. *Schmatta*."

"A rag, but also the clothing business."

"*Shiksa*."

She gave me a look. "A non-Jewish woman who is either romantically interested in a Jewish man or is the object of a Jewish man's affection."

"Or obsession." I smiled.

"Or obsession." She smiled back then kissed me.

"*Schmuck.*"

"A dick. Not exactly a word I would drop into a conversation with your mother."

"Are you kidding? She uses that word all the time. *Schlong.*"

"Adam . . ."

"Come on. *Schlong.*"

"A big dick."

"*Schmeckel*"

"A little dick."

"*Shtup.*"

"To fuck."

"*Schlemiel.*"

"A jerk."

"*Schlimazel.*"

"A bigger jerk than a schlemiel."

"*Shayna.*"

Martha hesitated before answering, so I repeated the word: "*Shayna.*"

"I love you."

"That's not what it means," I said. "It means 'beautiful.'"

"I know what *shayna* means," she said. "I love you."

"I love you, too."

Those words came out of my mouth as I sat there in the therapist's waiting room, my mind so far away, then slowly coming home to refocus on where I was.

"I love you, too."

It was ten thirty. Clearly there would be no session today, but I couldn't get up. I didn't want to. I didn't want to walk out the door and back to the reality of my life, the nightmare in slow motion. There were two nature paintings on the wall to my right. Both had monarch butterflies in them—one sitting on a tree branch, one flying past a hibiscus flower.

If only I knew when this would all be over. It would be so much easier.

38

LOOKING FOR MARTHA

I HAD BEEN WALKING AROUND in a funk for well over a month. It wasn't like before—the first six months after she died. Back then I'd be all down and depressed, but then I'd come out of it and start to feel better. I'd be hit by a grief tsunami that would take me down, only to subside so that I could feel the sunshine again. This time a tidal wave had hit me weeks before and I still felt like I was underwater, walking around in some sort of fog. I tried to get back to nature, I tried surfing and walks in the hills, but nothing was helping.

The grief counselors said that's just the way it worked, that it was going to be like this for a while, that there was no point in fighting it. "The grieving never really ends," they said, "it just changes over time." I almost never cried before Martha died; I was never able to let myself go. I was always hiding my feelings, pushing them down. Finally, after Martha, I was crying all the time. At least I let myself cry whenever I was alone and felt the need. It was a whole new experience to be sober and crying. It gave me some relief from the tsunami, the latest one that kept trying to keep me under.

The grief counselors gave us an exercise, one of many to help us process what we were going through. This was at Our House, a grief support center in West L.A. All twelve of us in our group had recently lost our spouses, and we were given a prompt to read then fill in the blank. My prompt read, "I still can't believe that . . ."

I could've taken the easy road and said, "I still can't believe that four and a half months after we were married, Martha would be diagnosed with cancer, and that eighteen months later, she'd be gone."

Too easy. I was determined to at least begin the discussion by saying something positive about my experience with Wonder Woman.

"I still can't believe that I met Martha when we were both in our fifties, that we were both divorced with kids we were dedicated to, and that even at that stage in our lives, it felt like we were in our twenties starting all over again. There was just this constant crazy energy between us, this attraction that was there all the time. We were driving in her car one Saturday afternoon when she pulled over on a secluded street. She got out of the car and walked around the front. Through the windshield I yelled, 'What are you doing?' Then she opened my door, pulled me out of the passenger seat, opened the back door, threw me in, and jumped me. It was like that all the time; it was just nuts with her. One weekday I was driving to meet her for lunch near where she worked. While I was looking for a parking space, I noticed this knockout brunette walking down the street. Of course, as she came closer I realized it was Martha and I literally blurted out, 'Holy shit, that woman is my girlfriend!' That's how we felt about each other. All the time.

"And now, yeah, I still can't believe I have to deal with these brutal tidal waves that drown me and crush me with the reminder that my gorgeous wife is now sleeping with the angels at Holy Cross Cemetery. That last tsunami still will not let up, making me feel like I'm dragging myself around all the time like I'm the walking dead and somebody should get a shotgun."

I think my share made an impression, because the two counselors looked a little shell shocked, not quite knowing how to deal with my rant.

Michael, another widower, saved the day by jumping in: "Wait a minute, Adam, can I ask you a question?" Of the six men in the group, Michael was one of the three of us who no longer wore a wedding band, and he had openly shared that he was happily involved in a new relationship. "Didn't you already start dating and didn't that have any positive effect on you?"

"Yes, I did, and she was really good for me."

I had met Cheryl, a single mom, in an Al-Anon meeting. After weeks of sharing our experience, strength, and hope, I finally asked her out. For a while, it was working and we had fun. It was a relief to have someone to spend time with after all the turmoil and tragedy of the previous two years. Thankfully, we were never actually together when the waves of grief hit me, and when they did arrive and tried to drown me, I just dealt with it on my own or with my family and friends or in grief group. Then again, sometimes I'd be walking with Cheryl and a butterfly would cross our path and I knew Martha was close, but I never said anything. Even though Cheryl seemed sensitive about my loss and we did occasionally talk about what happened, if Martha popped into my head when I was with her or something made me sad, I just held on to the feeling until I could deal with it later.

"Are you still seeing Cheryl?" Michael asked.

He was the only other guy in the group who had started dating. Some of the other men and women were still holding on to their spouses, not ready to move on, which I totally respected. In fact, there was no sense of judgment among us at all. The counselors pointed out that everyone dealt with their grief differently; the unifying factor was that we all wanted to process it, feel it, live through it, with the implicit understanding that we'd all somehow be stronger as we continued on through our lives. But it was nice for me to know there was another widower who felt it was OK to want to be with someone else this early in the grieving process. I felt strongly that Martha would want me to find someone new.

"No," I said to Michael. "I'm not with Cheryl anymore."

One morning when Cheryl was at my house, she had noticed something was wrong. "Are you OK?" she asked. "What's going on?"

"I was just, *ummm* . . . I'm so sorry, for some reason I was just thinking about Martha."

I thought by then it was safe to be honest with her, but I was wrong. Cheryl got up to leave. "I don't want to stick around and watch you wallow," she said as she was pulling her things together. "I think maybe it's time you moved on with your life, because it sure feels like you're stuck in some kind of rut."

I wasn't expecting that at all; she seemed so patient and kind. It shocked me, because I thought if anything she'd find it endearing that I wasn't willing to just dump all of my feelings about Martha and act like she didn't exist anymore and just move on. I mean, who would want to be with a guy like that? Martha just died in December 2012 and this was

April 2013, four months later, and maybe I was dating too soon and/or maybe, just maybe, Cheryl was being incredibly callous.

When I finally got my bearings, I had an emotional relapse—instead of counting to ten, I told her exactly what I was thinking: "Yeah, maybe you should take off, 'cause I think I'll just sit here and *wallow* for a while."

"Look, I know what you're going through," she said.

"You have no idea what I'm going through. Until you've lost a spouse who up and dies on you, and you are still very much in love with that person, you don't have a *clue* as to what I'm going through. Oh, and by the way, *why don't you get the fuck out of my life?*"

OK, just for the record, I did not actually say that last part. But losing my cool was bad enough. I had worked hard to learn not to say things that popped into my head in the heat of the moment, because I knew I'd end up regretting it later and would have to make an amends.

That same week I stumbled on what looked like an interesting British detective show. While investigating a murder, the young inspector comes across a woman who is an old acquaintance from college. She asks him if he has gotten over his college sweetheart and he says he isn't sure. She tells him she's willing to play second best if he will love her "just a little—a little would be enough." The evening after they sleep together, she meets up with him and tells him she's changed her mind, that he isn't ready.

When I met up again with Cheryl, she immediately stated her case. "You still have pictures of Martha on the mantel, and I know the flowers you bought for the house were really a tribute to her. I think we need to be clear that I deserve to be the top priority. I don't want to be made to feel like I'm competing with her."

"You're right, you shouldn't have to put up with all that, and I owe you an apology. You do deserve to be number one." This seemed to put her immediately at ease.

"Someday I'm going to have to move on," I said, "but I'm not sure I'm there yet. Maybe we should just take a break and revisit this situation in a few weeks to see where we're at."

Cheryl clearly didn't see that coming and seemed to be searching for words to possibly backtrack, to find a way to keep us going. But it was too late. I had no intention of revisiting the situation, because after having dated for several weeks, I was forced to admit to myself that I was not in love with Cheryl, *not even just a little.* If I were, I might have tried to defend myself and explain my predicament with the grief tsunamis and ask if she could work with me. I might have been much more apologetic and asked if she could be more patient with me. If I had been in love with Cheryl, those are the things I would have said. Then again, if I had been in love with Cheryl, it would have probably been in part because she understood all of that already.

Sharing all this in grief group—my feelings for my late spouse, my relationship with someone new—was what we were all there to do no matter what stage we were at in the grieving process.

"It's interesting that Cheryl reacted that way," said Jena. She was one of the widows. She was close to my age, had long brown hair, and wore glasses with black frames. She had lost her husband to a heart attack a week after I lost Martha. "I wouldn't want to be with someone who wasn't at least somewhat sympathetic to my losing my husband at this stage in my life."

"Oh, I totally agree," I said. "I want to be with someone secure enough with themselves that the mere mention of Martha is not going to cause a problem. The issue I'm struggling with is that what I had with Martha was way off the charts. Even though I do believe I'm going to find love again—I have to believe it—trying to *replace Martha* is something I'm going to need to look at and deal with. Cheryl was not necessarily a good match for me, and maybe it is too soon to be getting involved with someone new. What I want to be careful about, what I want to be mindful of, is that when I do find someone I'm comfortable and happy with, she shouldn't have to compete with my memories of Martha."

Jena and Michael and some of the others in the group nodded in agreement, which made me feel good—like I was actually doing the work of processing what I was going through and that I wasn't alone, I wasn't the only one dealing with these issues.

I thought about the woman in recovery when I was newly sober who told me, "In a year's time your life will look totally different." I thought about how, before he relapsed, Justin used to say, "The universe is conspiring at this very moment for your happiness." It was moments like this, when I would have a breakthrough and things started to look better—that I was able to look at the big picture and realize that Martha coming into my life was no accident, because there are no accidents in recovery and that there was still so much to look forward to. All in good time, because during the following months, I would often find myself at Holy Cross Cemetery.

Martha's gravesite is high on a hill overlooking the green lawn that slopes down toward a statue of Saint Francis. Afternoons are often sunny and breezy there. To find my way to her all I have to do is remember *Drive past the flower shop, count four trash cans up the hill, park and head to the right, stop in front of the two trees.*

When I saw Martha's headstone for the first time, it was just perfect—it came out more beautiful than I had imagined. Her sister and I designed it. It had a pink patina with roses engraved on both sides and it read LOVING AND JOYFUL, MARTHA NIMOY. I would bring fresh roses to her gravesite, and always a pair of clippers and a whisk broom to keep the edges clean. Then I'd stand there or sometimes sit nearby and rifle through the memory file, the highlights of all the things we did together, the day I proposed to her on the Inspiration Loop trail at Will Rogers Park, the times we walked along the beach together, our trips to Yosemite, our trip to Hawaii. In my mind's eye I'd often end up with her on her parents' service porch that morning when she held me and kissed me so deeply to the point where it felt like she would never let me go.

39

STAR TREK X:
THE FRANTIC SEARCH FOR SPOCK

I WAS REALLY MISSING JUSTIN. I had so much trouble understanding why he couldn't get his shit together and stay sober. He was going in and out of rehab and bouncing from one girlfriend to another. The Big Book says we are "not a glum lot," and Justin made recovery so entertaining. He was just an all-around amusing guy, like a character in his own movie. I remember the night he showed up to the Wednesday meeting wearing a sport coat, red silk shirt, black pants, and flip-flops. He had two blondes with him, one on each arm. His Hugh Hefner phase. And the night I saw him at the Good Hurt, a club on Venice Boulevard—a hired hand playing bass with these older R&B guys. There he was in a black collared shirt, love beads, and leather straps on his wrists, nail polish and just a hint of eyeliner. With his thick, jet-black hair, you just couldn't take your eyes off the guy as he banged away on that bass. Justin was such a rock star, such a cool cat. I had no doubt that kid was gonna make it someday. I just loved him so much.

He even sometimes helped me out with my mom. After going out on a supply run at her request, he left me this voicemail: "Hello, Mr. Nimoy, this is Watch Command Officer Justin Valdivia with Westland Security Services. I just wanted to inform you that this morning at 11:46 AM your mother, Mrs. Sandra Nimoy over at the Cashmere Street Estate, at 11:46 AM this morning Mrs. Nimoy hit the panic button and sent out an APB for an extra-large ice-blended mocha and a box of Almond Roca STAT. I was dispatched to respond to the emergency and want you to know that said items were procured and delivered at 12:22 PM. A Mr. Santiago signed for them. We sent a follow-up car over at 9:37 PM along with a bag of gummy bears to secure the perimeter at the Cashmere Street Estate, and we've had no trouble since that time. Just wanted you to be aware. Again, this is Watch Command Officer Justin Valdivia at Westland Security Services, badge number 248732. You have a good night."

Shortly after Martha and I were married at the Miramar, I got this message in a high-pitched voice: "Hello, Mr. Nimoy, this is Justin, I'm the senior desk clerk here at the Miramar Hotel and Resort in beautiful downtown Santa Monica. I just wanted to make you aware that your wife was reported swinging from the chandelier in our main ballroom and kindly request that you come collect her. Security is standing on high alert, but we usually like to have our guests deal with such matters privately if possible. Again, this is Justin at the front desk, but if I'm not here Alonzo can also help you out."

Why couldn't I get that guy back? Then again, I'm just your run-of-the mill recovering pothead who doesn't know shit about opioid addiction. But my old friend Chris Kelton knew.

"Remind me how you met Justin again," I said to Chris.

"A friend of mine brought him over to the house when he was just a few days sober. I had just come back from Costco with a bunch of bacon-wrapped filets, and I busted them out and threw them on the grill and fed him and we were friends ever since. It was like feeding a hungry cat—they never go away and you have a friend for life."

"But what's with all the relapsing? I mean, he seems to want to pull it together. He keeps reassuring me he's gonna do it."

After he checked himself into one of his rehabs, he'd called and said, "Don't worry Ishi, Little Crow will be coming back to you soon." He started calling me Ishi after one of my heroes, the last Yahi Indian who stumbled out of the California wilderness and into the modern world in 1911. Justin called himself Little Crow after the chief of the Dakota people who, like many others, met a tragic, untimely death. Justin apparently wasn't concerned about cultural appropriation.

"Yeah, a lot of us relapse," said Chris. "Sometimes it's just a part of recovery."

"But he keeps doing it and hasn't made it back."

"That's the point—there are those who are committed to recovery and there those who aren't. You never know. That's why it's one day at a time which has brought me closer to taking a twenty-year chip this year. But I constantly have to do the work."

"How do you think you did it?"

"I did the work and got to a position of neutrality with drugs and alcohol. I'm not fighting the temptation anymore—it's all in the Big Book. I don't care if I see it, smell it, hear about it, I'm neutral about it all, I just don't care."

"But Justin went out on tour and picked up again and you've been out on tour with bands plenty and didn't pick up."

"That's because I'm clear in my head about what happens to me when I pick up that may not happen to my friends. I have friends on the crew, and when we're out on the road they get shitfaced and are hurling or have fumes coming out of their head, and the next day they may do a shitty job but they show up standing at their station when it's time to go. I don't know if that would be my case. And then they'd say, 'Oh, I'm gonna quit when I get home,' and I'd say to myself, *What the fuck is up with that?* That's just crazy to live that way.

"If you're clean, you will be able to behave in difficult situations with a sense of integrity and morality that you learn in the program. Once you pick up, all bets are off. If you say, 'Oh, I'll just pick up tonight and go back tomorrow and raise my hand as a newcomer,' if you're a junkie it's highly unlikely that's going to happen and stick. I mean, I've done that like a dozen times, and one night, when I had a commitment the next day, I picked up that night and the next day I got to the meeting an hour early and dropped off the ashtrays, which was my commitment, and I didn't go back to a meeting for eight years while I was strung out on heroin and methadone. That's when I got down on my knees and begged God to either kill me or make it better.

"It's funny we're talking about this now, because today is September 1, and it was on this date twenty years ago when I got down on my knees. Then I checked into rehab on September 20 and got out on October 15. Then I used one more time. I was with some friends about to use again when there was a knock at my door. It was my roommate from rehab, who said he was about to go score and came over hoping I could talk him out of it. He was literally on the other side of my door when I had a syringe in my hand about to shoot up. That was October

20, and that's when I made my decision to squirt the syringe out on the floor. My friends were yelling at me for wasting the hit: "What the fuck did you just do!" I went out with my roommate. He didn't get stoned that day and I've been clean ever since, and I can't believe it's been almost twenty years.

"The point is, once you pick up you never know. Sometimes it's 'Oh man, I fucked up. I'll go back tomorrow,' but sometimes that becomes the next day after the next day after the next. The hard part is that if you're just a pothead like you and you kick, you're going to be cranky for a while, you're going to be restless, irritable, and discontent. With kicking heroin it's a much steeper climb, because you're going to be in physical hell having things like convulsions."

"Maddy, can you get Tinder on my phone for me?"

"Are you serious, Dad?"

"Yeah, my therapist told me to do it. Why, is it totally bogus?"

"No, some of my friends are on it and they've got all these hookups going. It really works. Here, give me your phone and I'll set it up."

We had just finished dinner at the Galley, an old-style steak and seafood restaurant on Main Street. Established in 1934, it's been designated the oldest restaurant and bar in Santa Monica. Maddy downloaded the Tinder app and started swiping. I moved over to sit next to her, watching her swipe at breakneck speed as a blonde woman with a golden retriever flew by then a brunette in a yoga pose then a curvy redhead behind an office desk. She came across a woman in a bikini who looked like a stripper and swiped left.

"Maddy, what was the matter with that one?"

"Dad, you can't be serious. That is so super unchill. You're not going to date someone who puts those kinds of pictures online." She continued swiping away. It was sort of exciting. It felt like maybe my old self was coming out of the fog.

Our dessert arrived: an apple torte and two peppermint teas.

"So what happened to Justin after that crazy night in New York when I saw him drinking? You never told me."

"Oh, Maddy, where to begin. After New York he went to some rehab facility in the Valley."

"Did the rehab work?" asked Maddy, having paused with the Tinder. I moved back to my seat, leaving her to annihilate that torte.

"Not really. He didn't seem to be able to kick his opioid habit, which he's had most of his life. He just wasn't the same after that, and then he relapsed again."

"Oh. Wow. I wonder how he got so messed up in the first place."

"I don't really know, honey; it could have been lots of things. Justin had a very difficult family life, but who knows what really happened."

It felt good to talk about this with Maddy, to be open and even matter-of-fact about everything that had been going on with Justin. "After rehab and his relapse, things got *really* messed up, because he called me to tell me he was going to marry a young woman from England even though I knew he had totally lost interest in her."

"Why'd he want to marry her?"

"Because she had a house and he thought she could provide the stability he needed."

Justin had called to tell me all this because he was trying to prove that he was back on track, that he was finally getting his life together and trying to be responsible. I didn't even try to argue him out of it. I just had to let go on that one. I didn't cause it, I can't control it, and I can't cure it, as we like to say in Al-Anon about loved ones lost in their addiction. I knew at this point I couldn't save Justin.

"I found out later he had left her before they tied the knot. Then he called me to say he was moving to Costa Rica with some new girlfriend to start a boating company."

After he moved to Costa Rica, he sent me an amends in an email that he said he was writing because his sponsor told him to. It was an *I'm so sorry if I said or did anything to upset you but you haven't been very supportive of me these past months* kind of amends. It didn't look anything like the amends he had sent me years before when I called him out on not showing up to meetings when he said he'd be there. That amends also arrived in an email and began with a story about how he had been channel surfing and happened on to what he described as "*Star Trek X: The Frantic Search for Spock.*" (It was actually *Star Trek III: The Search for Spock.*) As he was watching, he realized that he was Kirk and I was Spock and that he had left me, his best friend, on the Genesis planet when he should have saved me. That was seven years prior to his decision to go to Costa Rica. That was a Justin I didn't know anymore.

I knew I had to let go of any resentment toward him and forgive him for his latest lame attempt at an amends. After all he had done for me, I knew I had to accept him as he now was and pray that his Higher Power would take care of him.

As Chris put it, "He was like a brother to you, but his disease got the best of him, and it becomes so painful to be a failure to your family and friends. You get to a point where you think, *I'll never get out, I'm never going to be able to kick*, and you just want to get the fuck out, to pull a geographic, to go somewhere where you don't have to deal with people, because you don't want to face them or you don't want to fuck them over anymore. That, plus he doesn't have to bump into anybody—unless of course his Higher Power intervenes and he bumps into somebody from back home who asks him if he can go with them to a meeting."

Maddy was astounded by all this. She had no idea what had gone on with Justin and, like me, was having trouble reconciling the guy she thought she knew with the guy he turned out to be. "It's too bad you don't have Justin to talk to any more about everything that happened to you, about Martha and everything. I don't really get it, because when we first met him, he was so cool and fun to be with. Then there was that show in New York where he was acting weird and drinking, and everything changed. It was like I didn't even know him anymore."

"Yeah, me too."

"Have you talked to Justin at all lately, or no?" Maddy asked.

"No, honey, and I won't be talking to him again."

"Why not?"

"Because Justin died about three weeks ago."

"Wait, what? What do you mean?"

"Last weekend Chris Kelton called me to tell me Justin was dead."

"How did Chris find out?"

"Facebook."

"Oh my God, Dad, are you serious? Oh my God, this is really freaky. What happened to him?"

"No one knows exactly, but he was reported missing and several days later they found him floating in the water."

"Oh my God. Were drugs involved?"

"I can't say for sure, honey. It wouldn't surprise me, but I just don't know."

"How does it make you feel? Are you sad?"

Feelings. When Maddy was seven or eight, she always wondered about feelings, especially other people's feelings, when sad things happened. "Do you feel sad?" she would say. Like the time I lost my key chain with the dog tag from Bear, the dog I had when I was growing up in Westwood. Bear was the best dog, and I lost that key chain and Maddy asked me how it made me feel. "I feel really sad about it, Maddy." Other people's feelings were a total mystery to her when she was young; she was always trying to make sense of them.

How does it make me feel now? Am I sad?

"Yes, of course I'm sad, Maddy, very sad—but I'm also grateful to be out to dinner with you talking about this stuff."

The Galley was super old school: low light, sawdust on the floors, old-fashioned bar, twinkling lights hanging from the ceiling with plenty of other kitschy stuff on the walls. Traditional upholstered booths that are ridiculously blue. A feeling of another era. Just like M'Goos.

"Come sit next to me, honey. I need a hug."

She moved over to my side of the booth and put her arms around me.

"We are so lucky, Maddy. We have so much to be thankful for."

"I know, Dad. And I feel so bad for you."

"That is so sweet of you, Maddy, thank you. I think this was something that had been coming for a long time. We were just lucky to know Justin when we did."

40

BOYS FROM BOSTON

THE TOUR DRIVER PICKED UP his microphone. "We are now in the North End of Boston and about to pass the home of silversmith and patriot Paul Revere, whose famous midnight ride warned the Boston militia of the arrival of the British army."

In 2013, Dad and I flew to the East Coast to film *Leonard Nimoy's Boston*, a documentary about Dad's early life in that great city. I felt a sense of urgency to make this happen, because it was something I had been thinking about for some time and I was now concerned about Dad's health. Just the year before we'd attended the graduation ceremony at Boston University, where Dad was giving an address to the College of Fine Arts. As usual, he was in top form.

> This is true of any work in the arts: What is the work about? What does it say to a contemporary audience? What light does it cast on our lives and on the issues that concern us and connect us? Indeed, how does it help to heal the world? . . . Spock called for exactly the kind of work I was prepared to do. He was a character with a rich and dynamic inner life, half-human, half-Vulcan; he was the embodiment of the outsider like the immigrants who surrounded me in my early years. How do you find your way as the alien in a foreign culture? Where does your identity and your dignity come from and how do you make a contribution? . . . You are the creators and the curators of your own lives. You create

your own life and your work. Give us your best. Give us
the best of your art. We crave it. We hunger for it. Help us
to see ourselves, to know ourselves, to illuminate our lives.
And keep in mind what Victor Hugo said: "Popularity is the
crumbs of greatness."

That afternoon Dad was to receive an honorary degree at the general
commencement ceremony for the entire school, which took place on the
athletic field. The dignitaries had to walk around the track in procession
before ascending the stage. Dad accepted his degree, then gave the Spock
salute with both hands. The crowd went wild saluting him back—all
those students in their black caps and red gowns with their hands raised
high and their big grins. Just an amazing trajectory for a boy from the
West End of Boston who barely made it through high school.

When it was over, I was floored when Dad told me he didn't think
he was going to make it around the track. One lap is a quarter mile,
and they only walked about three quarters of that. It was difficult to
reconcile what he said with how good he looked. My mother thought
she had COPD. Even hoped she had it. But it was my father who would
ultimately receive the diagnosis. Smoking cigarettes for thirty years will
do that to you. I didn't realize how serious his condition was until that
commencement ceremony.

When we returned to Boston in 2013, I hired a camera crew and a
van so we could drive to my father's old neighborhood in the West End.
We stood in front of St. Joseph Church, which Dad said he had walked
past almost every day of his early life. From there we looked at what
used to be Chambers Street, where he lived with his family. I held up
a picture of what it once looked like, a long block of three-story walk-
up brick facade apartments, and compared that photo to the expensive
high-rise apartments that stand there today.

Dad pointed at the picture. "That's it," he said, "87 Chambers Street.
There were six of us in this apartment. One bathroom."

It was a two-bedroom apartment that Dad lived in with his parents;
his brother, my uncle Mel; his maternal grandparents; and occasionally
his uncle Meyer. My grandparents ultimately managed to buy the building and lived there until 1959, when the city took it by eminent domain
as a part of an "urban renewal" project in which the entire West End
was demolished to make way for the high rises.

I asked Dad if he shared a room with Uncle Mel. "Shared a room? We shared a bed!"

We drove to Beacon Hill, where he sold newspapers, and to the Hatch Shell, the bandstand where he folded chairs after performances by the Boston Pops. As we stood near the Boston Common, Dad pointed to a storefront where he used to sell vacuum cleaners. He also sold them door to door to come up with the extra cash he needed for the trip out to Hollywood after his parents declined to help him. His boss warned him not to sell the cheap demonstration model—he had to convince customers what they really needed was the deluxe model at twice the price. Dad was a tough kid from the streets, and by the age of seventeen had already become well versed in the art of the bait and switch.

During a break in the filming of our documentary, Dad and I took a duck boat tour, where they drive you around the streets of Boston in these ridiculous-looking amphibious landing vehicles from World War II. Then you splash into the Charles River for a little boat ride, then back onto dry land.

The tour driver grabbed the microphone. "On your left is the site of the Boston Massacre, where British troops fired on an angry crowd of protestors. Just around the corner and on the right is the Granary Burying Ground, where the parents of Benjamin Franklin are laid to rest, as well as three signers of the Declaration of Independence."

The bus was three quarters full. We sat in the back, just the way we liked it. Dad was incognito, in a baseball cap and sunglasses. We looked like tourists, which is what we were.

"We are now passing Beacon Hill, home to John Kennedy, John Hancock, and John Kerry, the three Johns. On our right on Cambridge Street is the Otis mansion, built in the Federalist style in 1796. Also on our right is Massachusetts General Hospital, and we're coming up on the West End of the city, formerly an immigrant neighborhood which was demolished to make way for quote-unquote 'urban renewal.' Of course, the most famous resident of the West End is none other than Leonard Nimoy, who starred as Mr. Spock on *Star Trek*. Do we have any *Star Trek* fans on board?"

At least a half dozen people in front of us raised their hands and yelped. I got all warm and fuzzy inside and turned to look at my father. He sat with his arms crossed over his linen jacket and nodded his approval. He was cool and almost as inscrutable as always. Paul Revere,

John Hancock, John Kennedy, and Leonard Nimoy. It just didn't make any sense, it seemed so . . . illogical.

We were the last off the bus. When Dad took off his hat and sunglasses and introduced himself to the driver, the poor guy went white, as if he was going to pass out.

After Martha died, I began studying Torah, the Five Books of Moses, with Rabbi Mark at Beit T'Shuvah. I had been regularly attending Friday-night services, had gotten to know Rabbi fairly well, and soon, every Friday at two o'clock I was in his office reading and discussing Torah. "God gave us free will; Torah is the manual on how to use it," Rabbi Mark would say, always emphasizing the importance of caring for "the poor, the widow, the orphan, and the stranger." During those weeks and then months together, we made our way through Genesis and into the time of the Hebrew patriarchs—Abraham, Isaac, and Jacob, and all the problems they had with each other as fathers and sons. It was during these sessions that he shared his perspective of how Abraham's test of faith was really a case of his failure to let go of resentments he held against Isaac. I told Rabbi Mark that despite making an amends to my father, he had never himself made an amends to me, even though he was sober. It was then that he explained that all the things my father had done for me during Martha's illness—making himself available at any time for the phone calls, bringing us food, regularly taking me to Beit T'Shuvah for Shabbat—all of that is what we call a *living amends*, and that I should recognize it for what it was. I had heard about a living amends before, but until then was never quite sure what it meant. Rabbi Mark also articulated something I had suspected deep down for some time: by making my amends and accepting my father for who he was, it allowed him to become the father I ultimately needed him to be.

Then the conversation with Rabbi went a bit deeper. He said that the amends I made to my father had far greater implications than just the incredible transformative effect it had on our relationship. He explained that the amends fell squarely within the philosophy of Rabbi Abraham Joshua Heschel and the miracle of t'shuvah (repentance, return). It's a concept I'm still grappling with, but it has to do with transformation and creation—that we can't go back in time but that somehow the power of t'shuvah "allows re-creation of the past to take place" and that through the forgiving hand of God, "harm and blemish which we have committed against the world and against ourselves will be extinguished, transformed into salvation." (Let's get Mr. Spock to weigh in on that one.) In this way, Rabbi Mark explained, the amends I made not only pertained to (and transformed) the lifelong troubles I experienced with my father, but it also applied to the troubles that existed between Abraham, Isaac, and Jacob. More specifically, the rabbi claimed that when I made the amends for myself, I was also making an amends on behalf of Abraham for putting the knife to Isaac's throat.

The trip to Boston gave Dad a chance to look back on where it all started and consider how far he had flown. It was part of the bookend of his life. It also gave me an opportunity to honor my father in a way that would have been impossible a few short years before. Arriving at the point where we could love each other unconditionally came about for no other reason than the power of twelve-step recovery. Prior to our reconciliation, most of my life with my father could be characterized as many happy memories marred by regular episodes of miscommunication, negative feelings, and conflict. With my amends to my dad and his living amends to me, everything changed, and we never again looked back at the wreckage of our past.

41

HALF-A-CENTURY ICON

BECAUSE THE BOSTON DOC was such a satisfying experience, the following year, in November 2014, I approached Dad about the possibility of producing a documentary film featuring Mr. Spock. I thought it would be a nice contribution to help commemorate the fiftieth anniversary of *Star Trek*, which was coming up in 2016.

"OK, let's do it," was his immediate response.

I put together a rough outline of what I thought the film should look like and drove up to his house to make my pitch. I had originally envisioned Dad narrating and hosting the project on camera in a way reminiscent of his work on *In Search of . . .* as we looked at Spock and *Star Trek* over the years. I thought it might be cool if we re-created the bridge of the *Enterprise* and Dad walked from station to station delivering his commentary before and after various clips from the original series, the animated series, and the feature films. When I arrived at his house for our first official meeting, I discovered he had already started pulling stuff off the internet. He googled "Spock's ears," which came back with over a hundred thousand entries. He loved that.

During this time, things had been going well with our extended family. Julie and I and our kids and Susan's son Aaron were all over there on a regular basis for holidays, birthdays, and Shabbat dinners. This meant a lot to Dad. He would give toasts about how happy he was to have the family together and would sometimes get emotional, which was always an eye opener for me. Dad usually sat at the head of the table during Shabbat dinners, which reminded me of Don Corleone, the

Godfather. I would sometimes play the role of Michael, the dutiful son, by sliding into the seat next to him and whisper silly things like "Luca Brasi sleeps with the fishes." He'd respond by saying, "Don't worry about it. I'm gonna make him an offer he can't refuse."

Several weeks after our first meeting to discuss the Spock documentary, I was at Dad and Susan's for lunch to present a more detailed outline. When I arrived, Dad seemed out of sorts.

"What's going on?" I asked.

"Oh, I'm really depressed," he said. That was interesting. A word, a feeling, I had never heard him express before.

"What are you depressed about?"

"This week I got a call about my availability to appear in the next *Star Trek* movie."

Dad took great pride in the fact that he was the only cast member who had appeared in the original *Star Trek* pilot (which began shooting fifty years before, in November 1964) and in the newest iteration of the film series from J.J. Abrams.

"What are you depressed about? That sounds great," I said.

"I'm depressed because I have to turn it down," he said.

"Why are you turning it down?"

"Because they're going to start shooting in April, and I don't think I'm going to be around by then."

I was shocked by this revelation, because he still seemed in relatively good health. We were sitting opposite each other at the breakfast table in the kitchen. Susan was on the phone in the background, against glowing windows that looked out on their beautiful backyard. We were sitting in the same location we were all in four years before, when Maddy and I went there for that lunch to work out some of our family issues. Suddenly this particular meeting with my dad took on a whole different color. Dad was anything but alarmist, so to hear him talk about his impending demise was disconcerting. To hear him talk about anything relating to his feelings was disconcerting. Then he went all withdrawn and introspective on me, just like the good ol' days. He was so deep in thought, he didn't notice me take out my phone and shoot a picture of him lost in Spock contemplation, with Susan on the phone in the background.

A few weeks later, just after New Year's 2015, we met again to talk about the documentary.

"Dad, we've got to get a camera crew in here right away to get your final thoughts about your *Star Trek* experience."

"What's your hurry?" he asked. "We have until September next year to finish this thing."

"You just told me weeks ago you couldn't be in the next *Star Trek* feature because you didn't think you were going to be around in the spring."

He brushed it off. "Ahhh, no, no, no. Forget what I said. I was just having a bad day, that's all."

It didn't seem like he was just having a bad day. At the time he looked like a guy who could see the white light at the end of the tunnel, and it was coming soon to a theater near Leonard.

In deference to my father, I did not call in a camera crew.

Seven weeks later he was gone.

"Can you confirm that Leonard Nimoy has passed away?"

It was the Associated Press on the phone.

"Are you serious? It's been in the news all day," I said.

"I need independent confirmation from a family member."

"Yes, Leonard Nimoy passed away this morning."

Like several times before, Dad had gone to the hospital because he was having trouble breathing. After being there for a couple of days, he decided enough was enough and wanted to stop the treatments for his COPD—he was going to spend his last days at home. As soon as they sedated him and put him into an ambulance, he fell into a coma. The entire family gathered at the house in Bel Air to be with him as he lay on a hospital bed that had been set up in his and Susan's bedroom. The following morning, he stopped breathing.

Soon the entire family left the room and I sat next to my dad. Just me and him alone together in the bedroom. It was quiet and peaceful. Ambient morning light came in from the bay windows that looked out on the yard.

As word spread around the planet that Leonard Nimoy had died, the phone started ringing. A news helicopter hovered overhead. Shutting all that out, I sat alone with my father. I just sat there focusing on my breath as I sometimes do in meditation. Suddenly I was overcome with these intense feelings of love and gratitude and satisfaction and what can only be described as a sense of oneness with him. I felt totally connected to Dad. In that moment, I thanked God or my Higher Power or whatever it was that enabled us to finally figure it out, so that we could get it right in the last years of his life, so that we could end our relationship with grace and style and love and connection. Even if at times he could still be Spock-like; even if at times he could still be confoundingly inscrutable.

Thank God, we finally figured it out.

———————————

There is one other aspect of my father's passing I'd like to share. Although Dad spent plenty of time in shul and was well steeped in Jewish culture, I would not call him a religious man. He was very much in touch with his cultural roots, but my mom and dad were low key on religious practice, having both been raised by parents who observed more orthodox life-styles. We always went to shul on the High Holidays, we always celebrated Passover and Hanukkah, and Mom and Dad refused to get a Christmas tree even though Julie and I begged them. (We ultimately settled for an ornamented Hanukkah branch.) But we didn't keep kosher, we didn't have separate plates for meat and dairy, and having bacon at home was not a problem. Dad could speak Yiddish; he and Susan did often attend services and helped establish a preschool at Temple Israel of Hollywood, where they had become members. They created a charitable foundation that was originally designed to support Jewish philanthropic organizations like Beit T'Shuvah.

And, of course, Dad had repeatedly said that the Vulcan salute derives from the hand gestures of the rabbis as they administer the priestly blessing to the congregation during Yom Kippur. In fact, if you look up "priestly blessing" online, you will likely find a reference to its use by Leonard Nimoy on *Star Trek*. (It's remarkable how many people are still learning about this connection between Spock and Judaism for the first time. On December 31, 2022, almost eight years after Dad died, the *New York Times* printed this as number one on their list of favorite facts of the year: "1. The 'Star Trek' hand gesture for 'live long and prosper' is derived from part of a Hebrew blessing that Leonard Nimoy first glimpsed at an Orthodox Jewish synagogue in Boston as a boy.")

Despite all these deep connections to our Jewish heritage, I never considered my father to be religious. Reading or studying Torah was not something he pursued, we never discussed his views on God, and we never took a family trip to Israel. I had even known my dad to work on Yom Kippur, the holiest day of the Jewish calendar. In 1972, feeling flush from three years on *Star Trek* and two on *Mission: Impossible*, my father called me into the living room, where he was sitting like a king in a big yellow chair. He announced that he was sending me on a student tour of East Africa for the summer. The idea of working on a kibbutz, an agricultural community in Israel, greatly appealed to me, but for some reason Dad had Kenya and Tanzania in mind. Sometimes I just could not figure the guy out. I had some idea of my dad's love for the cultural and ethnic traditions of Judaism (his knowledge of Yiddish, his reading of Jewish stories), but other than the Vulcan salute, I had no clue as to my dad's views on the religious and spiritual aspects of Judaism.

With all that in mind, I had a strange experience at the Jewish cemetery the day of Dad's memorial. The director of the mortuary offered us a chance to see my father in his open casket in a small room adjoining the chapel where the memorial was to take place. Not a single family member expressed an interest in seeing him, preferring to remember him "as he used to be." I, on the other hand, was a definite yes. I went back to the room, and there was his casket, open at the top, and there was my father. His head and body were wrapped in a smooth purple cloth almost like a tunic, with his face exposed. He looked regal. He looked like he could have been a Jewish prince, a patriarch, a king, or a prophet. (He did, after all, play the prophet Samuel in a TV movie about King David.) He was so impressive, as if he were ready to be buried in the cave at Machpelah—the burial place purchased by Abraham that is known as the final resting place of the Hebrew patriarchs. He was just so perfect, so at peace, so majestic. I had this weird sensation that I wasn't just looking at Dad, I was also looking back through time at an ancient ancestor of the Jewish people.

I immediately went to get the family. "You guys have got to come see this."

We all stood in awe of the figure lying before us. An appropriately dramatic ending, I thought, to the life of a man who had so much impact on so many generations.

42

HONOR THY FATHER

After Dad died, the show did indeed go on—my producing partners and I continued with our documentary film about Mr. Spock. The incredible outpouring of emotion over the loss of Leonard Nimoy (even President Obama weighed in!) made clear that the documentary had to focus not only on the pointy-eared alien but also on the multitalented artist who portrayed him.

Working on the film was a great way for me to process his loss—looking at all the old footage, the publicity stills, the family photos gave me an opportunity to grieve the loss of a parent in a way that few might experience. And then there were the interviews we conducted with friends, family, and colleagues who told incredible stories about Dad, the best of which I believe we included in the film. As we continued to piece the Spock doc together, more and more people involved with the project felt we should include the story of my own journey with my father, both the bad and the good.

Having settled on *For the Love of Spock* as the title, we took great pains to make sure that the father-son part of the story took a backseat as we focused mostly on the lives of Mr. Spock and Leonard Nimoy. Still, I struggled with just how much of my journey with Dad to include in the film. I showed a rough cut to several people, including ex-wife Nancy, who liked the film but was concerned there was too much of me in it. I immediately took her concern to Janice Hampton, our senior editor.

Janice came highly recommended and was hired when we were well into postproduction, the previous editorial staff having been let go for independently taking the film in a direction I had never intended. (They also asked the coproducers to limit my access to the editing room until they had completed their handiwork.) I wanted Janice on the project because: (1) I felt that there were too many men making this movie and that we needed to get a woman's perspective, (2) Janice had a significant amount of experience, having been an editor since the days when movies were actually shot and edited *on film*, and (3) Janice confessed at our first meeting that she knew absolutely nothing about *Star Trek*.

"Boom! You're perfect. You're hired."

She was relentless in keeping us on track, on point, and on theme (and she never once banned me from the editing room). When I told her about Nancy's comments and suggested we might need to make some changes, she resisted. I asked her to sit with me and review every cut involving the father-son storyline to see if there was anything we could curtail or cut out.

"How about this?" I asked.

"No."

"What about that?"

"No."

"This?"

"No, no, and no. We've been very austere with the story about you and your dad, and everything has to stay or it makes no sense. Your ex-wife is not the demographic we're appealing to."

The movie was in postproduction on the Paramount lot, which led to a couple interesting connections. The first was that the offices our producer David Zappone was using were in the Dreier building, which sits right above soundstages 8 and 9, where they shot *Star Trek: The Next Generation*.

The second was that shortly after my father died, my daughter Maddy, who had been working in production in the film and television industry, landed a job at Paramount Television Studios. During *For the Love of Spock*'s postproduction at Paramount, Maddy was promoted and received an office bigger than ours. Her Poppi would have been proud to know that she's still at Paramount Television and is now a vice president of production. The facilities manager at the studio had a still photo of Kirk and Spock blown up, mounted, and delivered to Maddy's office.

While we were working on the movie, I was going through some old boxes of keepsakes, letters, and photos that had been stored in that darkroom at my mother's house. It was in one of those boxes that I found a long letter from my dad, written to me on yellow legal paper.

I had long forgotten the letter even existed, and finding it was, as my father would say, "bashert," (often translated from Yiddish as "destiny"—as in, "there are no accidents in recovery"). Much of the letter is included in the Spock documentary. It was dated October 1973, when I was seventeen, and it was in response to an argument we had. He sent the letter to try to put our relationship into perspective, and it was a real eye-opener. He wrote about his relationship with his own father—that he "loved and feared him" but that they had little personal contact; most of his interactions were with his mother and neither of his parents was giving of approval. Because of this, he was always looking for approval, and when he became successful on *Star Trek*, he expected to receive that approval from the producers and the studio. He was shocked to find the opposite was the case, because they were worried he'd ask for more money, which he did. The letter confirmed what I had witnessed firsthand: that his parents delighted in his success but never said an approving word to him.

This whole issue of approval kept coming to mind in the years after we made the documentary. To get some clarity, I put in a call to my dad's older brother, Uncle Mel. By then, my uncle was ninety-four years old.

"Uncle Mel, I want to check on something. You went to Boston Latin, which was the premier grade school, but dad went to Boston Public because he wasn't a great student. Is that right?"

"He went to Boston English, and that's right. He might have done better in school if he applied himself, but he wasn't interested. All he cared about from a very early age was acting. He was always busy with theater productions. Like the time he spent the summer at Boston College in the theater department."

"OK but Nana and Papa never approved of all that, right?"

"No, they wanted him to go to college to get a professional degree."

"But you went to college, you were at Northeastern and then MIT. While you were in college, some of that time living at home, were they supportive? Did they express any happiness that you were living their dream of getting a diploma?"

"You know, this is interesting, because just the other night, before I went to sleep, I was thinking about this. While I was at Northeastern, I made dean's list every semester I was there. They never said anything. Not a word. This was especially true of my dad. I never knew what he was thinking. Never."

The letter from 1973 also mentioned the competition Dad had with his father. Dad wrote that his father was a barber who was not an ambitious man and made $150 a week. Dad felt he had him "beat" when Dad was earning $8,000 to $10,000 a year and commented how sad it was to even concern himself with being in such a contest. Dad also acknowledged that competition between him and me could be very tough when we had a difference of opinion, because he could be very loud and verbal. He noted that he had been very lucky, had made good money, and was famous. (With all those adoring fans, who was I to come along and say, "Hey, I think you might, on occasion, be wrong"?) He realized that my competing with him was "a lot tougher to deal with than competing against a $150 a week barber."

This whole idea of competing with Dad had never consciously entered my mind. How do you compete with a pop culture icon? Dad was so identified with Spock, who could pop up anywhere at any given moment. How was I going to compete with that? The motivation to go to college and law school was in part because I wanted to walk my own path that had nothing to do with my father, that was something he never could have done. No competition there. Or so I thought. He even wrote me a note once that when people asked him about me, he was proud to tell them about my academic career.

Then again, this competition issue raised in Dad's letter harked back to something my sister said years ago when I told her about how Dad walked out on me the night he came to Berkeley. "He's being passive-aggressive because he's in competition with you."

"What are you talking about?" I had no idea how Dad could possibly see me as a threat.

"Dad barely made it through high school, and being Russian immigrants, Nana and Papa always dreamed he would go to college. Now that you're at Cal, he's flat-out jealous."

Even when I quit the law and started directing, it was never with the intention of competing with Dad, it was more like *I'll be lucky and grateful if I can follow in any of his footsteps.*

Dad's competitive nature might help explain his up-and-down relationship with my favorite starship captain, Bill Shatner. For years my sister Julie and I heard stories about the problems between the two of them during the making of the original series. Bill was apparently quite competitive too, which was a problem when it became apparent that Spock was more popular and the press were showing up in the makeup trailer to interview Dad. This pissed off Bill, who insisted on having his makeup applied in his dressing room. There were several other incidents that my father described to me in great detail. Bill even interviewed Dad and asked him about some of these, and Dad just laughed them off. My father had a great fake laugh.

This all prompted me to ask Dad an obvious question. "With all the trouble between the two of you on set, how is it that you guys were so amazing together when the camera was rolling?"

My dad replied in typical Spock-like manner: "We were professionals."

Years later, in the '90s, Dad announced that Bill Shatner was his best friend. Julie and I were bewildered by this, but it was true. They seemed to be enjoying a nice, loving relationship with each other. Dad was right there to support Bill when his third wife, Nerine, tragically died in 1999. And on a much lighter note, they were terrific together in their Priceline commercials. Then, several years later, Bill was back to being persona non grata in my father's eyes. Sometimes I simply could not figure Dad out.

The competition issue was one of many ways in which we were living on different planets. I was never really the competitive type; team sports were definitely not my thing, I didn't care what my standing was in law school (I probably should have been paying more attention), and once Justin reminded me about "compare and despair," I rarely beat myself up over how well other people were doing. I think in many ways I may be more like Isaac rather than his rougher, tougher older half brother Ishmael. But in many other ways, I'm a lot like my dad, not the least of which is our genuine love for storytelling.

And then there was a part of my father's letter in which he expressed some sentiments that totally floored me. He said that he was proud that I was his son, that I have his approval and support, that I am priceless to him and that he deeply loves me. He said all those things about me way back then. How we could have so badly lost our way in the ensuing years is something I still struggle to understand.

————————

When the documentary was completed, we screened it at the Paramount Theater right on the lot. There were about 500 people in attendance: family members, friends, and several *Star Trek* cast members. When I introduced the film, I made mention of the fact that the original series was first produced at Desilu Studios, owned by Desi Arnaz and Lucille Ball, which became part of the west side of the Paramount lot when Paramount bought Desilu in 1967. Lucille Ball herself ran Desilu, and she was the one who made the call to go ahead and produce the *Star Trek* pilot, acting against the advice of her money men, who were worried about possible cost overruns. It has always amused me that the woman who played crazy redheaded Lucy Ricardo also played such a pivotal role in *Star Trek* history. I also mentioned that the street in front of the soundstages where they shot *Star Trek* had been renamed Leonard Nimoy Way, which I thought a fitting tribute to a man who gave so much of his life to *Star Trek*.

"My father never set out to create a popular character," I told the audience. "Instead, his genius was in finding a personal connection to all the roles he played. His intention in terms of Spock was to bring a dynamic and inner life to the character, and he did this by identifying with Spock, the only alien on the core *Enterprise* crew—the outsider trying to contribute to the society in which he found himself. This was exactly what Dad had experienced in Boston, where *he* was the outsider, the son of Russian immigrants trying to make his way and his contribution to the American society he was born into."

There was one other experience with my dad I shared that night. Its significance has become clearer to me as I reprocessed my life with him while working on this book.

Before production on *Star Trek* began in May 1966, Dad's last major acting role was as a guest star on *Gunsmoke*, a western that ran for twenty seasons on CBS. Dad was cast as John Walking Fox, a Comanche Indian. During the years before *Star Trek*, he had been cast in several westerns as a Native American. He once told me whenever he was asked a yes/no question in an audition the answer was always "yes." "Can you ride a horse?" "Yeah, I can ride a horse." He'd never been on a horse in his life.

Before they started shooting the *Gunsmoke* episode, "The Treasure of John Walking Fox," Dad was told to report to the Western Costume Company in Hollywood. The company was founded in 1912 by L. L. Burns, who had amassed a collection of hundreds of American Indian artifacts, weapons, costumes, and jewelry. Word of Burns's acumen for historically accurate western wear spread throughout the film industry, which had just started making movies in Hollywood, many of them westerns. For almost sixty years, his company was housed in a standalone five-story building on Melrose Avenue, right about where the Paramount Theater now stands. The building had been there from 1932 until 1990, when Paramount bought it and demolished it to expand the studio.

On a Saturday morning in 1966, my dad took me with him for the wardrobe fitting. As usual, we barely spoke as we drove into Hollywood. I was amazed to find that the Western Costume Company was crammed floor to ceiling with clothes from all eras and from all over the world. I sat in a waiting room with all that wardrobe while Dad was being fitted in the back. About twenty minutes later he jumped out from behind the door and yelled, "*Ta-da!*" with a huge smile on his face. It just blew my nine-year-old mind. He was decked out in buckskin from head to toe and was wearing a wig with shoulder-length hair. He was just amazing, and I was so happy to share in the joy and fun and to feel connected to him in a way that had otherwise, more often than not, been so incredibly difficult for us.

43

A HOME AND A DUMP

MADDY HAS ALWAYS BEEN very "organazized." She's also a tough nego-
tiator, which is probably why she's so good at her job overseeing how
budgets are spent on television shows produced at Paramount Television
Studios. When she started working at Paramount, she had been renting a
house with some roommates in Highland Park, north of downtown L.A.
The house was pretty worn out from years of renters, but it was built
on a hill called Mount Washington and had an incredible view of the
surrounding hills. Maddy was sent an eviction notice from her landlord,
who intended to fix the place and sell it. She had no intention of leaving
and told the owner she would buy the house "as is," without him needing to lift a finger.

Though run-down, the place was one of those with "incredible
potential." Just like Clarkson Road. Just like the house Martha and I
moved into. Because of the housing crunch in L.A., older areas were
being gentrified and Mount Washington was starting to become one of
them. At some point there would have to be an inspection, but in the
meantime I had Miguel, my Secret Weapon, come out and look at the
foundation to make sure it wasn't cracked. This house sat right on a
hillside, and we have little things in L.A. called "earthquakes" that shake
houses right off of hillsides. Miguel inspected and all good. The owner
knew the place needed upgrading everywhere—the paint, the plumbing,
the electrical—so that it would clearly have to be a "distress sale." We
asked him to name his price, hoping that he didn't know what the place
was worth even in its current state.

He didn't.

When escrow closed, we had Miguel working for two months to deal with badly needed repairs. Now the place is astounding. Good for you, Maddy.

Jonah's situation was another matter. In so many ways, he's loving and giving and sweet, and he's certainly talented. In other ways, he's totally challenged, and case in point was his apartment. He managed to find one within his price range in Silver Lake. When I went out there to look, it was clearly a dump with no potential. His mother agreed, but he insisted on living there, because it's in East L.A., where all the millennials are, and he was ten minutes from his sister, so I thought he'd be fine. And he was fine until a couple of years later when the city made the owners retrofit the place, turning it into a total construction (read, "war") zone. The project kept expanding to include renovating the pool and the parking lot. Jonah was constantly complaining about the dust in his apartment, the power outages, and the leaking porta-potty. The two of us went downtown for a meeting with his landlord to see about renegotiating the rent.

The landlord's office was a dump with no potential. It was a bona fide management company, but all the Yelp reviews said these guys were slumlords who didn't care about customer satisfaction or the upkeep of their buildings. At least they weren't in some high rise with plush offices. We were led into a conference room, where the carpet was stained from wall to wall. The conference table was made of laminated wood that was chipped everywhere. A young guy named Jeremiah came in to meet with us. He started the conversation by saying he was willing to let Jonah out of his lease and that he could move anytime he wanted to.

"That's very nice," I said, "but Jonah doesn't want to move. He wants you to live up to your end of the lease agreement—which, as it stands, you're not. He wants to stay there, but there has to be a rent adjustment, because the place is not what he bargained for."

"I can give him a $200-a-month break," said Jeremiah.

"Jeremiah, we appreciate the offer, but that's not going to cut it. The building is now a total construction zone leading right up to Jonah's front door. You've violated a number of housing ordinances by not giving him sixty days advance notice specifying the scope of the work, you didn't file a Plan of Construction with the Housing Authority, and my real estate attorney did a records search, and apparently you're missing several permits."

Most of that was bullshit. Having just built a house, I did talk to some guys about what might be missing from this tenement improvement project, and I did do some research on the internet. I still happen to be a member of the State Bar of California (although I'm on the inactive list) but know next to nothing about city ordinances dealing with construction. Nevertheless, I wasn't about to let three years of law school and seven years of practice go entirely to waste.

Jeremiah looked like a deer caught in headlights—he was totally dumbstruck. All he could think to say was "I'm not an attorney but . . ."

He agreed to cut Jonah's rent in half until the completion of all construction or for one year, whichever came later.

When we walked out of there, Jonah looked at me like I was the Messiah. "Dad, he looked like you just ate his lunch. That was awesome. You really humiliated that guy, which is great, because he's been giving me shit for months."

"Jonah, it was not my intention to humiliate him, the goal was to simply get you some rent relief. Jeremiah's just a small player in a slumlord management organization. His job is to try to make a buck just like everybody else. And what did you expect? Did you see those offices? Did you see that carpet? They're slumlords and you live in a dump, and you chose to live in a dump."

"Why didn't you tell me not to?!"

"Why didn't I tell you? Mom and I both tried to, but you wouldn't hear of it. And it should've been obvious to you. The building was a faded shade of pink and there were cracks and stucco patches everywhere. There were trash piles all over the place, and the so-called pool looked like a chemical waste site. You couldn't tell on your own that it was a dump? We tried to talk you out of it, but you were impossible, and Mom and I figured you still wanted to slum it for a while, which was fine by us. The fact that you were going to be living close to Maddy was literally the only advantage I could see to moving into that place."

Maddy had told me that one night while she was at home cooking and Jonah was at his apartment, she got a call from him.

"What are you doing?" asked Jonah.

"I'm at home making dinner," said Maddy.

"Oh, that's good," said Jonah, "because I'm hungry for dinner."

I took Jonah to Langer's Deli, an L.A. landmark, to celebrate his rent reduction. He ordered a corned beef sandwich and a side of eggs and bacon.

"Are you seriously going to eat all that?" I asked.

"That meeting made me hungry."

Then we went on to talk about his career. After years struggling to get his own band off the ground, Jonah was picked up by a little punk band from Orange County called the Offspring to join them on tour as a guitarist. The Offspring are actually *huge*. I used to listen to them when Jonah was a toddler, and I just adored those guys.

"We're going to South America at the end of the summer, then we have a short tour in Mexico and then we tour Canada during the winter."

This, of course, was all just before the pandemic.

"It's amazing what you've accomplished with those guys." I said. "I mean, I still can't quite believe you're tight with the guys who brought us 'Self Esteem.'"

In the summer of 2019, Jonah played with them on the last show of the final Vans Warped Tour. We had tried to get Jonah's solo band Furiosa on that tour a couple years earlier, but no go. The Warped Tour was a traveling rock show that had blasted through the US every summer since 1995. Now it was ending, and the Offspring headlined the last show in Mountain View, California. I happened to be visiting friends in Berkeley just fifty miles away, but told Jonah there was no way I would be going to that show if I couldn't watch from the stage. I'm much too old to be in a mosh pit with seven thousand crazy fans. It didn't look like he was going to be able to pull it off, and I was relieved that I could enjoy my quiet vacation in the Bay Area. Then I got the call that he managed to score me a backstage pass.

Watching from the wings reminded me of how much I really loved that band. And Jonah was right there rocking out with them. It was spectacular. I could not stop bouncing around I was having that much fun.

Jonah had been all over the world with these guys playing to venues of five to fifteen thousand people and had just been loving it. He was playing with guys who are almost twice his age, guys who had their first monster hit when he was two years old. He started playing a percussion rack as well as guitar on several songs, and the band was starting another tour of South America and Japan in the spring (although all of that would be cut short by the pandemic). I guess not doing any homework so that he could practice guitar to become a rock star had finally paid off.

"The thing is Jonah, playing percussion is great, because you're adding a whole new element to what you can do for the band," I told him. "Everything you've done has brought you to this moment. The writing, the recording, the rehearsing, the performing. All the bands you were in and all the gigs you played. And all those private lessons you took not because we made you but because you wanted to. You may not be as organazized as Maddy, but you worked very hard to get to where you are, and you did it on your own, and we're all very proud of you."

As for my own living situation, I tore down the house I had bought with Martha. I built a new home, with an incredible design by my good friend Bob Ramirez, who designed the addition to the Clarkson Road house we built so many years ago. The construction crew for my new home included my Secret Weapon, Miguel, whose incredible craftsmanship is visible inside and out. One of the backyard rosebushes Martha loved so much somehow managed to survive the two years of construction, so we built a planter around it. Sometimes I would sit in the sun in the backyard and a butterfly would happen by. In those moments, it felt as though I would be given another chance, that despite all that happened and whatever other challenges were ahead, that in the end everything would be OK or would turn out just the way my HP had planned.

I got myself a pandemic dog, a Labrador retriever, and named her Belle. I already had a cat named Sally that Krystal, from the Happy Destiny bookstore, insisted I adopt when I happened to be in there the year after Martha died. After catching up with her and telling her about losing Martha, Krystal proclaimed, "You didn't come here to buy AA literature, you came here to get this cat!" and she showed me a picture of Sally, a tortoiseshell kitty. (I also picked up a tabby named Crash. At night when I walk Belle, the two cats follow us down the street.) Every morning, Belle and I walk/jog through the neighborhood, and oftentimes we pass by that first house my dad bought on Palms Boulevard. Sometimes I stand there and consider it. It still looks sad and dilapidated and neglected, not like when we used to live there and Dad kept it in tip-top shape. I still sometimes have this fantasy that one day I'll buy that house and bring in my Secret Weapon to fix it up, still entertaining some vague notion that it would somehow make up for all the problems I had with my dad that started when I was very young. But then, of course, my second thought kicks in reminding me that with *this* house, there is simply nothing to be done, and I am just going to have to let it go.

The other thing that sometimes comes to mind about that house is that for my father, the fans and the paparazzi and the limos and the red carpets were all very fine, but he never forgot where he came from. The old West End of Boston, that tenement neighborhood in which he grew up, was always a part of him that kept him grounded and gave him a sense of humility and gratitude. I often like to think that for me, it was our little house on Palms Boulevard.

44

THE BOOK OF JONAH

As with the end of every summer, in 2022, Yom Kippur was upon us. The Day of Atonement had arrived. A day of fasting and prayer. The holiest day of the Jewish year.

I was invited by the new rabbi at Beit T'Shuvah to talk about the Book of Jonah. By this time, I had become a board member at that organization, and for many years we had been enjoying services in our new sanctuary. The sanctuary is spacious and lit from spotlights anchored in a beautiful wood-panel ceiling that must be twenty-five feet high. There's carpeting everywhere, comfy seats, and more wood paneling behind the bimah. There is a stage section where the Beit T'Shuvah band is permanently parked. A wonderful, spiritual space whose primary purpose is to service the residential community as well as alumni and friends and family who make up the congregation. There are usually well over a hundred residents in recovery at Beit T'Shuvah, the House of Return, and the mission created by Harriet Rossetto and Rabbi Mark Borovitz continues through our motto: "Recover your passion. Discover your purpose."

My talk about the Book of Jonah was not going to be a straight reading of the story as my father used to do, but a midrash or drash, which is a discussion or interpretation of the possible meaning of the story. Since Beit T'Shuvah is a residential addiction treatment facility and the afternoon Mincha service would include most if not all of the residential community, the drash also needed to explore how the story of Jonah and the Whale might shed some light on the experience of recovery. My presentation that day pulled together so many elements I have been exploring in this memoir, it seemed logical to include it as the closing chapter of this book.

———————

Hello, my name is Adam and I'm a grateful member of this community.
Hi, Adam!

I also have the honor of being a board member here at Beit T'Shuvah, and I am a person in recovery. I'd also like to mention that when I was growing up, my parents were members at Adat Shalom, which is not far from here and is the temple where I was bar mitzvahed. And quite often on Yom Kippur, my dad would come up to the bimah and read the entire story of Jonah. I used to go with him, and it was an incredible experience, because my father had such a great voice and he read the story with so much depth and feeling. I remember being with him in the early '80s, just about forty years ago, and I was thinking, *If* Star Trek *fans knew they could just walk in here and watch Leonard Nimoy read from the Book of Jonah, the place would be packed.*

I love the Book of Jonah, because in addition to being a story about atonement and forgiveness, which is why we read it on Yom Kippur, there's also so much about recovery in this story.

Jonah was told by God to go to Nineveh and prophesy against the people because they were "wicked," but there are no details about their sinful behavior. Instead of going to Nineveh, Jonah got on a ship headed in the opposite direction. God created a huge storm on the sea, and Jonah told the frightened sailors to just throw him overboard to stop the sea from raging. While Jonah was sinking to the bottom of the sea, God commanded a "dag gadol," a large fish that we interpret to be a whale, to go and save him. Jonah spent three days and three nights in the belly of that whale, and that's when he appears to have finally hit bottom. He reaffirmed his faith in God, expressed gratitude for being saved, and promised to take direction if he ever got out of there. It seems to be a full-on t'shuvah, an amends, a return, a transformation. God then commands the whale to spew Jonah out on dry land, and anyone who's had a hangover can easily imagine what he must have looked like and felt like when he finally got out of that whale. But he got his second chance when God called on him again, and this time he went immediately to Nineveh.

When Jonah arrived in Nineveh, his prophecy was short, just eight words: "Forty days more and Nineveh shall be overthrown." The people heard him and made *their* amends by fasting and praying. The king himself put on sackcloth and sat in ashes and issued a decree that they should turn back from their evil ways and their injustices so that God will relent and so that they might not perish. God saw all of this, and the city was spared. Happy ending, right? Wrong, because Jonah was angry that the city was not destroyed. He was so upset that he actually begged God to let him die. Most prophets complain that people don't listen to them. Jonah uttered just eight words and everyone in town changed their behavior, so what is his problem?

To understand why Jonah has such a resentment toward these people, we need to zoom out and take a look at the historical context of this story. Because the story was probably written in the eighth or seventh century BC, and at that time Nineveh was the capitol of the Assyrian Empire. The Assyrians were the military superpower in the region who conquered all the neighboring cities in Mesopotamia, and in 721 BC they swept down from the northeast and destroyed the northern Kingdom of Israel and laid siege to the southern Kingdom of Judah. It was their successors, the Neo-Babylonians, who came in and finished the job by taking Jerusalem and destroying the Temple, which was the center of Jewish secular and religious life. The Jews were then taken captive and forced to move to Babylon. Jonah had good reason to despise these people who were, historically, the bitter enemies of the Jews. He had historical justification. But in the end, it didn't matter. The people repented, Nineveh was spared, and Jonah was devastated. That's what's so incredible to me about this story, because it shows God's love and mercy extends to all people, not just the Jews. God is always ready to forgive all who repent with no distinction between race, religion, or territory. It's a story of judgment and compassion, of repentance and mercy. And for the last eighteen years, during my recovery, what has also been of keen personal interest to me about this story is Jonah's emotional relapse, his inability to let go of his ill will towards these people, because learning to let go of resentments has been the cornerstone of my own recovery.

The Big Book of AA tells us that the fourth step, "Made a searching and fearless moral inventory of ourselves," is specifically designed to deal with resentments. The Big Book says, *Resentment is the number one offender, it destroys more alcoholics than anything else, and from it stems all forms of spiritual disease.* Step four then is our grudge list—who pissed us off, how they did it, how it affected us, and the famous fourth column of the fourth step: what was our part in it. It was this step that gave me so much trouble in my early sobriety, because I couldn't figure out what to do with the top dog on my grudge list. Just like Jonah, I had good reasons for my resentment toward my number one offender, and that person happened to be my father. I was four years into my recovery before I finally made an amends to my dad for my part in our dysfunctional relationship. Until that time, I really wasn't experiencing the miracle of recovery, the "promises," were not coming true and I was not "trudging the road of happy destiny." I was simply sober while carrying around a bunch of resentments. Just like Jonah.

Without going into too much detail, my relationship with my dad was doomed from the start. My father's parents were Russian immigrants, from Ukraine actually, who managed to make their way to Boston, where my father was born. My dad grew up during the Great Depression selling newspapers on the Boston Common when he was ten years old. When he told his parents he wanted to become an actor, they were devastated and said they wouldn't help him, because they expected him to go to college. My dad came to L.A. at age eighteen with no financial support and had to hold down numerous odd jobs just to make his way, all while pursuing his acting career. By the time he was just twenty-five years old, he was supporting our family of four.

I, on the other hand, was born in sunny Southern California and in 1966, when *I* was ten, *Star Trek* went on the air and suddenly things became pretty comfortable in the Nimoy household. Instead of delivering newspapers before or after school, I was reading Spider-Man comics, watching '60's TV, and listening to the Beatles. I was always proud of my dad, but we were worlds apart—planets apart, really—as he was much more of his parents' Old World generation than he ever was of mine. As a result, our relationship was always awkward and distant.

During my college years, when my pot problem kicked in and my dad's alcoholism was in full bloom, it was just a recipe for disaster, and for the next thirty years, we would often run into trouble, because we simply didn't have any tools to deal with the conflict. And when you get into an argument with a guy who has millions of Spock fans all over the world, it's just impossible.

I went into recovery in 2004, but there was no way I was going to make a ninth-step amends to my dad. My father had gone into recovery before me, but he had never made an amends to me, so why the hell should I make one to him? In 2006 I joined an Al-Anon group, where I learned about detaching with love, and that's exactly what I did—I detached with love, thinking that would solve my problem. And for several years my father and I were essentially estranged.

Back in the '90s when I had my own kids—my daughter Maddy was born in 1990 and my son, whom we appropriately named Jonah, was born in '92—back then my relationship with *my* kids was totally different, because for the most part we were close and loving and I was very involved in their lives. I took them to soccer, I took Jonah to softball and kung fu and to his drum lessons and his guitar lessons. I took Maddy to her piano and cello lessons and her math tutor and helped her with her homework and drove her and her friends all over this town. I would jam with Jonah while he played drums and I played guitar. I would pick Maddy up at 1 AM from broomball parties and was even dumb enough to get up at 5 AM to take Jonah and his buddies surfing at Point Dume. I did everything for those kids, *and they still found reasons to hate me!* Maddy was mad at me all the time because her mom and I split up when she was thirteen. She would send me little emails that read: "I hate you, I hate you, I HATE YOU." Jonah was a talented musician and from an early age was determined to become a rock star, so what was the point of eighth-grade history? He was similar to my dad in that respect: he was a nightmare in school and simply refused to do any homework. A traditional school setting was probably not the best place for him, but I couldn't get him to do anything. It got to a point where I finally came down on him like a ton of bricks, I was just so frustrated with his excuses. While I was laying into him, I could hear myself sounding just like my dad, but I couldn't stop myself. Jonah was twelve at the time, and he started crying and he turned to me and said, "You have no idea how much I hate you right now," and I thought, *You have no idea how much I hate myself.*

Then the kids' relationship with my dad went completely south, because they had no clue as to how to relate to each other. My dad finally decided to reach out to me by sending me a letter in which he listed all my character defects, all my failures, all the reasons why he was disappointed in me or just plain pissed off at me. I couldn't believe it. He had totally taken my inventory. Of course, I was not going to let this ruin my serenity. I had some recovery tools by then! So I practiced "restraint of pen and tongue" and "don't just do something, sit there," which meant that I didn't respond to his letter; I just let it go. I gave him the last word hoping he would calm down and praying that some day we might have a relationship.

Then a buddy of mine in recovery told me that this was a great opportunity, that because my dad had filled out the fourth column of my fourth step for me, I should take the letter to him and make an amends for everything in it. I fought him on this, because I had some terrific resentments of my own against my dad—I had "historical justification"! My sober buddy, who had known me most of my life, basically told me I was just like the prophet Jonah: I could be right about my dad and hold on to my resentments or . . . I could be happy, joyous, and free. But to "trudge the road of happy destiny," I would have to take that letter and make the amends. Although I wasn't really feeling it at the time, I took the direction and made the amends to my father. I "faked it till I made it," as we say in the program. My dad seemed to really enjoy the experience, so much so that when it was over, he invited me to Shabbat dinner. I really must give him credit, because after I made the amends his anger toward me disappeared—he himself was ready to let go of his resentments toward me and move on. All he really wanted, all he *needed*, was to be heard and seen and validated in a way that his parents could never do for him, nor could all those millions of adoring fans. In the end, I was ready to let go of my resentments as well.

And slowly but surely my dad and I began to rebuild our relationship. So much so that three years later, in 2011, I was sitting in my car in a parking lot, having just gotten off the phone with a doctor who told me that the cancer my new wife Martha had been diagnosed with, Martha whom I had just married four months before, that the cancer they found in Martha was terminal and she was not going to survive. And after receiving that earth-shattering news from the doctor, the first call I made was to my father.

"Dad, we're screwed. She's not going to make it," I said.

"How do you know?" he asked.

"I just talked to the doctor."

"Oh, Adam, I'm so sorry," he said. "Does Martha know?"

"No, and she doesn't want to. She thinks she can beat this, but the doctor is now saying the cancer has spread too far."

"Where are you?" he said. "I'll come to you."

"No, that's OK," I said. I just needed to tell someone, and that someone was you."

That conversation was unthinkable just a few years before. Unthinkable.

And for the next eighteen months my dad helped me get through one of the worst periods of my life. He helped me right up until the day Martha died. He used to bring me here to Friday-night Shabbat services at Beit T'Shuvah, just so I could take a break. It was Rabbi Mark Borovitz who told me my dad was making a living amends to me, that he was there when I needed him in a way that was simply impossible for him when I was a kid.

During this time my dad and my kids also reconciled. Dad was very proud of my daughter Maddy, because in part with his help she was pursuing a career in production. The year my dad died, Maddy was hired at Paramount Television Studios, the studio that made all things *Star Trek*. Now she's a vice president and she used to have an office right across the way from the Dressing Room building, where my dad had an office when he was co-starring in the original series of *Mission: Impossible*.

My dad and Jonah were definitely birds of a feather. The two of them were skyping into *Star Trek* conventions all over the country, because my father was too old to go in person. Dad would sing "Maiden Wine," this song that Spock sang on one of the original episodes, and Jonah would accompany him on guitar. It was just the most ridiculous thing, watching the two of them together while Dad tried to sing this song. It was almost embarrassing, but it was also brilliant. They were brilliant together. At one point I witnessed my dad telling Jonah that he was a true artist. It was like Dad was able to recognize in Jonah what his own parents could not see in him. During those last years of my father's life, we were all brilliant together. The family was together, and we were all one. It was amazing.

And all I had to do was let go of my resentment and make the amends.

And as for me and Jonah, my son Jonah, well, for the last five years, Jonah's been playing with a little punk band from Orange County called the Offspring.

I may be dumb but I'm not a dweeb.
I'm just a sucker with no self-esteem.

Some of you might have heard of that song. "Self Esteem" was a hit in 1994 when Jonah was two years old. Now he's touring all over the world with the Offspring, playing guitar and keyboards and percussion in that band. Last month I texted him because I knew they had just played Rock in Rio, this huge music festival in Rio de Janeiro.

"How was the show?" I asked.

He immediately texted back: "It was insane. Sold out one hundred thousand people. Just hung out with Dexter." That's Dexter Holland, the songwriter and lead singer of the Offspring. "Just hung out with Dexter and he said I've become the glue of the band. I am losing my mind!!!!"

I wrote back, "Jonah you are the man! I am so effing proud of you. I love you sooo much and am so happy for you."

"Thanks fasha!!!" That's what my kids call me when they're happy with me. "Thanks fasha!!! Love you too!!! It's a dream!! We did it!!"

To which I replied:

"Yes, we did."